CRITICAL INSIGHTS

Barbara Kingsolver

CRITICAL
INSIGHTS

Barbara Kingsolver

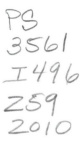

Editor
Thomas Austenfeld
University of Fribourg

Salem Press
Pasadena, California   Hackensack, New Jersey

Cover photo: AP/Wide World Photos

Published by Salem Press

© 2010 by EBSCO Publishing
Editor's text © 2010 by Thomas Austenfeld
"The *Paris Review* Perspective" © 2010 by Katherine Ryder for *The Paris Review*

∞ The paper used in these volumes conforms to the American National Standard for Permanence of Paper for Printed Library Materials, Z39.48-1992 (R1997).

Library of Congress Cataloging-in-Publication Data
Barbara Kingsolver / editor, Thomas Austenfeld.
　　p. cm. -- (Critical insights)
　　Includes bibliographical references and index.
　　ISBN 978-1-58765-642-2 (one volume : alk. paper) 1. Kingsolver, Barbara--Criticism and interpretation. 2. Women and literature--United States--History--20th century. I. Austenfeld, Thomas.
　　PS3561.I496Z59 2010
　　813'.54--dc22
2009027638

PRINTED IN CANADA

Contents

About This Volume, Thomas Austenfeld   vii

Career, Life, and Influence

On Barbara Kingsolver, Thomas Austenfeld   3
Biography of Barbara Kingsolver, Marilyn Kongslie and
    Karen L. Arnold   7
The *Paris Review* Perspective, Katherine Ryder for *The Paris Review*   11

Critical Contexts

The Political Is Personal: Sociocultural Realities and the Writings of
    Barbara Kingsolver, John Nizalowski   17
Barbara Kingsolver and the Critics, Rosemary M. Canfield Reisman   36
Cultivating Our Bioregional Roots: An Ecofeminist Exploration
    of Barbara Kingsolver's *Prodigal Summer*, Christine M. Battista   52
The Gothic and the Ethnic in Barbara Kingsolver's *The Bean Trees*,
    Matthew J. Bolton   69

Critical Readings

Gardens of Auto Parts: Kingsolver's Merger of American
    Western Myth and Native American Myth in *The Bean Trees*,
    Catherine Himmelwright   87
The Loner and the Matriarchal Community in Barbara
    Kingsolver's *The Bean Trees* and *Pigs in Heaven*,
    Loretta Martin Murrey   112
Trauma and Memory in Kingsolver's *Animal Dreams*,
    Sheryl Stevenson   123
Exploring the Matrix of Identity in Barbara Kingsolver's
    Animal Dreams, Lee Ann De Reus   152
Luna Moths, Coyotes, Sugar Skulls: The Fiction of Barbara
    Kingsolver, Amanda Cockrell   173
The Missionary Position: Barbara Kingsolver's *The Poisonwood
    Bible*, Elaine R. Ognibene   192

The Neodomestic American Novel: The Politics of Home in
    Barbara Kingsolver's *The Poisonwood Bible*, Kristin J. Jacobson   216
The Revelatory Narrative Circle in Barbara Kingsolver's
    The Poisonwood Bible, Anne Marie Austenfeld   246
Barbara Kingsolver and Keri Hulme: Disability, Family,
    and Culture, Stephen D. Fox   260
The Southern Family Farm as Endangered Species:
    Possibilities for Survival in Barbara Kingsolver's
    Prodigal Summer, Suzanne W. Jones   283

Resources

Chronology of Barbara Kingsolver's Life   303
Works by Barbara Kingsolver   305
Bibliography   306

About the Editor   311
About *The Paris Review*   311
Contributors   313
Acknowledgments   316
Index   319

About This Volume

Thomas Austenfeld

This volume in the Critical Insights series brings together a set of materials to serve both as an introduction to Barbara Kingsolver's writings and as a guide to scholarly readings of her work. The volume begins with a general introduction to Kingsolver's life and work that provides a context for the beginning reader. Biographical data shedding light on her fiction and essays are provided in the sketch by Marilyn Kongslie and Karen L. Arnold, and Katherine Ryder's sketch for *The Paris Review* shows us Kingsolver at her most political, especially in her essay collection *Small Wonder* (2002).

At the heart of the volume are two sections of essays. I have written a headnote for each essay to give readers a quick orientation and to allow them to read the essays in the order they find most useful. The first, shorter section, "Critical Contexts," opens a number of doors for the reader. John Nizalowski—the other author who references *Small Wonder*—traces the social and political engagement that is so characteristic of Kingsolver's work back to its many possible biographical roots, from the author's home and educational history all the way to her life experiences as an adult, including motherhood. Rosemary M. Canfield Reisman documents how early reviews shaped Kingsolver's reputation. She also locates Kingsolver's abiding concern for social issues in the years of the author's journalistic apprenticeship.

Christine M. Battista considers Kingsolver's contribution to ecofeminism. Given the ongoing national and international debates about climate change and sustainability, Battista's essay is highly topical. Matthew J. Bolton's essay invites readers to see Kingsolver in one of several literary contexts. He uses the tropes of the gothic novel to situate *The Bean Trees* in literary history, pointing out how Kingsolver playfully subverts the expectations of the genre. Together, these two initial essays with a distinctly literary focus delineate the large frame of reference in which Kingsolver's work needs to be seen; reaching from literary history to present-day progressive politics, this novelist's work is relevant and timely.

The second section of essays, "Critical Readings," assembles carefully selected, recently published essays placed together here for their ability to converse with each other and thus to engage the reader in the ongoing conversation about Kingsolver's work. The essays are arranged thematically, following roughly the chronology of Kingsolver's major publications. Most of the essayists are literary critics, but some come from such fields as rhetoric and psychology and bring their own disciplinary views to bear on the novelist's works. I suggest reading the essays with a view toward their potential to complement each other and to illuminate different aspects of the same works.

The Bean Trees (1988) and *Pigs in Heaven* (1993) are thematically linked. Catherine Himmelwright and Loretta Martin Murrey both examine Kingsolver's transformation of pervasive western American myths and consider the corrective impulses the author offers us with a female protagonist who unexpectedly discovers her maternal qualities. Mothering, in turn, connects Taylor Greer with her own part-Cherokee heritage and creates communities in the place of the lone western men we know from the cowboy tradition.

Kingsolver's 1990 novel *Animal Dreams* also takes place in Arizona and has moved specialists from several disciplines to interpret it. Sheryl Stevenson uses a "trauma studies" approach to help us understand Codi Noline's difficult process of identity finding, while Lee Ann De Reus uses psychology and family studies theory to arrive at slightly different conclusions. Not just *Animal Dreams* and *Pigs in Heaven*, but indeed all of Kingsolver's work is replete with animals, and Amanda Cockrell finds this biological absorption a key to Kingsolver's work as she writes about luna moths and coyotes, among other animals.

Kingsolver's 1998 novel about the Congo, *The Poisonwood Bible*, is particularly rich in interpretive contexts, and several essays in this section together investigate its key aspects. While Elaine R. Ognibene deftly teases out the connections between personal and political manifestations of colonialism in her essay, Kristin J. Jacobson reads the same novel through the lens of nineteenth-century American women's writing, especially against the foil of Louisa May Alcott's *Little Women* and the conversations about "neodomesticity" surrounding Alcott. Anne Marie Austenfeld analyzes the multiple narrators of the novel, who come together as a circle of tale-tellers to render the complex history of the Price family abroad. Austenfeld shows that a rhetorical appreciation of *The Poisonwood Bible* also illuminates some of Kingsolver's journalistic and reportorial work. Extending the context into further corners of the English-speaking world, Stephen D. Fox compares Keri Hulme's *The Bone People* with *The Poisonwood Bible* to determine how the authors render key characters with disabilities.

Suzanne W. Jones brings Kingsolver home, as it were, to the American South, where the novelist currently resides. Jones's essay is both a critical appreciation of the sheer literary power of *Prodigal Summer* (2000) and a recognition of Kingsolver's place in the circle of southern writers who have made preservation and local sustainability issues their central concerns. The essay thus connects back to Battista's opening observations.

These essays will reward readers who have a desire to discover aspects of Kingsolver's work they have not yet fully seen, or simply inspire readers to go back and read their favorite Kingsolver texts again. Since Kingsolver is not just a writer but an activist as well, readers may even want to do something about their fascination!

CAREER, LIFE, AND INFLUENCE

On Barbara Kingsolver_____

Thomas Austenfeld

Now that Barbara Kingsolver has been an established writer for a little more than twenty years, one may attempt to look at her place in literary history—a history that she continues to assist in shaping. The 1988 publication of *The Bean Trees* was a seemingly instant success, but Kingsolver had in fact been perfecting her writing skills for a long time, both as a journalist and as a science writer. While the settings of her novels have shifted over the years from the American Southwest to Africa and, finally, to the Appalachian South, Kingsolver has never abandoned her clear sense of place or, for that matter, her clear sense of direction. When we read her fiction, the firm feeling of place, touch, smell, and taste remain with us even after we have put down the book. The sparse vegetation of the Southwest and its sagebrush smell emerge as poignantly from her texts as do the rivers and snakes of the Congo, as do the rich and varied flora and fauna of the American South, its pine trees and its butterflies.

What I call Kingsolver's clear sense of direction has to do with both where she is coming from and where she is taking her reader. The American landscape—desired, admired, settled, mined, abused, cherished—has given rise to both literature and criticism at every point of contact between European settlers and aboriginal inhabitants. The precise description of places has been a hallmark of American literature since Columbus and the Puritans, although those early writers arrived with a marked sense of the distinction between themselves as owners and the places they perceived and described as their possessions, whether geographical or spiritual. Kingsolver, by contrast, seeks out the connections among herself, her characters, and the places they inhabit—and the notion of "inhabiting" is more important to her than the notion of "occupying." Kingsolver's literary ancestors, then, are not Columbus and the Puritans; instead, they are writers who encounter their landscapes with wonder and admiration and concern, writers like John

Muir, Aldo Leopold, and Rachel Carson. These and others like them share with Kingsolver a fierce commitment to a deeper appreciation of the complex interconnectedness of all living things. Whether in Muir's California mountains, Leopold's Nebraska sandhills, Carson's birdless forests, or Kingsolver's vegetable patches, human beings participate in, rather than own, biological activities.

A firm consciousness of landscape is also a constituent feature of the American Western, a genre in which (usually) men traverse a (usually) hostile space and transform a lawless territory into a place of order through the exercise of violence. Kingsolver has offered her readers both thoughtful and terrifying variations on this topic, both in her southwestern novels and in *The Poisonwood Bible*, where Nathan Price's attempt to transform a place fails utterly while the women of the family, each in her own way, test ways of engaging with place. Women are key to Kingsolver's fiction, and their sense of place can be directed toward a place in the mind as much as toward a place on the map. Codi Noline's search for herself in *Animal Dreams* is a search as much for interior placement as for a geographical location, such as the "home" that suggestively begins her father Homer's name. Adah's home in *The Poisonwood Bible* is the linguistic landscape of her mind. And the sanctuary that is so important in *Pigs in Heaven* is a home offered to the homeless.

Places, relationships, vegetation, homes, the interconnectedness of all living things—these might have become the ingredients of a highly conventional package of a traditional woman's sphere of literary activity. Barbara Kingsolver won't have it that way. Keenly alert to the times in which she lives, she makes all of her fictional places come alive with the real political and ecological challenges they face. A place one knows well is also a place of work in Kingsolver's writing. Whether it be the picket line in the Arizona mining strike of 1983, U.S. immigration policy in *The Bean Trees*, American foreign interventions in *Animal Dreams* and *The Poisonwood Bible*, or Deanna's work for the Forest Service in *Prodigal Summer*, a place always exists in the present and has the power to demand engagement. The "real" feelings that create the books and that are communicated to readers contribute to the force that emerges from a Kingsolver text. It is the sense of being there oneself.

Now, creating a sense of "being there oneself" is a task that imaginative literature has set for itself since its beginnings, but it is particularly operational in the tradition of realism. Whether the domestic realism of Louisa May Alcott or the muckraking realism of Upton Sinclair or the ethnic ecologies of Willa Cather, multiple versions of American realism flourished during the last third of the nineteenth century and first years of the twentieth, and part of Kingsolver's literary history resides in this tradition. More precisely, however, she is what, more than one hundred years ago, was called a "novelist with a purpose." This designation is no longer fashionable, but it describes precisely the particular form of engagement that calls to us from Kingsolver's work. Though Kingsolver's literary skills have evolved from one text to the next, she has never set aside the mission of her writing—"mission" not in the sense misunderstood by Nathan Price, but "mission" as a form of truth telling, "mission" as a drive to educate her readers. Before she became a best-selling author, Kingsolver's mission took the form of journalism. Each of her novels foregrounds a political, social, psychological, religious, or environmental state of affairs that animates the characters as they discover who they are and where they belong.

In recent years, her mission has been more documentary in character. The essays in *Small Wonder* (2002) and especially the 2007 *Animal, Vegetable, Miracle* signal another line of inheritance in American literature that goes back to the mid-nineteenth century. *A Year of Food Life*, the subtitle to *Animal, Vegetable, Miracle*, calls to mind Henry David Thoreau's *Walden*, one of the most famous American chronicles of a year, a book known perhaps even more abroad than in the United States. Thoreau's testimony to living simply—and proving it possible!—was balanced by his serious engagement with the social and political causes of his time, whether war with Mexico or the adoption of the Fugitive

Slave Law in Massachusetts. Thoreau's essays, always conscious of the "I" that is speaking, never abdicating responsibility toward others, resonate within Kingsolver's present work. Her quintessentially American themes, as well as her knowledge of American literary traditions, make her as relevant and purposeful as any author writing today.

The twenty years that have elapsed since the publication of *The Bean Trees* have seen one millennium give way to the next. Barbara Kingsolver has accompanied us on this journey and will continue to do so. What is true in plant and animal biodiversity, however, is also true in interhuman relationships. The American problems of racial identity and racial prejudice, perhaps the largest historical burdens of this nation, now slowly beginning to resolve themselves, have been consistent topics of Kingsolver's mission, especially in reference to Native Americans. By 2042, just a few years down the road, the ethnic makeup of the United States will no longer allow any group to claim majority status. Instead, census officials tell us, the country will have achieved a "minority majority" status, with European-origin whites, African Americans, and Hispanics all being minorities in their own rights, with smaller minorities such as Native Americans and Asian Americans completing the picture, but without any numerical majority dominating the mix. Ethnic unity is generally fostered by a sense of shared traditions, places of origin, religious affiliations, and blood ties. When these traditional ties weaken as members of ethnic groups increasingly intermingle, other means of bonding and of building community must take their place. Beginning with *The Bean Trees*, Barbara Kingsolver has imagined communities that cut across ethnicity and kinship in anticipation of the expected "minority majority" status now foreseen by demographers. In this contribution, I think, lies one of her most important truths, if "truth" will remain the province of the realistic writer with a purpose.

Biography of Barbara Kingsolver

Marilyn Kongslie and Karen L. Arnold

Born in Annapolis, Maryland, on April 8, 1955, Barbara Kingsolver grew up in Kentucky. Her father, Wendell, was a physician, and her mother, Virginia, was a homemaker. Kingsolver, who has kept a journal of personal revelations since the age of eight, learned a sense of community in small-town Kentucky. Later, she would write that community means a place where people "grow their own food and know who they could depend on for help." Part of her heritage is Cherokee, and her stories include American Indian characters, history, and issues.

The bulk of her stories center on community, but after leaving Kentucky for college she discovered that the reality of community is relatively rare in other parts of the United States. At the same time, she deliberately lost her "hillbilly" accent, which prompted ridicule wherever she went. "People made terrible fun of me for the way I used to talk, so I gave it up slowly and became something else. It was later in life, about ten years later, that it occurred to me this language was a precious and valuable thing."

Kingsolver began her university studies with a piano scholarship but then switched to biology because it was more practical. She earned a B.A. magna cum laude in biology from DePauw University (1977) and an M.S. in biology from the University of Arizona (1981); she has completed additional graduate study. Throughout her life she has written, everything from childhood journals to scientific and technical writing after college. Before publishing her first novel, *The Bean Trees*, Kingsolver was a research assistant in the department of physiology at the University of Tucson (1977-1979), a technical writer in the Office of Arid Lands Studies (1981-1985), and a freelance journalist (1985-1987). Her late-1970s activity in the sanctuary movement to help Central American refugees led to writing pamphlets for the cause. Writing gratified Kingsolver, and when she realized that she might make a living doing something that she loved, she turned to fiction.

Her writing has been marked by her political and social convictions, covering everything from U.S. political policy in Latin America to human rights issues. In her first novel, *The Bean Trees* (1988), a young woman leaves home, adopts a child, and becomes politically enlightened. The novel achieved both critical and popular success, as did *Animal Dreams* (1990), a story of a woman's search for place, and *Pigs in Heaven* (1993), a book about children's rights, loneliness, and poverty. Kingsolver's *Homeland, and Other Stories* (1989) consists of twelve short stories. Her first collection of poetry, *Another America/ Otra America* (1992), with parallel English and Spanish texts, reveals her sense of being a citizen of the world. Her nonfiction work *Holding the Line: Women in the Great Arizona Mine Strike of 1983* (1989) features the bravery and persistence of women protesting copper mining practices during difficult and violent strike years in southern Arizona copper-mining towns. *The Poisonwood Bible* (1998) details missionary lives in a prerevolutionary Belgian Congo. The novel narrates the Price family's experiences from five distinct points of view. *Prodigal Summer* (2000) tackles the problems of how an inherited sense of place and land complicate a family's acceptance of an outsider who marries into a rural, agricultural clan. *Small Wonder* (2002), a collection of essays, revisits Kingsolver's concerns with ordinary events, writing, and patriotism in the wake of the terrorist attacks of September 11, 2001.

Kingsolver's many awards include the Enoch Pratt Library Lifetime Achievement Medal in 2005, the 2002 International IMPAC Dublin Literary Award for *Prodigal Summer*, an award for the Best American Science and Nature Writing in 2001, a National Humanities Medal in 2000, the 1999 Patterson Fiction Prize, a *New York Times* Ten Best Books selection for *The Poisonwood Bible* in 1998, American Library Association awards for *The Bean Trees* in 1988 and *Homeland, and Other Stories*, the Mountains and Plains Booksellers Award for Fiction for *Pigs in Heaven*, a citation of accomplishment from the United Nations National Council of Women in 1989, and a PEN/Faulkner

Award for Fiction and an Edward Abbey Ecofiction Award for *Animal Dreams* in 1991.

Kingsolver's subjects come from her heart and from real-life experiences. Her Native American heritage, her southern upbringing, her activities in support of human rights, and her coverage of the Arizona mine strike all inspired her books. Critics continue to praise Kingsolver's sensitive portrayals of average people facing everyday victories and losses as well as extraordinary challenges.

From *Magill's Survey of American Literature*. Rev. ed. Pasadena, CA: Salem Press, 2007. Copyright © 2007 by Salem Press, Inc.

Bibliography

Aay, Henry. "Environmental Themes in Ecofiction: *In the Center of the Nation* and *Animal Dreams*." *Journal of Cultural Geography* 14 (Spring, 1994). Comparative study of Kingsolver's novel and *In the Center of the Nation* (1991) by Dan O'Brien is one of few early scholarly discussions of Kingsolver's work.

DeMarr, Mary Jean. *Barbara Kingsolver: A Critical Companion*. Westport, Conn.: Greenwood Press, 1999. Provides a good overview of Kingsolver's work, emphasizing her ecofeminism.

Fleischner, Jennifer, ed. *A Reader's Guide to the Fiction of Barbara Kingsolver: "The Bean Trees," "Homeland, and Other Stories," "Animal Dreams," "Pigs in Heaven."* New York: HarperPerennial, 1994. A good resource for the student new to Kingsolver's work.

Gaard, Greta. "Living Interconnections with Animals and Nature." In *Ecofeminism: Women, Animals, Nature*, edited by Greta Gaard. Philadelphia: Temple University Press, 1993. Discusses the implications of a personal/political commitment to the natural world.

Kingsolver, Barbara. "CA Interview." Interview by Jean W. Ross. *Contemporary Authors*. Vol. 134. Ed. Susan M. Trotsky. Detroit: Gale Research, 1992. Brief biographical and professional information sections are followed by an interview covering Kingsolver's writing methods, the sources of some of her characters, the importance of her background, and some of her nonfiction writing.

_____. Interview by Robin Epstein. *Progressive* 60 (February, 1996): 33-38. In this informative interview, Kingsolver states her belief that most readers do not think her writing is overly political and notes that she feels that she has a responsibility to discuss her beliefs with the public.

_____. Interview by Lisa See Kendall. *Publishers Weekly* 237 (August 31,

1990): 46-47. Kingsolver discusses her early literary influences and her research and writing methods.

Marshall, John. "Fast Ride on *Pigs*." Review of *Pigs in Heaven*, by Barbara Kingsolver. *Seattle Post-Gazette*, 26 July 1993: 1. Presents an overview of Kingsolver's writing.

Pence, Amy. "Barbara Kingsolver." *Poets and Writers* 21, no. 4 (July/August, 1993): 14-21. Discusses Kingsolver's writing and her commitments to political activism and family.

Ryan, Maureen. "Barbara Kingsolver's Lowfat Fiction." *Journal of American Culture* 18, no. 4 (Winter, 1995): 77-123. Ryan compares Kingsolver's first three novels and first short-story collection.

Wagner-Martin, Linda. *Barbara Kingsolver's "The Poisonwood Bible": A Reader's Guide*. New York: Continuum, 2001. An in-depth guide to Kingsolver's most popular novel.

the PARIS
REVIEW

The *Paris Review* Perspective

Katherine Ryder for *The Paris Review*

Barbara Kingsolver writes with an abiding sense of responsibility. She calls herself a political writer; to be anything less would be an abdication of duty. Her fiction and nonfiction, ranging from an early journalistic account of female mine workers in Arizona to an erotic novel set during an Appalachian summer, are united by her rage against economic and social injustice, the inequality that marks the relationship between colonizer and colonized, men and women, rich and poor.

Those who criticize Kingsolver—and she's had quite a few critics—are clearly uncomfortable with this novelist who fancies herself a pundit. Her response to the American invasion of Afghanistan, an op-ed for the *Los Angeles Times* called "No Glory in Unjust War on the Weak," provoked strong rebukes from publications ranging from *The New Republic* to *The Wall Street Journal*. Yet a careful reading of her work reveals a carefully nuanced thinker. Her novels, her essays, and her journalism are all ultimately narratives driven by character, not dogma. The mostly marginalized, working-class women who populate her books—like Codi Noline in *Animal Dreams* and Deanna Wolfe in *Prodigal Summer*—are far from mere archetypes; they are struggling with the complexities of family and love relationships, historical circumstances, and the stifling environments in which they live.

Kingsolver was trained as a biologist, and for all of her impassioned prose, some of the scientist's sense of detached fascination with the natural world survives in her work. Whether it's the Congo, Arizona, or her native Appalachia, her characters have to share the world with a menagerie of other species. Nature is constant and inescapable, and it always has the upper hand. Even her personal memoir, *Animal, Vegetable, Miracle*, about the year her family spent eating primarily food grown on their Virginia farm, dwells as long on the natural wonder of a ripening tomato as on the concerns of the farm's inhabitants (and convincing her family to live so basically was a formidable challenge).

Her works are haunted by the memories of the places where she grew up—by Kentucky and the Congo especially. The latter provided the setting for *The Poisonwood Bible*; the book is built upon Kingsolver's deft ability to place the reader in that striking landscape. Told from the varying perspectives of a mother and her four daughters, the novel follows an American missionary family as they confront the bitter consequences of the colonial legacy in Africa. As in much of the author's work, no two perspectives are ever identical; each is a call and response of repeated language and overlapping themes. And again, the political becomes the personal, as Kingsolver attacks the legacy of Western involvement in Africa while building a home for the characters in the reader's mind. We are all innocent, we are all guilty, nobody has clean hands—that is Kingsolver's world. "We are all beasts in this Kingdom" as she puts it in *Small Wonder*, her book of essays published in response to the attacks on the World Trade Center. But her vision is not bleak; Kingsolver remains stubbornly optimistic, although it is an optimism born of resilience rather than romanticism.

In "What Good Is a Story?" an essay in *Small Wonder*, she writes that in her work she is trying to "carve something hugely important into a small enough amulet to fit inside a reader's most sacred psychic pocket." That her writing can be both a precious object and a politically relevant broadside is a tribute to Kingsolver; that it remains perennially popular is a tribute, in a way, to us.

Bibliography

Faludi, Susan. *The Terror Dream*. New York: Macmillan, 2007.

Kingsolver, Barbara. *Animal Dreams*. New York: HarperCollins, 1990.

_____. *Animal, Vegetable, Miracle: A Year of Food Life*. New York: HarperCollins, 2007.

_____. *Holding the Line: Women in the Great Arizona Mine Strike of 1983*. Ithaca, NY: ILR Press, 1989.

_____. *The Poisonwood Bible*. New York: HarperCollins, 1998.

_____. *Prodigal Summer*. New York: Perennial, 2000.

_____. *Small Wonder: Essays*. New York: Perennial, 2002.

CRITICAL CONTEXTS

The Political Is Personal:
Sociocultural Realities and the
Writings of Barbara Kingsolver_____

John Nizalowski

Barbara Kingsolver's work is not merely shaped by its author's convictions; more specifically, argues John Nizalowski, this author embraces her politics proudly. This essay traces the origins of Kingsolver's political convictions to her childhood, her parents' home, her college years, and her lived experiences in the American Southwest. Drawing an arc backward to the politically engaged writing that marked the 1930s in the United States, Nizalowski sees Kingsolver as much in the tradition of John Steinbeck as in that of Frank Waters or Edward Abbey.   — T.A.

Barbara Kingsolver is a political author, and, unlike many American writers who emerged during the 1980s, she proudly embraces the label. As she said in a 1993 interview with Donna Perry:

I'm only going to write a book if it's addressing subjects I care about. Otherwise, why write a book? It's not worth the time, and it's not worth the readers' time, and it's not worth burdening the world with another pile of pages. It surprises me constantly that almost everybody else in the United States of America who writes books hates to be called a political writer. As if that demeans them. (154)

Throughout the two decades of Kingsolver's literary career, she has followed this calling to be the progressive social conscience of her times, and her political interests are largely rooted in her personal experiences. Therefore, such thematic concerns as environmentalism, class structure, race, feminism, labor rights, immigrant rights, American Indian rights, U.S. foreign policy, postcolonialism, organic agriculture, and ecological diversity all arise from a life lived in the pursuit of wisdom, social justice, and creative fire.

In the 1930s, Kingsolver's political focus would have been well within the literary mainstream. With the Great Depression, American authors, faced with the nation's stark economic conditions, turned from "art for art's sake" to social realism—literature steeped in the political issues of the day. John Dos Passos's *U.S.A.* trilogy (1930-36), Josephine Herbst's *The Executioner Waits* (1934), John Steinbeck's *Grapes of Wrath* (1939), and other works of the day unrelentingly portrayed the failings of capitalism. As explained by David P. Peeler, "Depression fiction was more concerned with economic forces and social action than with the individual psyche, with the collectivity as opposed to the individual, and with the poor rather than with the middle or upper classes" (153), a description that nicely fits Kingsolver's books, despite their being written half a century or more later.

However, after World War II, politically motivated fiction waned in the United States. Peeler notes that once the Depression passed, so did the anticapitalist vision of American writers: "By the 1950's, those prospects of losing the self in a community became less appealing. It increasingly seemed that, rather than adding a vital dimension to life, groups actually detracted from it" (282). In *The Dream of Golden Mountains*, Malcolm Cowley explains that after the dream of an American communistic utopia died, what remained was "a widely pervading mood . . . of suspicion, acrimony, and accusation, a foreshadowing of the McCarthy era" (314). In an interview with Robin Epstein of *The Progressive*, when asked what had caused the separation of art and politics in the United States, Kingsolver also raised the specter of Senator McCarthy's anticommunist witch hunts of the 1950s: "I don't know whether it was because of McCarthyism, or whether there was some evil humus in this country from which sprang Joseph McCarthy and people who supported him and this idea that art and politics should separate themselves" (35).

However, in the mid-1960s, a distant conflict in Asia would transform the American political landscape. On August 7, 1964, the Tonkin Gulf Resolution gave President Lyndon Johnson the power to send combat troops into Vietnam. By 1967, tens of thousands of U.S. troops were committed, casualties soared, and the antiwar movement was in full swing (Gosse 88-94). In response, many American writers turned leftward and once again embraced political subjects with books like Norman Mailer's *Miami and the Siege of Chicago* (1969) and Kay Boyle's *The Long Walk at San Francisco State* (1970). Alongside the antiwar movement, the earlier civil rights movement gained momentum, and the counterculture flourished. By 1970 the feminist and environmentalist movements had also emerged. All these movements would shape the early political consciousness of Barbara Kingsolver.

Born on April 8, 1955, Kingsolver would come of age in a nation undergoing profound transformations. She grew up in the small town of Carlisle, Kentucky, a locale that would shape her social-political views in a number of ways (Snodgrass 7). First, there was the example of her father, Wendell Kingsolver. As a physician, Dr. Kingsolver could have developed a financially remunerative practice in a city. Instead, he chose to work in a poor rural county, at times accepting vegetables instead of cash from his patients (Snodgrass 8). Barbara Kingsolver would later state that her father showed her to do "what you think is right regardless of whether or not that's financially or otherwise regarded" (quoted in DeMarr 2). Also, when Barbara was eight, her father, in order to offer his services as a doctor to a new African nation, took the Kingsolver family to the Congo. Living without electricity or running water on a continent where she was in the minority revealed to Kingsolver the inherent tensions and contradictions in American privilege and international relationships (Snodgrass 9).

Kingsolver did not, however, need to go to Africa to learn the bitter lessons of class structure and racism. Her home country provided many examples of the damages caused by these social ills. As she explained in her interview in *The Progressive*, her town was racially segregated, as was her school until the second grade. It also had a sharply divided class structure: "I never read Marx until I was about eighteen, but the first time I read *Grundrisse* and *Capital* I said, 'I know this stuff. I grew up with this stuff'" (34).

Not all of Kentucky's lessons were about social divisions and repression. There was the landscape's beauty to inspire Kingsolver, planting the seeds of her environmentalism. Southern Appalachia in the 1960s remained largely undeveloped, and Nicholas County was given over primarily to farming and woodlots. The power of Kingsolver's childhood landscape comes through in this passage describing Zebulon Mountain, a fictional version of Virginia's Walker Mountain, from her novel *Prodigal Summer*:

> Now it was only the damp earth that blossomed in fits and throes: trout lilies, spring beauties, all the understory wildflowers that had to hurry through a whole life cycle between May's first warmth—while sunlight still reached through the bare limbs—and the darkness of a June forest floor. . . . In a few more weeks the trees would finish leafing out here, the canopy would close, and this bloom would pass on. Spring would move higher up to awaken the bears and finally go out like a flame, absorbed into the dark spruce forest on the scalp of Zebulon Mountain. (8-9)

While Kentucky brought about her ecological awakening, the region did not help to bring out her latent feminism. In "Letter to My Mother," Kingsolver describes how at the age of thirteen she asked her mother, "Name one good thing about being a woman." Her mother hesitated before answering, "The love of a man." Because of the hesitation, Kingsolver knew she "didn't have to believe it" (*Small Wonder* 164). This was 1968, the women's movement was in its earliest stages, and the National Organization for Women had just formed (MacLean 14). It is highly unlikely that a thirteen-year-old living in rural Kentucky was aware of the feminist movement just reaching the national political stage, yet, with her teenage challenge to traditional feminine roles, Kingsolver was already becoming aware that there could be alternatives to that role.

Later, in her high school library, Kingsolver discovered Doris Lessing's *Martha Quest* (1952), and her nascent feminism deepened. As she explained in an interview with Donna Perry, "I loved the fact that [Lessing] was writing about something real and important—the frustration of women who had absolutely no choices in their lives but to marry these hideous men who treated them badly" (150). However, it was not until college that Kingsolver "read everything of Lessing's," along with feminist authors such as Germaine Greer, Robin Morgan, and Gloria Steinem.

Kingsolver embraced more than feminism at DePauw, a liberal arts college in Greencastle, Indiana. It was 1973, and the student movements formed in the 1960s were still going strong. Kingsolver marched against the war in Vietnam, worked to better the conditions for Indiana's Spanish-speaking farm laborers, and joined a women's group (Wagner-Martin 33-34). In a creative-writing class she began work on a short story about a Cherokee woman that would eventually become "Homeland," thereby establishing her interest in American Indian issues (Wagner-Martin 36). She even changed her major from music to biology, a field of study she would later call her "religion" (Interview, Perry 147).

The following year, Kingsolver ventured to Greece to study at the Hellenic-American Union in Athens; she spent her weekends hitching around the Aegean. She found in Europe a congenial culture. By the mid-1970s, European nations had largely embraced democratic socialism, with its universal health care, comprehensive unemployment coverage, generous maternity leave, and educational benefits. For Kingsolver, these aspects, along with Europe's deep appreciation for the arts, made the Continent a near utopia, healing many of the societal ills produced by the individualistic capitalism of the United States (Kingsolver, *High Tide* 109).

In 1979, after nearly a year in France and a brief stay in Kentucky,

Kingsolver left for Tucson (Wagner-Martin 39). For nearly a century, the American Southwest has attracted artists and utopians of all stripes with its magnificent desert landscape and American Indian and Spanish cultures. In the 1970s the region still held its romantic appeal, and cities such as Tucson, Flagstaff, Santa Fe, and Taos swelled with the ranks of youth still following the previous decade's countercultural ideals. Kingsolver certainly fit this mold, and she settled happily in southern Arizona, becoming a science writer for the Office of Arid Lands Studies and a freelance journalist (Wagner-Martin 47). Everything about southern Arizona appealed to her. At first she lived in the Spanish barrio, and there the lessons she had learned in Kentucky and Indiana about poverty, class, and race deepened. Also, the desert granted her a new ecological system to understand and strive to protect, furthering her environmental consciousness (Wagner-Martin 42).

Political movements new to Kingsolver awaited her in Tucson as well. American backed right-wing terror in Central America, with roots stretching back to Theodore Roosevelt's presidency and beyond, soared with the election of Ronald Reagan in 1980 (Grandin 427-28). The response in Tucson was the birth of the Sanctuary Movement, a loose confederation of churches and progressive groups that sheltered Central American political refugees. Since the Reagan government supported the state-sponsored sectarian bloodshed taking place in such countries as El Salvador and Nicaragua, these refugees could not claim political exile status and were therefore in the United States illegally (Bau 10). Kingsolver became an active member of the Sanctuary Movement, its political activism reviving the feelings from her early protest days at DePauw. In 1979 she became an organizer for the Tucson Committee for Human Rights in Latin America, which was affiliated with the national Committee in Solidarity with the People of El Salvador (Wagner-Martin 43). These groups, formed to protest American involvement with Central American dictators during the Carter administration, joined the Sanctuary Movement during the early 1980s.

Another aspect of Kingsolver's political worldview developed through her freelance reporting on the 1983 strike at the Phelps Dodge Mining Company's Morenci copper mine in southeastern Arizona. The strike began on July 1, 1983, when workers refused management's demands to give up cost-of-living raises and accept reduced medical benefits (Wagner-Martin 53). It was a bad time for labor. Since the early 1970s, the power of unions had declined owing to a decrease in industrial jobs and falling wages. Fearful of an uncertain job market, workers were beginning to back away from unions, and an abundance of nonunion labor and management's threats of relocating to other countries caused union workers to hesitate before calling a strike. This trend climaxed when President Reagan fired eleven thousand striking air traffic controllers in 1981. The federal government was leading the way in breaking strikes, and employers took full advantage of the growing antilabor mood. The 1983 Phelps Dodge strike was the next key battle against union power (Freeman 203).

When the strike began, Phelps Dodge wasted no time finding fourteen hundred replacement workers who would cross picket lines. Within weeks, nonunion workers charged that union members had committed acts of violence, and Arizona governor Bruce Babbitt sent in seven hundred National Guard troops and state troopers. What followed was an eighteen-month stalemate between the union and mine management (Wagner-Martin 54-55). As Kingsolver explains in *Holding the Line*, her book on the Phelps Dodge strike, "It's impossible to point to a single day on the calendar and declare, 'This is when the copper strike ended'" (191), but by December 31, 1984, as strikers held one of their last rallies, it was clear that between the likely decertification of the union by the National Labor Relations Board and the wholesale shutting down of the Arizona mines by Phelps Dodge, the union had lost (173-74).

Despite the strike's failure, Kingsolver took a hopeful narrative from the experience. One of the unique aspects of the Phelps Dodge strike was that primarily women occupied the picket lines, because the men were either involved in the negotiations with Phelps Dodge management, and thereby barred by law from being on the picket lines, or were finding part-time jobs to supplement the inadequate forty-dollar-per-week strike pay (Kingsolver, *Holding* xv). For Kingsolver, therefore, the strike was proof that women, through their organized strength, could challenge society's traditional gender roles, elevate their own political consciousness, and achieve social-cultural change.

Long after, in the introduction to the 1996 reprinting of *Holding the Line*, Kingsolver described the strike as "a watershed event for me because it taught me to pay attention: to know the place where I lived" (xiv). The strike was certainly a literary watershed as well, becoming a major inspiration for her Arizona novels, especially *Animal Dreams*. Also, her coverage of the strike for *The Progressive* magazine resulted in her first national publication.

One more facet needed to come into place before Kingsolver's Arizona-era political matrix was complete: the experience of motherhood and alternative family structures. In 1985, Barbara Kingsolver married Joseph Hoffmann, a professor of chemistry at the University of Arizona, and a year later she was pregnant with her first child, Camille. As all the pieces of her creative world coalesced, her first novel, *The Bean Trees* (1988), emerged (Snodgrass 15). In "Letter to My Mother," Kingsolver describes giving her mother the manuscript of *The Bean Trees*, declaring that in it, "I've explained everything I believe in, exactly the way I always wanted to: human rights, Central American refugees, the Problem That Has No Name, abuse of the powerless, racism, poetry, freedom, childhood, motherhood, Sisterhood Is Powerful" (*Small Wonder* 170). The novel tells the story of Taylor Greer as she adopts a Cherokee girl, Turtle, who has been sexually and physically abused.

With this rich fictive template, Kingsolver realized her political voice, referencing at last the sociocultural narratives of her life's arc. Mary Jean DeMarr views *The Bean Trees* as a feminist bildungsroman about a woman learning to be empowered and independent (66).

Catherine Himmelwright finds in *The Bean Trees* a unifying of the standard male narrative of the adventure west with the classic female narrative of creating a home. "By combining these two figures," Himmelwright states, "Kingsolver fashions a new American mythology that unites both male and female imaginative constructions" (120). Himmelwright also notes that Turtle's Cherokee identity "evokes the forced removal of . . . the Cherokee, along the Trail of Tears (1813-1855). Allusions to this historical event intensify Kingsolver's questioning of an American mythology of conquest and control" (127).

On the day she returned from the hospital with her newborn daughter, Kingsolver signed the contract with HarperCollins for the publication of *The Bean Trees* (Wagner-Martin 65). Now that she was a published author, she set out to finish her book-length account of the Phelps Dodge strike, and, on the advice of her agent, a collection of short stories. Both books were published in 1989. Of the two, Kingsolver completed the strike narrative first. She shaped *Holding the Line* from the narratives of key women involved in the Phelps Dodge strike, and it is through their eyes that the reader encounters important events, such as the arrival of the nonunion labor force, the state troopers' intimidation of union members, and the indifference by the National Guard to the suffering of workers caused by the October 1983 flood of the San Francisco River. The short-story collection *Homeland, and Other Stories* continues Kingsolver's exploration of many of the social-political themes found in *The Bean Trees* and *Holding the Line*, including the displacement of the Cherokee in "Homeland," child abuse in "Extinctions," feminism and contemporary family realities in "Quality Time," and labor issues in "Why I Am a Danger to the Public."

With *Holding the Line* and *Homeland* completed, Kingsolver plunged into *Animal Dreams* (1990), her second novel. In an interview with L. Elisabeth Beattie, Kingsolver revealed that *Animal Dreams* began with a question:

Why is it that some people are activists who embrace the world and its problems and feel not only [that] they can, but that they must, do something about the world and its problems, while other people turn their back on that same world and pretend it has no bearing on their lives? Why is it, moreover, that these two kinds of people can occur in the same family? (164)

Animal Dreams covers familiar Kingsolver territory, including U.S. government policy in Central America, feminism, environmentalism, class structure, and race issues. The novel begins when Codi Noline leaves Tucson and returns to her hometown of Grace, a remote mountain village in Arizona, to teach high school biology and tend her father, Doc Homer Noline, who is suffering from Alzheimer's disease. Meanwhile, Hallie, Codi's sister, heads for socialist Nicaragua, where government forces are fighting a bloody civil war with the American-backed right-wing Contras. In Nicaragua, Hallie plans to work in the cotton fields of Chinandega, but Contra forces kidnap and murder her soon after she arrives.

In Grace, Codi begins a relationship with Loyd Peregrina, a Pueblo Indian who was her high school lover. Loyd takes Codi on journeys to Pueblo Indian ruins and to his home village of Santa Rosalia Pueblo. These encounters with the Pueblo world reveal to Codi an alternative view of the universe and humanity's place in it, in the same way that the matriarchal structure of the Hispanic community opens her to a family structure different from the individualistic, patriarchal mainstream American one. The novel's ecological crisis arises when Codi's biology class cannot find microbes in the town's river water because of upstream toxic discharges from the Black Mountain Mining Company.

Commenting on the novel's environmental theme, Patti Capel Swartz writes, "In *Animal Dreams* . . . making connections between cultures and connections with the earth is a part of political commitment: a political commitment that calls for civil disobedience if the prevailing governmental or industrial policies and laws are unjust" (66). Linda Wagner-Martin emphasizes the spiritual implications of this concept, which derives from the Pueblo Indian vision articulated in the novel by Loyd Peregrina: "Leavened with the heart-stopping beauty of the deer dance, of the millennia-old pueblos, of the unpoisoned natural farms, the discourse between the meaninglessly intellectual Codi and the wise, yet proud, Loyd draws the reader further and further into the distinction, which the novel shows to be arbitrary, between human and animal" (82).

Kingsolver's next book was her poetry collection *Another America/ Otra America* (1992). The bilingual poems in this book, English and Spanish, cover much of the same political ground as the rest of her Arizona works. In an interview with Donna Perry, Kingsolver explained that the title refers to the Spanish-speaking part of the Americas, which "starts at the Mexican border and goes south," as well as to the poor in the United States, who so seldom get a voice in the national discourse (162). However, since many of the poems are about Kingsolver's experiences, the collection takes on a more personal weight. For instance, she includes "This House I Cannot Leave" and "Ten Forty-Four," poems examining the rape she suffered as a student at DePauw. "Deadline" describes an antiwar vigil in which Kingsolver participated the night before the start of the Gulf War, the 1991 conflict that pitted the United States against Iraq over Iraq's occupation of Kuwait.

Kingsolver's opposition to the Gulf War, and her reaction to the waves of unconstrained patriotism it inspired, are subjects more thoroughly examined in *High Tide in Tucson* (1995), her first book of essays. In "Paradise Lost," she explains that she left the United States for the Canary Islands in response to the Gulf War and the noxious patriotism it unleashed: "It was 1991, and in the U.S., a clamor of war worship had sprung like a vitriolic genie from the riveted bottles we launched on Baghdad" (108). The essay "Jabberwocky" also begins with a critical examination of the Gulf War, then goes on to discuss the pressures in American culture to conform to blind patriotism while writers feel they must avoid politics, a form of censorship. Many of the essays in *High Tide in Tucson* clarify the political stances Kingsolver takes in her novels through the direct expression of her political beliefs without the disguise of fictional characters or invented plots. As she stated in her interview with Robin Epstein in *The Progressive:* "Everything in *High Tide in Tucson* I think I've said before behind the mask of fiction, but this time I stepped out from behind the mask and said, 'I, Barbara Kingsolver, believe this'" (36).

Before *High Tide in Tucson*, Kingsolver wrote one more novel with an Arizona setting. *Pigs in Heaven*, which appeared in 1993, the same year in which she was divorced from Joseph Hoffmann, is the sequel to *The Bean Trees*. While its political territory is quite similar to the earlier novel, Kingsolver adds a new element. As she explained in an interview with L. Elisabeth Beattie, after writing *The Bean Trees*, Kingsolver witnessed a custody case in Tucson involving an American Indian child adopted by Anglo parents. This case brought to her attention the Indian Child Welfare Act. Passed in 1978, it provides for the right of an Indian tribe to keep its children. A tribe even has the legal ability to retrieve children who have already been adopted by non-Indians. The dynamic between two opposing viewpoints intrigued Kingsolver. Mainstream American culture, with its individualism, sides with the mother, claiming that the best interests of a child lie with his or her adoptive parents. From the tribe's standpoint, "the fundamental good is what's good for the community." Fascinated by this conflict, Kingsolver realized she had a ready-made story in Taylor's adoption of Turtle to explore the impact of the Indian Child Welfare Act (170).

In *Pigs in Heaven*, Turtle appears on *The Oprah Winfrey Show* because she saved a man's life at Hoover Dam. Annawake Fourkiller, a Cherokee lawyer, sees the segment and realizes that Turtle is a member of her tribe. When she tracks down Taylor in Tucson and challenges her right to keep Turtle, Taylor grabs Turtle and flees to Seattle, where the two struggle in poverty. In the end, encouraged by her mother, Alice Greer, who has entered into a relationship with Turtle's grandfather, Johnny Cash Stillwater, Taylor realizes she should approach Fourkiller and work out what is best for Turtle. An agreement emerges that gives Taylor custody during the school year and Cash and Alice custody during the summer.

A number of critics have attacked *Pigs in Heaven* as unrealistic and unconsciously racist. Maureen Ryan writes: "The problem with Barbara Kingsolver's fiction is that the big subjects, the looming dangers, are always dismissed. Everyone in her books turns out inherently good and well-meaning; the men sensitive and sexy, the women intrepid and resilient (and *always* perfect mothers)" (81). Melissa Schoeffel proposes that linguistic clues in *Pigs in Heaven* indicate that Kingsolver possesses an unintended but discernible favoring of individualistic, Euro-American motherhood over the collective, Cherokee vision of family (34-35). And Kathleen Godfrey criticizes the author of *Pigs in Heaven* for her idealized, stereotyped Indians: "By creating an idealized image of Cherokee community, an image with little crime, selfishness, or negative circumstances (beyond poverty), Kingsolver runs the risk of promoting misunderstanding of Native people who do not fit the stereotype" (269).

Still, other critics have answered these charges by championing Kingsolver's political vision as enlightened and nuanced. Most notably, Magali Cornier Michael defends *Pigs in Heaven* as presenting a fresh, progressive vision for human society that justifies its lapses in realism: "I would argue that formulating positive alternatives to dominant conceptions *requires* a leap into the realm of utopia. Blaming the novel for not being 'realistic' enough ignores the potential of utopia to offer alternatives that move significantly beyond the already known and already experienced" (108).

In terms of political vision, Kingsolver's next novel, *The Poisonwood Bible* (1998), is the most sophisticated in her oeuvre. With *The Poisonwood Bible*, Kingsolver returned to her childhood sojourn in Africa as a source for her fiction. When Kingsolver was in the Congo in 1963, the country had recently undergone a horrific upheaval as a consequence of Western interference in the newly independent nation.

After decades of struggle, the Congo attained its independence from Belgium on June 30, 1960. Elections brought Patrice Lumumba to power. Lumumba, a charismatic leader, was a hero of the Congolese people (Haskin 20-21). He had communist leanings and turned to the Soviet Union for help when the Belgian-trained army, the Force Publique, rebelled (Haskin 23-24). President Eisenhower, fearing a strong Soviet presence in the heart of Africa, gave the CIA permission to assassinate Lumumba. Before the assassination could take place, however, Joseph Mobutu, the chief of staff of the Force Publique, declared military rule. The U.S. government, delighted at the elimination of a communist threat, gave Mobutu one million dollars in aid (Haskin 26-27). Later, Mobutu would help engineer Lumumba's execution (Haskin 29).

Over the next five years, which included the time Kingsolver spent in the Congo, power shifted back and forth. Finally, on November 24, 1965, Mobuto seized the country once and for all, and his brutal dictatorship would last until 1997, when he finally died in exile (Haskin 81). During this time, he received two billion dollars in assistance from the American government, with an additional twenty-five million dollars for his personal use (Haskin 48-49). This history forms the backdrop to *The Poisonwood Bible*.

The novel's main characters are Nathan Price, a conservative Christian missionary from Georgia, his wife, Orleanna, and his four daughters, Rachel, Leah, Adah, and Ruth May. The story of Price's tyranny over his family and his failed, misguided mission to bring Christian American culture to the Congo becomes an extended metaphor for the immorality of American intervention in the region, the disaster of Mobuto's rule, and the tragic consequences of conservative, patriarchal Christianity. Susan Strehle illuminates the novel's political and historical depths as well as its complex, allegorical method:

> The novel focuses . . . on the reproduction of an exceptionalist national ideology in the American home, together with the passivity that enables it.

Through allegory, the novel narrates the logic that sustains an imperialist mission to impose American doctrine on other lands; it also dramatizes the patriarchal mission to create a network of support by disciplining young Americans as quiescent domestic subjects. (415)

In her fifth novel, *Prodigal Summer* (2000), Kingsolver returns to the familiar themes of love, human interconnection, and our relationship to the earth. A number of significant differences exist, however, between this pastoral novel and her Arizona novels. First, this one is set in southern Appalachia. Changes in Kingsolver's life partly explain this shift in setting. In 1994, Kingsolver married her second husband, Steven Hopp, an ornithologist from southwestern Virginia. The new family began using Hopp's ancestral home near Walker Mountain, on the Virginia-Kentucky line, as their summer residence. This return to the Appalachia of her youth—as well as her increased interest in agricultural issues, organic farming, and biodiversity—all led up to *Prodigal Summer*, a novel about three relationships. The first concerns Deanna Wolfe, a ranger in the Zebulon National Forest, and Eddie Bondo, a hunter. The second, a marriage, is between Lusa Maluf Landowski, a young researcher of moths and butterflies, and Cole Widener, an Appalachian farmer. The third centers on Garnett Walker, a farmer fond of pesticides and chemical fertilizers who is attempting to bring back the blight-destroyed American chestnut tree, and his neighbor, Nannie Rawley, an advocate of organic farming.

Suzanne W. Jones notes that with *Prodigal Summer*, Kingsolver pulls together a lifetime of knowledge on botany, farming, and the environment:

In *Prodigal Summer* Kingsolver's academic training in evolutionary biology and ecology, her abiding concern for community and family, and her intimate knowledge of a particular place combine to produce no less than a blueprint for saving the small family farm and for restoring the ecological balance in a southern Appalachian bioregion that is struggling to survive. (84)

A year after the release of *Prodigal Summer*, on September 11, 2001, nineteen members of al-Qaeda, a radical Islamist movement, hijacked four American airliners and flew two of them into the World Trade Center towers in New York City. A third jet slammed into the Pentagon, and the fourth crashed in a Pennsylvania field. In a matter of hours, nearly three thousand Americans along with citizens of other countries had perished in the terrorist attacks. As Kingsolver explains in the foreword to *Small Wonder*, a newspaper asked her for a response to the tragic events. "Within a month I had published five different responses to different facets of a huge event in our nation's psychology— little pieces that helped me to see the thing whole and try to bear it" (xiv). These essays formed the core of *Small Wonder* (2002), which, along with *The Poisonwood Bible*, is the most overtly political of Kingsolver's books. It is also her most controversial, containing pieces that caused a firestorm of criticism.

Kingsolver's antiwar stance and criticism of American foreign policy, born in the anti-Vietnam War protests of her college days and honed during the 1991 Gulf War, had not diminished when the 9/11 attacks took place. Thus her responses were highly critical of the United States. In "Flying," she notes the many countries that the United States has bombed in the past half century and states, "It has *always* been happening to us—in Nicaragua, in the Sudan, in Hiroshima, that night in Baghdad—and now we finally know what it feels like" (188). In "And Our Flag Was Still There," she states, "When fear rules the day, many minds are weak enough to crack the world into nothing but 'me' and 'evildoers,' and as long as we're proudly killing unlike minds over there, they feel emboldened to do the same over here" (237). Finally, in "God's Wife's Measuring Spoons," she sums up the negative reactions from the press to her criticism of American foreign policy: "It seems a certain sector has been led to associate my name with treason and sedition" (250).

Kingsolver covers other subjects as well in *Small Wonder*. In "Life Is Precious, or It's Not" she responds to the 1999 Columbine High School shootings. "Household Words" portrays the tragedy of homelessness. "Seeing Scarlet" and "Setting Free the Crabs" examine the loss of wildlife habitat. "A Fist in the Eye of God" and "Lily's Chickens" discuss the dangers of genetically engineering agricultural seed stock and express support for organic farming and the growing local food movement.

Such essays provide a bridge to Kingsolver's next book. Published in 2007, *Animal, Vegetable, Miracle* covers a year during which the Kingsolver family lived on their Virginia farm and either produced their own food or bought what they ate locally from farmers they knew. The book's primary purpose is to champion the local foods movement, both as a pathway to a healthier diet and as a way to reduce human beings' global environmental impact.

Through her writings, Barbara Kingsolver has shown that creative work can be political in intention and content and still succeed as literature. She has also, through her work, demonstrated that there is a strong connection between everyday life and the social-political sphere. While Kingsolver has rightfully pointed out that American literary writers and critics tend to disdain creative texts with overt political themes, this tendency is less pronounced in the Southwest. Frank Waters and Edward Abbey, Kingsolver's Tucson neighbors in the 1980s, blazed a trail of socially concerned writing with novels such as *The Man Who Killed the Deer* (1942) and *The Brave Cowboy* (1956). Both authors have literary prizes named in their honor, and it is no surprise that Barbara Kingsolver has won them both. Closer to Kingsolver's generation, the American Southwest has produced a legion of writers who embrace political content, including N. Scott Momaday, Rudolfo Anaya, John Nichols, Leslie Marmon Silko, Linda Hogan, Jimmy Santiago Baca, and Terry Tempest Williams. All of them, like Kingsolver, write not only to relate good stories and express their love for the Southwest's landscapes and peoples but also to further their hope that the world can be made better through powerful, artistically rendered words. This is a hope that Kingsolver's Depression-era forbears would have warmly embraced.

Works Cited

Bau, Ignatius. *This Ground Is Holy: Church Sanctuary and Central American Refugees*. New York: Paulist Press, 1985.

Cowley, Malcolm. *The Dream of Golden Mountains*. New York: Penguin Books, 1981.

DeMarr, Mary Jean. *Barbara Kingsolver: A Critical Companion*. Westport, CT: Greenwood Press, 1999.

Freeman, Joshua B. "Labor During the American Century: Work, Workers, and Unions." *A Companion to Post-1945 America*. Ed. Jean-Christophe Agnew and Roy Rosenzweig. Malden, MA: Blackwell, 2002. 192-210.

Godfrey, Kathleen. "Barbara Kingsolver's Cherokee Nation: Problems of Representation in *Pigs in Heaven*." *Western American Literature* 36.3 (2001): 259-77.

Gosse, Van. *Rethinking the New Left: An Interpretive History*. New York: Palgrave Macmillan, 2005.

Grandin, Greg. "Off the Beach: The United States, Latin America, and the Cold War." *A Companion to Post-1945 America*. Ed. Jean-Christophe Agnew and Roy Rosenzweig. Malden, MA: Blackwell, 2002. 426-45.

Haskin, Jeanne M. *The Tragic State of the Congo: From Decolonization to Dictatorship*. New York: Algora, 2005.

Himmelwright, Catherine. "Gardens of Auto Parts: Kingsolver's Merger of American Western Myth and Native American Myth in *The Bean Trees*." *Southern Literary Journal* 39.2 (2007): 119-39.

Jones, Suzanne W. "The Southern Family Farm as Endangered Species: Possibilities for Survival in Barbara Kingsolver's *Prodigal Summer*." *Southern Literary Journal* 39.1 (2006): 83-97.

Kingsolver, Barbara. *The Bean Trees*. New York: HarperPerennial, 1988.

_____. *High Tide in Tucson: Essays from Now or Never*. New York: HarperCollins, 1995.

_____. *Holding the Line: Women in the Great Arizona Mine Strike of 1983*. 1989. Ithaca, NY: Cornell UP, 1996.

_____. Interview. *Backtalk: Women Writers Speak Out*. Ed. Donna Perry. New Brunswick, NJ: Rutgers UP, 1993. 143-69.

_____. Interview. *Conversations with Kentucky Writers*. Ed. L. Elisabeth Beattie. Lexington: UP of Kentucky, 1996.

_____. "An Interview with Barbara Kingsolver" by Robin Epstein. *The Progressive* 60.2 (1996): 33-38.

_____. *Prodigal Summer*. New York: HarperCollins, 2000.

_____. *Small Wonder*. New York: HarperCollins, 2002.

MacLean, Nancy. *The American Women's Movement, 1945-2000: A Brief History with Documents*. Boston: Bedford/St. Martin's Press, 2009.

Michael, Magali Cornier. *New Visions of Community in Contemporary American Fiction: Tan, Kingsolver, Castillo, Morrison*. Iowa City: Iowa UP, 2006.

Peeler, David P. *Hope Amongst Us Yet: Social Criticism and Social Solace in Depression America*. Athens: U of Georgia P, 1987.

Ryan, Maureen. "Barbara Kingsolver's Lowfat Fiction." *Journal of American Culture* 18.4 (1995): 77-82.

Schoeffel, Melissa. *Maternal Conditions: Reading Kingsolver, Castillo, Erdrich, and Ozeki*. New York: Peter Lang, 2008.

Snodgrass, Mary Ellen. *Barbara Kingsolver: A Literary Companion*. Jefferson, NC: McFarland, 2004.

Strehle, Susan. "Chosen People: American Exceptionalism in Kingsolver's *The Poisonwood Bible*." *Critique* 49 (2008): 413-28.

Swartz, Patti Capel. "'Saving Grace': Political and Environmental Issues and the Role of Connections in Barbara Kingsolver's *Animal Dreams*." *ISLE* 1.1 (1993): 65-80.

Wagner-Martin, Linda. *Barbara Kingsolver*. Philadelphia: Chelsea House, 2004.

Barbara Kingsolver and the Critics_____

Rosemary M. Canfield Reisman

Beginning with an accounting of the laudatory reviews for King-solver's first novel, *The Bean Trees*, Rosemary M. Canfield Reisman tracks how the author's reputation grew incrementally with each of her published works. Reviews often set the tone for how a book was received. Critics did not always approve of the neat endings of King-solver's plots and occasionally detected what they considered to be too much unfounded optimism about human nature. After the publication of *The Poisonwood Bible,* Kingsolver's reputation was cemented, and her works became the subjects of entire critical studies. She has earned her celebrated status by developing her talents ever further with each novel and by continuing to produce texts of high quality that engage the reader in pertinent issues of social change.   — T.A.

When she was named a 2000 National Humanities Medalist, Barbara Kingsolver was commended for producing novels written to a high literary standard whose purpose is to bring about social change. The four novels thus described included her first published work, *The Bean Trees* (1988), *Animal Dreams* (1990), *Pigs in Heaven* (1993), and *The Poisonwood Bible* (1998) (Towler, Reichers, and Gerard 20-31).

While it is hardly surprising that Kingsolver's sense of purpose did not alter throughout the decade, or indeed that it has not changed since, it is somewhat unusual for a writer's first book to be praised so highly. In *The New York Times Book Review*, Jack Butler called *The Bean Trees* "an accomplished first novel," as "richly connected as a fine poem." Butler concluded his review by describing *The Bean Trees* as a "remarkable, enjoyable book, one that contains more good writing than most successful careers" (15). Other reviewers also admired Kingsolver's style, commenting that it is a unique combination of lyricism, particularly in the passages describing nature, and realism, given the novel's setting in the blue-collar world of poverty, seedy bars, and sudden violence and among frightened illegal aliens. As a Tucson, Arizona, teacher pointed out, neither the realistic setting nor the very real social problems Kingsolver mentions, such as child abuse, make *The Bean Trees* less captivating for his students. He characterized the novel as "engaging, heartwarming, poignant, surprising, and hopeful" (Mossman 85). *Ms.* and the *Women's Review of Books* praised Kingsolver, a feminist by conviction, for her skill in tracing the development of relationships between women and in dramatizing the ongoing struggles of women to survive. Several critics were troubled by what they saw as a tendency toward formula writing: the good characters—those who agree with the author's views—behave so impeccably that they seem less than human. Moreover, not far into the novel, it becomes obvious that it is proceeding toward a predetermined happy ending. Most reviewers, however, welcomed the upbeat tone of *The Bean Trees*.

During the early 1980s, while working as a freelance journalist, Kingsolver reported on a series of strikes against the Phelps Dodge Mining Company that ended in a victory for the company. After miners were banned from striking, the women in their families took over the picket lines. Among the audiotapes that Kingsolver had accumulated, those that most interested her were the ones showing the transformation of docile housewives into activists. In her first nonfiction book, *Holding the Line: Women in the Great Arizona Mine Strike of 1983* (1989), Kingsolver focuses on these changes among the women she interviewed, though she also deals with economic injustices in general and, more specifically, with the mistreatment of Mexican Americans. Although *Holding the Line* did not appeal to as wide an audience as did *The Bean Trees*, the book was applauded in such publications as the *Industrial and Labor Relations Review*, the *Labour History Review*, and *Contemporary Sociology*. Reviewers in these journals agreed that the scope of Kingsolver's study, her meticulous research, and the high quality of her writing make her work a valuable addition to the academic literature, a good supplementary text for students, and a book that should interest many members of the general public. *Holding the Line* prompted only a few negative comments. Marc W. Steinberg, writing in *Contemporary Sociology*, would have liked to see Kingsolver pay more attention to ethnic issues, particularly as the strike affected Mexicans and Native Americans (237). A reviewer in *Labor Studies Journal* agreed with Steinberg that the study was extremely valuable but felt that, by voicing her own anger with Phelps Dodge, Kingsolver had weakened the effect of the women's testimonies (Tischler 82-83). Again, it seems that the author's passion for a cause led her into what some saw as excesses that marred what would otherwise be an almost flawless artistic work.

In her review of Kingsolver's second published work of fiction, *Homeland, and Other Stories* (1989), Wendy Brandmark took issue with such criticisms. She argued that one of Kingsolver's virtues is that despite her empathy for characters caught in difficult situations, she "cannot forgive those who cramp the vitality of others, who watch with indifference the destruction of the earth's bounty." Brandmark concluded that "the power of these stories rests as much with their moral awareness, their righteousness, as it does with their charm and the ease of her story-telling" (22). Earlier, another *Times Literary Supplement* reviewer found the collection more carefully crafted than *The Bean Trees* but still uneven: the strongest stories, she insisted, are those in which the narrators are children, as in the title story, and the weakest are those narrated by "young, educated adults" (Neuhaus 956). However, Russell Banks called all of the stories "interesting" and most of them "extraordinarily fine." He expressed admiration for the author's "Chekhovian tenderness toward her characters," her sense of the comic where male foibles are concerned, and her unusual style, which "mixes argot with aphorism, sexual frankness with delicate high-mindedness" (16).

By the time *Animal Dreams* was published, Barbara Kingsolver was becoming acknowledged as one of the best new American regional writers. Her first two books of fiction were popular, and both *The Bean*

Trees and *Homeland* won awards from the American Library Association. However, her new novel was judged far superior to *The Bean Trees*. In an interview with Lisa See Kendall, Kingsolver herself suggested that the problem with *The Bean Trees* was that, like many first novels, it was essentially autobiographical: despite her best efforts, Kingsolver kept hearing her own voice in that of Taylor Greer, the heroine of the novel. Recognizing this problem, Kingsolver said, she experimented with various voices while she was working on the *Homeland* stories. As a result, by the time she began *Animal Dreams*, she could turn over the narration to her heroine, Codi Noline, who shares some of the author's attitudes but has her own distinct personality. What does not change in *Animal Dreams* is the thematic content. As Kendall points out, again Kingsolver feels compelled to draw the attention of her readers to unresolved family relationships, abuse of the environment, the exploitation of Native Americans, systematic injustice in the treatment of the labor force, and sinister American schemes in other countries, in this case support of the Contras in Nicaragua. Kingsolver admitted to the interviewer that at one point she feared she had so many themes that perhaps *Animal Dreams* should be five novels instead of one. However, upon consideration, she realized that all these issues are actually manifestations of a pervasive flaw in human nature: the failure to recognize that everyone is a part of the larger world. This epiphany made it possible for her to proceed with *Animal Dreams* and, indeed, to return to most of these themes in her subsequent publications (46-47).

However, reviewers again regretted that a novel they agreed was beautifully written was too predictable. As Carolyn Cooke commented, not only does virtue triumph at the end of *Animal Dreams* but also none of the major characters seems to suffer from moral uncertainty. Thus Codi's Native American lover does not hesitate to give up cockfighting simply because both Codi and his mother disapprove of it (653-54). This incident also reflects a pattern evident in all of Kingsolver's novels: it is not men but women who possess the moral compass, and it is not men but women, and very ordinary women at that, who effect re-forms. As Kendall points out, in *Animal Dreams* it is the women of the Stitch and Bitch Club who save the river that runs through their town from being contaminated by the poisonous by-products of the Black Mountain Mining Company (46-47).

Writing in *Time* magazine, Paul Gray argued that Kingsolver's con-sistent elevation of women as saviors of their communities and of the planet, usually through the "adoption of older, often Native American ways," is another instance of "eco-feminist fiction," a new subgenre developed in the 1980s by such writers as Ursula K. Le Guin, Lou-ise Erdrich, and Alice Walker. Gray described Kingsolver's *Animal Dreams* as an "entertaining distillation of eco-feminist materials." The novel has a "fragile landscape," a "doughty heroine," some wise and virtuous Native Americans, and, most important of all, a set of strong-willed matriarchs more than capable of taking on the white males who represent the mining company (87).

Gray agreed with earlier reviewers of Kingsolver's work that her heroines can be "preachy"; in fact, he stated that the novel has a "rather hectoring tone." However, he found that defect balanced by the au-thor's use of humor (87). *Animal Dreams* was popular with readers and critics alike. In addition to being a best seller, in 1991 the novel won the Pen/USA West Fiction Award and the Edward Abbey Ecofiction Award. It was also named the Arizona Library Association Book of the Year.

Kingsolver's first volume of poetry, *Another America/Otra America* (1992) was not as widely reviewed as her earlier works, and the few re-views that appeared were fairly perfunctory. Critics pointed out that Kingsolver's reason for including a Spanish translation of each poem was obviously her desire to make a political statement about social and political injustices in the Americas. However, though they found some of her poems impressive both in form and in content, reviewers agreed that Kingsolver is at her best when she is writing fiction.

Though Kingsolver's next novel, *Pigs in Heaven*, had a first printing of one hundred thousand copies and was chosen as a Book-of-the-Month Club alternate, some critics dismissed it as simply another of the author's "feel-good fables for the politically correct" (Young 9). There was no doubt that the book would sell well: as a sequel to *The Bean Trees*, *Pigs in Heaven* had a ready-made audience. Moreover, readers could expect the same folksy humor and the same types of admirable, strong-willed women that had pleased them in Kingsolver's earlier fiction. However, though even her most severe critics had to admit that Kingsolver "is vivid, animated and amusing," they could not forgive her for suggesting simplistic answers to complex problems or for depending on "idealistic feminist theory" instead of attempting to "illuminate human behavior," which Young calls the real task of literature (9). In *The New York Times*, Christopher Lehmann-Haupt was gentler in his criticism, admitting that Kingsolver is talented and praising her in particular for the empathy revealed in her treatment of her characters. Nevertheless, he found some of the passages of *Pigs in Heaven* unbearably "treacly," and he also faulted the book for its lack of tension and its predictability (C16).

By contrast, a *Library Journal* reviewer insisted that *Pigs in Heaven* surpasses *The Bean Trees* primarily because it demonstrates that family problems can be resolved only by love. Similarly, a *Publishers Weekly* critic commended Kingsolver for her emphasis on the importance of family ties and on the need for wisdom, insight, and compassion in dealing with others. In a *Newsweek* review, Laura Shapiro pointed out that in *Pigs in Heaven*, for the first time Kingsolver "challenges her own strong, 60's-style politics." Instead of applying the tenets of political correctness to every moral issue, as she had previously done, Kingsolver presents a complex situation in which neither side is wholly right or wholly wrong. Clearly the politically correct decision would be to turn over the Cherokee child to her own people. However, Kingsolver understands that the consequences of breaking a bond between a child and a mother, or the person she has come to regard as her mother, can be devastating. Shapiro was not particularly happy with

Kingsolver's use of coincidence to work out a solution to the problem, but she was impressed by the fact that in the course of the novel what begins as a confrontation ends with compromise and understanding. Appropriately, Shapiro's review was titled "A Novel Full of Miracles" (61).

Karen Karbo, too, saw *Pigs in Heaven* as a marked improvement on Kingsolver's earlier books. Having expected the novel to turn into a "morality play," in which Turtle's fate is based on the principles of political correctness, Karbo was surprised to find it a "resounding achievement" in which the author "somehow manages to maintain her political views without sacrificing the complexity of her characters' predicaments." Karbo agreed with Shapiro that the denouement, while a bit far-fetched, does not in any way mar the book. The only flaw she saw in *Pigs in Heaven* is that the author fails to pass moral judgment on the relatives, themselves Cherokee, who are indifferent to Turtle's plight. Karbo praised Kingsolver for her narrative gift and for her skill in blending "a fierce and abiding moral vision with benevolent, concise humor" (9). A Canadian reviewer agreed; as she put it, by refusing to brand either side as "wrong," Kingsolver ends up with a "charming positivism" that is unusual in present-day fiction (Daurio C16).

With the publication of her first fictional work, Barbara Kingsolver had won both the hearts of the reading public and the respect of the critics, and over the six years that followed, she retained the attention of both groups. One of the first attempts to account for Kingsolver's appeal is an essay by Maureen Ryan titled "Barbara Kingsolver's Lowfat Fiction," which appeared in 1995 in the *Journal of American Culture*. Ryan observes that, on a superficial level, one can explain the popularity of Kingsolver's novels by noting that they have compelling characters, well-crafted plots, and an easy, often colloquial style. However, more poignantly, Ryan sees them as "the exemplary fiction for our age: aggressively politically correct, yet fundamentally conservative" (77). Although the causes Kingsolver embraces are not the same as those of the nineteenth-century reformers whom she admires, such as Charles Dickens, she does pride herself on being an "old-fashioned" writer, not only because of her emphasis on social issues but also because her fiction is meant to appeal not just to the few but to everyone. What disturbs Ryan is that "for all their apparent attention to the pressing social problems of our time, Kingsolver's light and lively books—which purport to give us food that's both nourishing and appetizing—leave all of us feeling just a bit too fine" (78).

In *The Bean Trees*, Ryan argues, while Kingsolver does send Taylor Greer out of a secure rural environment and into contemporary society, the emphasis is not on the real dangers that lurk there but instead on "the characters' resilience and the inherent goodness of the world." *Pigs in Heaven* is similarly optimistic, for though the Cherokee do threaten to remove Turtle from her adoptive mother's care, in the end it is their community that takes in not just Turtle but also Taylor and even her mother, thus providing them with an extended family and, by insisting on preserving ancient customs and traditions, giving them an antidote to the temptations and dangers of the outside world. Again, the characters have moved easily to a happy ending and a secure environment (78-79). Ryan admits that the dangers in *Animal Dreams* are more worrisome than those in the other two novels; certainly Kingsolver does not gloss over the fact that the heroine's sister, who has been helping the Nicaraguan peasants, is kidnapped and then murdered. However, that takes place at a distance; in Grace, Arizona, the villainous mining company is defeated by a group of Mexican American women who thus avert disaster and rescue their community.

Despite her consistent advocacy for nontraditional families, Kingsolver often reveals herself as adhering to traditional values. As Ryan puts it, the author believes in the "sanctity of motherhood." She also offers her readers an easy faith: "if we love our children and our mothers, and hang in there with hearth and home, the big bad world will simply go away." Thus, Ryan concludes, Kingsolver does indeed adhere to the "conventions of traditional realistic fiction," and though that practice has made her popular, it can leave a thoughtful reader unsatisfied (81).

Kingsolver herself has often expressed concern that her readers

---

might be reading her novels purely for pleasure and ignoring their political content. This motivated her to select twenty-five of her essays, many of which had previously been published, and bring them together in an edited, somewhat expanded form in a miscellany titled *High Tide in Tucson: Essays from Now or Never* (1995). Though she had feared that she would lose readers by being too outspoken, Kingsolver told Robin Epstein in an interview for *The Progressive* that *High Tide in Tucson* was an even greater immediate success than any of her novels. Reviewers, too, were enthusiastic, praising Kingsolver for her warmth, her humor, and her poetic style, the same qualities that they had admired in her fiction, and several wrote that they had found the personal anecdotes in the collection especially appealing. One of the few dissenters was a British critic who was repelled by Kingsolver's self-dramatization, particularly in some "cringe-making vignettes of American life," such as the account of her jazz tour. That reviewer's conclusion was that Kingsolver should abandon personal essays and express herself instead in "her fine novels" (Barker 36).

If some reviewers found Kingsolver too "preachy," their objection was to style, not to content. Very few readers would object to the author's passion for the environment, her reverence for nature, or her pleas for social justice, whether the downtrodden are women, children, or specific ethnic groups. With *The Poisonwood Bible*, Kingsolver ventured into riskier territory, for the novel is meant to serve not only as an indictment of American foreign policy but also as an exposure of the stupidity, the insensitivity, and the hypocrisy of Christian evangelical missionaries. In a review for *Christianity Today*, Tim Stafford called the voices of the women in the novel "unforgettable" but expressed his disappointment that in a novel supposedly about religion, "neither faith nor doubt has any punch." He added, "This makes me wonder whether Kingsolver has ever known a fundamentalist missionary" (88). Alan Neely also worried about troubling "incongruities" in *The Poisonwood Bible*, such as the fact that Nathan, a Southern Baptist, is "a devotee of the Apocrypha." A former missionary himself,

Neely also pointed out that no church's mission board would have allowed someone like Nathan to go into a field where he would have to work with people of other cultures.

The Poisonwood Bible is also an attack on the patriarchal system of family governance, for, as a *Publishers Weekly* reviewer pointed out, the Reverend Nathan Price, an evangelical missionary who has decided to convert a village in the Congo to Christianity, has no more respect for women than he does for the natives and, in fact, is both physically and mentally abusive to his wife and his four daughters. By using these five women as narrators, Kingsolver shows the extent to which they have been brainwashed by Nathan and the system that he represents. Through their eyes, the author reveals truths not only about the disastrous results of Nathan's bungling efforts but also about the effects of past colonial rule and of more recent American intervention, effects that Nathan is too blind to see. Reviewer Liane Ellison Norman noted that after exposing American "imperialism" and the persistence of "habits of racial superiority," Kingsolver ends her book by having four of her female narrators deliver a sermon. To those who might object to this intrusion on the narrative, Norman responded that by writing "so big, so important, and so engrossing a novel," Kingsolver had earned the right to end the book in any way she liked (59).

Even critics and reviewers who were annoyed by occasional authorial intrusions in the book agreed that *The Poisonwood Bible* was Kingsolver's best novel to date. Certainly it inspired a much wider variety of critical approaches and interpretations than any of her previous books. In the *Women's Review of Books*, for example, Gayle Green argued that the novel is about "what these characters see, fail to see, learn to see" and about how all of us may come to think differently about other cultures (8-9). Another writer suggested that the novel shows the difference between "Nathan Price's narrow definition of salvation" and true "redemption" (Warren C5).

Writing in the *National Catholic Reporter*, Judith Bromberg called the book Kingsolver's "best to date" in both style and content, though she did find the political comments at the ending "a bit belabored." She also contrasted Nathan's "self-serving" use of Christianity with the efforts of his predecessor, a priest gone native, who continues to serve his people in the true spirit of Christianity (13). Tim Stafford in *Christianity Today* stated his admiration for Kingsolver's creation of a "finely wrought, distinctive voice" for each of the Price women, but he found Nathan no more than a "stick-figure" whom the author herself does not seem to understand. He also deplored the fact that none of the characters has a profound faith or even a profound doubt, leading Stafford to "wonder whether Kingsolver has ever known a fundamentalist missionary." Though the book has its merits, he concluded, it is basically a "cartoonish story of idiot missionaries and shady CIA operatives" (88). Alan Neely, a theologian and former Southern Baptist missionary, worried that readers of what he described as an "exquisitely written, engaging book" will not see the "incongruities" in the novel, such as the impossibility of a church mission board's sending out someone as ill suited to deal with other cultures as Nathan Price. Neely was also troubled by the fact that Kingsolver does not permit Nathan a voice, thus depriving him of his humanity, and he wondered whether readers will realize that the fundamentalist missionary presented to them is not a realistic representation but merely a caricature (138).

Even its severest critics, however, cannot deny that *The Poisonwood Bible* is a major literary achievement. Prior to the novel's publication, Kingsolver was considered an extremely talented writer who produced entertaining novels with political overtones. Like her earlier novels, *The Poisonwood Bible* was a best seller; in fact, it had sold more than one million copies before June 2000, when Oprah Winfrey chose it as the thirty-fifth selection for her on-air book club. *The Poisonwood Bible* also impressed the literary world, however; with its publication, Barbara Kingsolver established herself as one of the most important writers of her era. Soon several book-length studies of Kingsolver were published, among them Mary Jean DeMarr's *Barbara Kingsolver: A Critical Companion*, Mary Ellen Snodgrass's *Barbara King-*

solver: A Literary Companion, and Linda Wagner-Martin's biography *Barbara Kingsolver*. Essays on *The Poisonwood Bible* also began to appear frequently in scholarly journals. They included comparisons of *The Poisonwood Bible* to Joseph Conrad's *Heart of Darkness* (1902) and to Louisa May Alcott's *Little Women* (1868) as well as one study of the similarities between Kingsolver and the New Zealand author Keri Hulme in their treatment of disability. *The Poisonwood Bible* has been viewed as a political allegory, as a feminist protest, and even as a systematic refutation of the Platonic concept of absolute truth. The very fact that *The Poisonwood Bible* can be approached in so many different ways is further proof of its superior quality.

In 1999, Barbara Kingsolver made a unique contribution to her chosen field by establishing the Bellwether Prize for Fiction, which is awarded biannually for an unpublished novel by a relatively unknown writer with a commitment to social change. Her own efforts in that area, as well as the high quality of her writing, were recognized when it was announced that Kingsolver would receive the National Humanities Medal in 2000, sharing that honor with such world-famous writers as Ernest Gaines and Toni Morrison.

Kingsolver's next novel, *Prodigal Summer* (2000) was much lighter in tone than *The Poisonwood Bible*. However, as Paul Gray commented in his review in *Time*, though its subject is not institutionalized evil but "the rhythms of nature and man's misguided attempts to interfere with them," *Prodigal Summer* is at least as didactic as any of the author's previous works. "It can be no accident," Gray continued, "that three of the four main characters in the novel have worked as teachers in the past and aren't at all shy about giving lectures" (90). However, as Suzanne W. Jones explains in her examination of the novel, the enlightened characters do not merely voice their beliefs; they also live them. Thus Lusa Landowski, the city girl whose husband's death left her with a farm to run, shows the community how to save the small family farm while she herself learns how important it is to "understand both the human and nonhuman ecology" of the place where one lives

(90). Jones expresses admiration for the way in which Kingsolver carries her emphasis on interconnections into seemingly casual details and even into the "braided narratives" (94) that constitute the structure of the novel, which justify a second and even a third reading.

Some reviewers of *Prodigal Summer* were disturbed by Kingsolver's vision of "a utopia of sex and fecundity ruled over by glorious nature and wise females" (Bush 1245). Even though the coyote hunter Eddie Bondo wins the heart of Deanna Wolfe and then departs, leaving her to rear their child, thus fulfilling the pattern of male behavior one would expect in a Kingsolver novel, it has been pointed out that there is a sympathetic male character in *Prodigal Summer*, the elderly widower Garnett Walker. Though he refuses to stop using herbicides, at least Walker has a noble purpose: to bring back the American chestnut tree. His presence suggests that Kingsolver's "range is certainly expanding" and underscores her theme, "how important dependency is for human survival" (Gibson 17).

Barbara Kingsolver's second essay collection, *Small Wonder* (2002), was not as well received as *Prodigal Summer*. The five essays that Kingsolver wrote as responses to the terrorist attacks of September 11, 2001, and the subsequent military action taken by the United States were labeled unpatriotic by some reviewers and naive by others. According to one reviewer, even when Kingsolver is dealing with other subjects, her pronouncements in *Small Wonder* contain "errors of fact" and "mistakes and lapses in logic" (Mesic 70-71). The reviewer for *The Economist* concluded that nonfiction is not the best genre for Kingsolver and expressed the hope that her "crusading optimism" will "launch more consistently affecting fiction in future" ("Little" 363). However, Kingsolver's next work, *Animal, Vegetable, Miracle: A Year of Food Life* (2007) was not another novel; instead, it was an account of a year during which Kingsolver's family lived on local food, most of it from their own Appalachian farm. One reviewer commented that by indulging her "glorious wit," in this book Kingsolver finally manages to avoid being "preachy" (Hughes 8). *Animal, Vegetable, Miracle* received an enthusiastic reception from critics and readers alike. On February 15, 2008, *Booklist* included it as one of the "Top Ten Books on the Environment."

Although readers and reviewers may disagree with Barbara Kingsolver's views, none of them denies her command of the language, her gift for creating characters, and her skill in developing plots. Even though her works are sometimes marred by didacticism or self-righteousness, her many readers seem to recognize that these flaws are merely evidence of the passion for human rights, social justice, and ecological responsibility that motivates her to write. As Snodgrass puts it, Kingsolver is a "master writer blessed with moral vision and an innate certainty of place and character. . . . As a result of her courageous stands, her works enlarge reader compassion for the earth as well as for the poor and beleaguered" (3).

Works Cited

Banks, Russell. "Distant as a Cherokee Childhood." Rev. of *Homeland, and Other Stories*, by Barbara Kingsolver. *The New York Times Book Review* 11 June 1989: 16.

Barker, Elspeth. "With Buster the Hermit Crab." Rev. of *High Tide in Tucson*, by Barbara Kingsolver. *The Independent on Sunday* [London] 23 June 1996: 36.

Brandmark, Wendy. "Kinship with the Earth." Rev. of *Homeland, and Other Stories*, by Barbara Kingsolver. *Times Literary Supplement* 24 Jan. 1997: 22.

Bromberg, Judith. Rev. of *The Poisonwood Bible*, by Barbara Kingsolver. *National Catholic Reporter* 19 Mar. 1999: 13.

Bush, Trudy. Rev. of *Prodigal Summer*, by Barbara Kingsolver. *Christian Century* 22 Nov. 2000: 1245.

Butler, Jack. "She Hung the Moon and Plugged in All the Stars." Rev. of *The Bean Trees*, by Barbara Kingsolver. *The New York Times Book Review* 10 Apr. 1988: 15.

Cooke, Carolyn. Rev. of *Animal Dreams*, by Barbara Kingsolver. *The Nation* 26 Nov. 1990: 653-54.

Daurio, Beverly. "A Rare, Bracing Tonic for a Cynical Age." Rev. of *Pigs in Heaven*, by Barbara Kingsolver. *Globe and Mail* [Toronto] 10 July 1993: C16.

DeMarr, Mary Jean. *Barbara Kingsolver: A Critical Companion*. Westport, CT: Greenwood Press, 1999.

Gibson, Sharan. "Family Values on the Farm; People Need People as Barbara

Kingsolver Returns to Her Roots." Rev. of *Prodigal Summer*, by Barbara Kingsolver. *Houston Chronicle* 3 Dec. 2000: 17.

Gray, Paul. "On Familiar Ground: Barbara Kingsolver Returns with Another Novel of Strong Women, Noble Issues and Love of the Land." Rev. of *Prodigal Summer*, by Barbara Kingsolver. *Time* 30 Oct. 2000: 90.

_____. Rev. of *Animal Dreams*, by Barbara Kingsolver. *Time* 24 Sept. 1990: 87.

Green, Gayle. Rev. of *The Poisonwood Bible*, by Barbara Kingsolver. *Women's Review of Books* 16.7 (1999): 8-9.

Hughes, Kathryn. "Kathryn Hughes Finds a Chronicle of Living Off the Land Is Saved from Being Preachy by Glorious Wit." Rev. of *Animal, Vegetable, Miracle*, by Barbara Kingsolver. *The Guardian* [London] 7 July 2007: 8.

Jones, Suzanne W. "The Southern Family Farm as Endangered Species: Possibilities for Survival in Barbara Kingsolver's *Prodigal Summer*." *Southern Literary Journal* 39.1 (2006): 83-97.

Karbo, Karen. "And Baby Makes Two." Rev. of *Pigs in Heaven*, by Barbara Kingsolver. *The New York Times Book Review* 27 June 1993: 9.

Kingsolver, Barbara. "Barbara Kingsolver: Her Fiction Features Ordinary People Heroically Committed to Political Issues." Interview by Lisa See Kendall. *Publishers Weekly* 31 Aug. 1990: 46-47.

_____. Interview by Robin Epstein. *The Progressive* 60.2 (1996): 33-38.

Lehmann-Haupt, Christopher. "Community vs. Family and Writer vs. Subject." *The New York Times* 12 July 1993: C16.

"Little Big Voice: New Essays." Rev. of *Small Wonder*, by Barbara Kingsolver. *The Economist* 11 May 2002: 363.

Mesic, Penelope. "Earth Mother." Rev. of *Small Wonder*, by Barbara Kingsolver. *Book* May-June 2002: 70-71.

Mossman, Robert. Rev. of *The Bean Trees*, by Barbara Kingsolver. *English Journal* 79.6 (1990): 85.

Neely, Alan. Rev. of *The Poisonwood Bible*, by Barbara Kingsolver. *International Bulletin of Missionary Research* 24.3 (2000): 138.

Neuhaus, Denise. "On Dependable Ground." Rev. of *Homeland, and Other Stories*, by Barbara Kingsolver. *Times Literary Supplement* 7 Sept. 1990: 956.

Norman, Liane Ellison. Rev. of *The Poisonwood Bible*, by Barbara Kingsolver. *Sojourners* 28.2 (1999): 59.

Rev. of *The Poisonwood Bible*, by Barbara Kingsolver. *Publishers Weekly* 10 Aug. 1998: 366.

Ryan, Maureen. "Barbara Kingsolver's Lowfat Fiction." *Journal of American Culture* 18.4 (1995): 77-82.

Shapiro, Laura. "A Novel Full of Miracles." Rev. of *Pigs in Heaven*, by Barbara Kingsolver. *Newsweek* 12 July 1993: 61.

Snodgrass, Mary Ellen. *Barbara Kingsolver: A Literary Companion*. Jefferson, NC: McFarland, 2004.

Stafford, Tim. Rev. of *The Poisonwood Bible*, by Barbara Kingsolver. *Christianity Today* 11 Jan. 1999: 88.

Steinberg, Marc W. Rev. of *Holding the Line: Women in the Great Arizona Mine Strike of 1983*, by Barbara Kingsolver. *Contemporary Sociology* 20.2 (1991): 236-38.

Tischler, Barbara L. Rev. of *Holding the Line: Women in the Great Arizona Mine Strike of 1983*, by Barbara Kingsolver. *Labor Studies Journal* 17 (1992): 82-83.

Towler, Katie, Maggie Reichers, and Chrissa Gerard. "Making a Difference: The 2000 National Humanities Medalists." *Humanities* 22.1 (2001): 20-31.

Wagner-Martin, Linda. *Barbara Kingsolver*. Philadelphia: Chelsea House, 2004.

Warren, Colleen Kelly. "Family Tragedy Plays Out in Congo." Rev. of *The Poisonwood Bible*, by Barbara Kingsolver. *St. Louis Post-Dispatch* 18 Oct. 1998: C5.

Young, Elizabeth. Rev. of *Pigs in Heaven*, by Barbara Kingsolver. *The Guardian* [London] 23 Nov. 1993: 9.

Cultivating Our Bioregional Roots:
An Ecofeminist Exploration of
Barbara Kingsolver's *Prodigal Summer*_____

Christine M. Battista

Christine M. Battista situates Kingsolver's life and work in the emerging critical paradigm of ecofeminist criticism. Starting with the observation that both women and the land have traditionally been on the losing end of Western dualistic thought patterns, Battista looks at the philosophical tenets undergirding *Animal, Vegetable, Miracle* and at the lives of the three women protagonists of *Prodigal Summer*, who practice alternative modes of living and learn new ways of interacting with the natural world, sometimes at the expense of their ability to interact with the human-centered world. Through the example of Kingsolver, Battista shows that advocacy for the natural world must have consequences for one's personal life and one's choices. The recognition of the ecological interdependence of the earth's biological inhabitants leads both the writer and the critic to a radical questioning of traditional assumptions about sustainability.   — T.A.

My connection to the region is completely personal. I grew up in rural Kentucky with a love for the language, music and forested mountains that rose just to the west of us. When I left the region to go to college and live in other places, I was stunned to discover the world knows almost nothing about "hillbillies," and respects them even less. An undercurrent of defensiveness about this has guided my writing and my life, I think, as I've tried to seek out the voices of marginalized people. I've lived in three continents and all over the U.S., but no place outside of the rural eastern deciduous woodlands has ever truly and wholly felt like home.

— Barbara Kingsolver, personal interview

The decision to attend to the health of one's habitat and food chain is a spiritual choice. It's also a political choice, a scientific one, a personal and a convivial one. It's not a choice between living in the country or the town; it is about understanding that every one of us, at the level of our cells and respiration, lives in the country and is thus obliged to be mindful of the distance between ourselves and our sustenance.

—Barbara Kingsolver, foreword to Norman Wirzba's
The Essential Agrarian Reader

As the farmers go under, as communities lose their economic supports, as all of rural America sits as if condemned in the shadow of the "free market" and "revolutionary science," the economist announces pontifically to the press that "there will be some winners and some losers"—as if that might justify and clarify everything, or anything. . . .

It seems that we have been reduced almost to a state of absolute economics, in which people and all other creatures and things may be considered purely as economic "units," or integers of production, and in which a human being may be dealt with, as John Ruskin put it, "merely as a covetous machine."

—Wendell Berry, *The Art of the Commonplace*

Human beings have a singular access to the earth that offers unlimited possibilities for our existence. The way in which we perceive and treat the land, therefore, has a profound impact on our own inhabitancy. Ecofeminist theory is a productive way to interrogate how we think about land and what kinds of discourses, or dominant ways of thinking, are embedded within Western, male-centered narratives of domination. For instance, ecofeminist scholars Heather Eaton and Lois Ann Lorentzen argue that "Euro-western cultures developed ideas about a world divided hierarchically and dualistically" (3). In other terms, the history of Western thinking has produced narratives that artificially divide the world into opposing dualisms; these dualisms create an unequal divide between women and men and, consequently, have denied women equal access to emancipatory rights and justice. These dualisms have also created an unequal division between culture and nature, thus denying nature *living* agency. Ecofeminist scholarship asserts that we must interrogate these frameworks of oppression if we are to institute viable change for both women and ecology. In this essay, I argue that narratives such as Barbara Kingsolver's *Prodigal Summer* are important because they enforce, in Karen J. Warren's phrase, an "ecofeminist ethic" that "emerges from the voices of those who experience disproportionately the harmful destruction of nonhuman nature" (99). Following this ethic, Kingsolver illustrates how we can and must give voice to those who have been "disproportionately" harmed—namely, women and ecology. Kingsolver's focus on the rehabilitation of a southern Appalachian region attests to her own dedication as a committed biologist, environmentalist, artistic activist, and ecofeminist author. As I argue in the essay, Western modes of thinking have constructed a disproportionate framework through which humans relate to the nonhuman world.[1] In this regard, books such as *Prodigal Summer* are crucial because they prompt us to reconsider our ecological constitution so that we may inhabit the earth in more sustainable and ethical ways.

In her collection of ecological and political essays *Small Wonder*, Kingsolver makes a case for relearning kinship with the land. According to Kingsolver, the creation of a materialistic culture has created a divide between humanity and nature. As a result, Kingsolver emphasizes, we have forgotten how to appreciate and connect with nature. She argues that civilization, and its fast-paced agenda, muddles our minds and makes us forget what is important about life: *the living environment and all its harmonious living components*. I quote at length the following passage from *Small Wonder*, where Kingsolver articulates how she receives inspiration directly from nature:

I have come to depend on these places where I live and work. I've grown accustomed to looking up from the page and letting my eyes relax on a landscape upon which no human artifact intrudes. No steel, pavement, or streetlights, no architecture lovely or otherwise, no works of public art or private enterprise—no hominid agenda. I consider myself lucky beyond words to be able to go to work every morning with something like a wilderness at my elbow. In the way of so-called worldly things, I can't seem to muster a desire for cellular phones or cable TV or to drive anything flashier than a dirt-colored sedan older than the combined ages of my children. My tastes are much more extreme. I want wood-thrush poetry. I want mountains. (36)

As both an author and an environmental activist, Kingsolver argues that it is a necessity that we cherish and preserve our natural environment. If we become too immersed in our modern technological and materialist culture, we lose our "rooted sense" of the land itself: "What we lose in our great human exodus from the land is a rooted sense, as deep and intangible as religious faith, of why we need to hold on to the wild and beautiful places that once surrounded us" (39). These passages from *Small Wonder* exemplify the kind of environmental activism Kingsolver emphasizes in both her nonfiction and her fiction.[2]

Not unlike *Small Wonder*, *Prodigal Summer* elucidates some of Kingsolver's most prominent environmental, biological, and, in this case, feminist concerns.[3] The central narrative is centered on the stories of three Appalachian women, each of whom is committed to her relationship with the land. It is Kingsolver's project in *Prodigal Summer* to explore what exactly we have lost in our "great human exodus from the land" and how we can begin to foster our own individual land ethics. In her most recent nonfiction work, *Animal, Vegetable, Miracle* (2007), Kingsolver details her own exodus from Tucson, Arizona—a city that truly has, according to Kingsolver, lost its "rooted sense" of the land. Kingsolver emphasizes that her family wanted to live in a place "where rain falls, crops grow, and drinking water bubbles right up from the ground," and so they made the move to southern Appalachia, a region where her ancestors were born and raised (3). In this autobiographical chronicle, Kingsolver cultivates her own renewed sense of environmental justice and does so by raising and growing almost all of her own food, from the basil in spring to the green beans in summer to the apples in fall. Her winter is spent canning, freezing, and preserving the food she has raised as she prepares for the upcoming season of growing and harvest. Her family is committed to renewing their own land ethic and creating roots in and through their inhabitancy of the land. Kingsolver's personal commitment toward cultivating a renewed land ethic speaks to a kind of feminist agency that directly confronts our "great human exodus from the land." *Animal, Vegetable, Miracle* and *Prodigal Summer* illuminate the need to resist the forms of domination that have negative impacts on our relationship with the land.

Prodigal Summer is not only ecofeminist; it is also what we might call *bioregionalist*. Michael Zimmerman writes of bioregionalism in his theoretical treatise *Contesting Earth's Future: Radical Ecology and Postmodernity*:

> Bioregionalism maintains that a culture is most healthy when its practices, myths, and norms are tied up with the natural culture's geographical region. Because bioregional cultures would presumably be concerned with the flourishing of all life in the region, not just with human life, concern about short-term profit would be replaced by concern with long-term issues, ranging from protecting wild area to developing ecologically compatible agriculture and manufacture. (27)

Bioregionalism means that we should concern ourselves with our local region and how we inhabit it. The flourishing of a regional culture depends on our ability to produce an environmental ethics that contributes to the long-term sustainability of the region. This is quite different from what we are accustomed to in the twenty-first century, with the proliferation of large-scale agribusiness producing crops on a large scale and transporting them nationally and globally. Although this kind of industrial farming can keep food prices relatively stable except in times of global disaster, provides variety for many people, and yields a tremendous amount of crops, it has an adverse impact on regional economies and is detrimental to local ecology. *Prodigal Summer* care-fully addresses these issues and ultimately argues for a transformation to smaller-scale farming and localized economies. In addition, King-solver illustrates the dangers associated with the overuse of pesticides that are often associated with large-scale agribusiness and, through her characters, offers healthy alternatives that contribute to the vitality of a region and all of its inhabitants.

In the novel, each female protagonist uniquely contributes to Appa-lachia's bioregional development through her own narrative, a narra-tive that is woven into a rich ecological tapestry that encompasses the whole of the novel. The characters' relationships to the Appalachian landscape and one another are based on a "relational ethics" character-ized by "compassion and humility." This "relational ethics" resonates with Warren's definition, in which she remarks that it is a "loving per-ception of the nonhuman world . . . that maintains *difference*, a distinc-tion between the self and other, between the human and non-human, in such a way that perception of the other *as other* is an expression of love for one who/which is recognized at the outset as independent, dissimi-lar, different" (137). Each woman's relationship to her environment is based on this relational ethics—an ethics of profound concern for the other, whether human or nonhuman.[4]

In framing her narrative, Kingsolver "uses principles of ecology to question and to illuminate human behavior" (Jones 176), and these principles are particularly evident in the construction of each female character. The first character we encounter is Deanna, a woman who defines her own relational ethics through her self-invented job—a job that involves the ecological rehabilitation of Zebulon Mountain. In fact, "two years after her arrival, one of the most heavily poached ranges of southern Appalachia was becoming an intact ecosystem again" (59). Because Deanna makes the choice to live in the wilder-ness, her relationship to the earth, and to humans, significantly changes. In the opening paragraph of the novel, Deanna is described as a woman whose "body was free to follow its own rules, whose body moved with the frankness that comes from solitary habits" (1-2). In fact, her "long-legged gait [was] too fast for companionship," and "two years alone had given her a blind person's indifference to the look on her own face" (2). Deanna no longer feels tethered to a male-centered society that passes judgment on how she moves or the choices she makes. She is able to pursue her passion and is dedicated to the "return of a significant canid predator and the reordering of species it might bring about" (62). Once a "graduate student in wildlife biology" whose thesis was on the "coyote range extension in the twentieth century," Deanna creates her own place on Zebulon Mountain, which involves a struggle "against some skeptics" and a "rare agreement between the Park Service, the Forest Service, and the Department of Game and Inland Fisheries" (59). Deanna has to fight for her position and is able to define and create her own agency through her alternative relationship with the land.

One of Kingsolver's central concerns within *Prodigal Summer* is her depiction of the indissoluble relationship between humans and the land. A passage that occurs at the beginning of the novel and is repeated at the end speaks to this assertion: "Solitude is only a human presumption. Every quiet step is thunder to beetle life underfoot; every choice is a world made new for the chosen. All secrets are witnessed" (1). Kingsolver articulates that humans and nonhumans exist within a delicate web of ecological vitality. The "human" does not stand above or beyond nature; rather, nature is part and parcel to human functioning. Deanna, whose "body is free to follow its own rules," is no longer monitored by the constrictive limitations imposed by Western modes of thinking. In fact, she no longer exists according to traditional clock time:

> Deanna knew exactly when the morning ended. She never wore a watch, and for this she didn't need one. She knew when the air grew still enough that she could hear caterpillars overhead, newly hatched, eating through thousands of leaves on their way to becoming Io and luna moths. (58)

Deanna's ecological independence is interrupted, however, when she meets Eddie Bondo, a game hunter who is tracking coyotes on Zebulon Mountain—the very coyotes Deanna is helping to preserve. Upon meeting Eddie, Deanna realizes that "she'd forgotten how to talk with people, it seemed—how to sidestep a question and hide what was necessary" (10). As Kingsolver reveals, Deanna's commitment to the non-human world is complicated by the fact that she loses her ability to relate to the human world. While Deanna's isolation allows her to develop a deeply ecological sensibility, it does very little to help her understand and confront the human motivations that ultimately lead to ecological devastation. Eddie, therefore, serves as a reminder of Western patriarchy and its constrictive influences that need to be confronted, not simply ignored or evaded.

Although Deanna is unsure at first how to relate to Eddie and is frustrated with his immature sensibilities and his lust for hunting predators, he nevertheless awakens in Deanna sexual desires that mimic the beginning of spring:

> Spring would move higher up to awaken the bears and finally go out like a flame, absorbed into the dark spruce forest on the scalp of Zebulon Mountain. But here and now, spring heaved in its randy moment. Everywhere you looked, something was fighting for time, for light, the kiss of pollen, a connection of sperm and egg and another chance. (8-9)

Eddie and Deanna's sexual relationship follows the rise and fall of spring into early and late summer, further mimicking the indissoluble relationship between humanity and ecology. Deanna concedes to Eddie and allows him into *her* territory, claiming that "it was the body's decision, a body with no more choice of its natural history than an orchid has, or the bee it needs, and so they would both get lost here, she would let him in, anywhere he wanted to go" (24).

As Deanna's lust continues to blossom, however, so does her disdain for Eddie's passion to kill. Deanna knew the hatred of western ranchers toward coyotes; it was famous, maybe the fiercest human-animal vendetta there was. It was bad enough even here on the tamer side of the Mississippi. The farmers she'd grown up among would sooner kill a coyote than learn to pronounce its name. . . .

What might bring a Wyoming sheep rancher to the southern Appalachians at this time of year was the Mountain Empire Bounty Hunt, organized for the first time this year. It'd been held recently, she knew, around the first day of May—the time of birthing and nursing, a suitable hunting season for nothing in this world unless the goal was willful extermination. It had drawn hunters from everywhere for the celebrated purpose of killing coyotes. (28-29)

According to a 1999 article in *Audubon Magazine* by Mike Finkel, "every year 400,000 coyotes are exterminated in the United States" (52). Finkel argues that "some ranchers kill as many coyotes as they can," organizing game-killing contests in which ranchers are motivated through monetary rewards (54). Just to name a few, there is the "Coyote Derby in Montana, the Predator Hunt Spectacular in Arizona, the San Juan Coyote Hunt in New Mexico, and on the East Coast, the Pennsylvania Coyote Hunt" (54). In fact, these contests "are advertised in sporting-goods stores, gun clubs, and Varmint Masters magazine. It is all perfectly legal" (54). In a conversation with Eddie, Deanna refers to the Predator Hunt Spectacular in Arizona, remarking that "they have those hunts all over. It's no secret; they advertise in gun magazines. There's one going on right now in Arizona, the Predator Hunt Extreme, with a ten-thousand-dollar prize for whoever shoots the most. . . . Just pile up the bodies. Bobcats, coyotes, mountain lions, foxes—that's their definition of a predator" (321).

Unwilling to see Deanna's perspective that "predation is *honorable*" in that it "culls out the sick and the old, [and] keeps populations from going through their own roofs," Eddie remains committed to his animosity toward predators. In fact, he tells Deanna: "You can't and you won't change my mind. I'm a ranching boy from the West, and hating coyotes is my religion. Blood of the lamb, so to speak. Don't try to convert me and I won't try to convert you" (323). The opposition between Deanna and Eddie parallels the Western, male-centered understanding of women and ecology that I have mentioned. Kingsolver's ecofeminist revision of the relationship between predatory animals and human beings, however, calls into question this form of Western patriarchy.[5] Eddie is symbolic of Western modes of thinking that feminize (and hence pacify) the landscape for domination. Deanna, however, remains vigilant in her resistance against Eddie's patriarchal tendencies, continually emphasizing that humans and nonhumans are part and parcel of the same ecological web. She tells Eddie: "There's no such thing as *alone*. That animal was going to do something important in its time—eat a lot of things, or be eaten. There's all these connected things you're about to blow a hole in. They can't *all* be your enemy, because one of those connected things is you" (320). This passage again demonstrates the novel's ecofeminist concern to provide "not only a transformation of gender relations but also a radically *different* way for humanity to interact with nature" (Alaimo 9).

While Deanna realizes her potential on the mountain overlooking Zebulon Valley, the other female protagonists of *Prodigal Summer*, Lusa and Nannie, realize their agency from within the heart of the Valley. Lusa's story begins when her husband, Cole, dies and she subsequently inherits his farmhouse and the acres of land that accompany it. Overwhelmed at this unexpected turn of events, Lusa has the immediate inclination to return to her original home in the city. As events continue to unfold, however, she develops a kinship with the land. When she decides to stay, she immediately falls under the pressure of the paternalistic tendencies in Zebulon: "Life in Zebulon: the minute you're born you're trapped like a bug, somebody's son or wife, a place too small to fit into" (104). Lusa's agency, however, lies in her evasion of these traditional patriarchal patterns.

Lusa's first step toward her personal emancipation is her refusal to grow tobacco.[6] The men in Zebulon had expected that she would continue with the business because, as her in-law Little Rickie tells her, "Your tobacco . . . you hang it in the barn to cure, and then it can just go on hanging there as long as it needs to, till the time's good to sell. Everybody in the county can grow tobacco, but every leaf of it might get lit and smoked on a different day of the year, in a different country of the world" (108). Despite the social pressures that surround her, Lusa refuses to concede and commits, instead, to a life of subsistence farming.[7] No one, including Lusa's smothering sisters-in-law, can understand her stubborn refusal. In a conversation with Cole's sister Jewel, Lusa remarks: "Oh, I'm being stupid I guess. Farm economics, what do I know? But half the world's starving, Jewel, we're sitting on some of the richest dirt on this planet, and I'm going to grow *drugs* instead of food? I feel like a hypocrite. I nagged Cole to quit smoking every day of our marriage" (122). Eventually, Lusa decides to raise hormone- and antibiotic-free goats to sell for the Jewish, Christian, and Muslim holidays Passover, Easter, and Id-al-Adha. She struggles constantly with her decision, however: "Yes it was food, and people needed food and their merry feasts, but from this end it seemed like so much effort and loss just to repair a barn and pay off some debts on an old, sad farm. For the hundredth time Lusa tried and failed to imagine how she was going to stay here, or why" (239).

Lusa's character is representative of the struggle small farming communities face against a world that is becoming increasingly reliant on corporate agribusiness and industrial farming. Indeed, Lusa feels "despair . . . not only for the loss of her husband, but for all the things people used to grow and make for themselves before they were widowed from their own food chain" (293). Not unlike Deanna, Lusa struggles against a male-centered society. Although Lusa does not immediately choose to inherit the farm, she nevertheless makes it her mission to reconstitute the way in which the farm functions, thus providing a healthy alternative to a dwindling agricultural bioregion in southern Appalachia. Lusa's awareness of corporate agribusiness is shown in many of her conversations, particularly with Crys, her niece: "Everybody around here used to grow their own wheat and corn for bread, plus what they needed for their animals. Now they buy feed at Southern States and go to Kroger's for a loaf of god-awful bread that was baked in another state . . . because they can't afford to grow grain anymore" (292).

The town of Egg Fork has suffered severe impacts from the corporations, and local farming is under pressure. Lusa, however, represents Kingsolver's personal commitment to small, subsistence-based agriculture: "Kingsolver has Lusa think like a bioregionalist, rather than an agri-industrialist, and in so doing highlights current problems in agribusiness practices, which ignore bioregional differences in favor of supposed universal solutions" (Jones 180). Kingsolver herself was born and raised in a rural Kentucky community and, over the years, has seen what corporate agribusiness has done to destroy the land and the businesses of local ecological farming and sustainability.[8]

The narrative in the novel that is most concerned with the local farming practices in Zebulon Valley is that of Nannie and Garnett—two neighbors who have been at odds with each other for years over their opposing viewpoints concerning the land. Garnett's character represents a traditional male-centered perspective that assumes the land is a space situated for the manipulation of humans. For instance, Garnett insists, "A forest that obeyed the laws of man and geometry, that was the satisfaction" (270). Nannie, however, does not "really think of the woods as *belonging* to us, exactly" (339). While Garnett believes in the generous use of pesticides, herbicides, and other means of ecological control, Nannie believes that "everything alive is connected to every other by fine, invisible threads. Things you don't see can help you plenty, and things you try to control will often rear back and bite you. . . . There's even a thing called the Volterra principle . . . , which is all about how insecticide spraying actually drives up the numbers of the bugs you're trying to kill" (216). Nannie echoes Kingsolver's personal commitment to responsible and organic farming practices.[9] As Suzanne W. Jones asserts, "Kingsolver clearly shows throughout the novel that not understanding the interconnections between the natural and the human world damages the ecosystem, as Nannie's argument with her neighbor about broad-spectrum insecticides . . . demonstrate[s]" (181). By the end of the novel, Nannie and Garnett develop a kinship with each other, a kinship that is based primarily on Garnett's newfound respect for Nannie's agricultural activism.

As I have demonstrated, Deanna, Lusa, and Nannie all utilize their relationships with the land to resist a male-centered society that places women and ecology at the margins. Patrick D. Murphy supports such a claim in his essay "Nature Nurturing Fathers in a World Beyond Our Control":

> In *Prodigal Summer*, both male and female characters learn from each other, articulate ideas to each other, and engage in verbal and sensuous dialogues with each other and the interanimating world in which they grow physically, spiritually, and intellectually. In accepting a world beyond their control, these characters act and interact in constructive, nurturant ways with the kind of responsibility that refuses the fanciful escape routes of either fatalism or autonomy, passivity or isolation. (202-3)

The characters all learn from one another in and through their acceptance of a natural "world beyond their control" and their subsequent immersion in such a world. If we change the way we interact in the natural world, Kingsolver seems to emphasize, then we can change the way we interact with one another. *Prodigal Summer* functions as an artistic medium through which Kingsolver can express her own commitment to rural integrity.[10] As she elucidates in *Small Wonder*:

> It's a privilege to live any part of one's life in proximity to nature. It is a privilege, apparently, even to know that nature is out there at all. In the summer of 1996 human habitation on earth made a subtle, uncelebrated passage from being mostly rural to being mostly urban. More than half of

all humans now live in cities. The natural habitat of our species, then, offi-cially, is steel, pavement, streetlights, architecture, and enterprise—the hominid agenda. (38)

Despite claims to the contrary,[11] *Prodigal Summer* is an ecofeminist revision of Western, male-centered understanding toward women and nature. It is no accident that the protagonists are all female and must struggle for an alternative form of agency against an overwhelmingly patriarchal society. In *Prodigal Summer*, Kingsolver cultivates an eco-logically centered ethic of care that is concerned with rejuvenating local regional cultures. By giving voice and life to a small rural com-munity and propagating a need to rely on sustainable ecoculture, King-solver maintains that we need to resist large forms of agribusiness that threaten the stability of communities and ecosystems. As Wendell Berry remarks in *The Art of the Commonplace*:

> As the farmers go under, as communities lose their economic supports, as all of rural America sits as if condemned in the shadow of the "free market" and "revolutionary science," the economist announces pontifically to the press that "there will be some winners and some losers"—as if that might justify and clarify everything, or anything. . . .
>
> It seems that we have been reduced almost to a state of absolute econom-ics, in which people and all other creatures and things may be considered purely as economic "units," or integers of production, and in which a hu-man being may be dealt with, as John Ruskin put it, "merely as a covetous machine." (207-8)

Prodigal Summer chronicles the problems of large-scale industry, the threat such industry poses to small rural communities, and the im-pact it has on an entire bioregion; the novel also reveals the important changes we need to make if we are to create a sustainable future for hu-manity *and* ecology. Although these environmental issues may seem insurmountable, Kingsolver shows that there are always possibilities for resistance. In *Prodigal Summer*, it is the women who have the power to resist. For instance, although Lusa inherits a farm that has been controlled through generations of male property and male power, she nevertheless finds a way to resist these generations of control and inhabits the land in an alternative way. Similarly, Deanna and Nannie both create their own ecological niches, thus undermining the notion that women are mere vessels that function as vehicles for male desire. Deanna transforms Eddie's desire toward her into a means for her to re-investigate creatively her own subjectivity—a subjectivity that has been constituted largely through her isolation from any kind of human community—and makes the decision to rejoin Zebulon Valley and raise her child among Zebulon's women and men.

Prodigal Summer, through its commentary concerning ecology, gender, and corporate agribusiness, offers an alternative ecofeminist sensibility that enables women to find their agency through their relationship with the land itself. This does not mean that women are essentially closer to nature; rather, it means that, although women have disproportionately experienced the negative effects of a male-centered society, they can utilize their position to address and resist ecological destruction. Kingsolver's own personal commitment to ecological justice in Appalachia reveals that, although *Prodigal Summer* is a work of fiction, it nevertheless unveils what lies at the heart of Kingsolver's concerns for ecological stability, female emancipation, and bioregional resistance.

Notes

1. Karen J. Warren details the full importance of an ecofeminist ethic in her book *Ecofeminist Philosophy*, asserting, in particular, that an "ecofeminist ethic . . . presupposes and maintains difference—difference among humans as well as humans and nonhuman animals and nature—while also recognizing the commonality among these groups" (99).

2. See also Kingsolver's foreword to Norman Wirzba's *The Essential Agrarian Reader*.

3. In her article "The Southern Family as Endangered Species: Possibilities for

Survival in Barbara Kingsolver's *Prodigal Summer*," Suzanne W. Jones argues that Kingsolver's "academic training in evolutionary biology and ecology, her abiding concern for community and family, and her intimate knowledge of a particular place combine to produce no less than a blueprint for saving the small family farm and for restoring ecological balance in a southern Appalachian bioregion that is struggling to survive" (178).

4. See Stacy Alaimo's *Undomesticated Ground*. The term she refers to is "situated theorizing" and is influenced by Donna Haraway's phrase "situated knowledges," which, according to Alaimo, suggests that "writings that are not explicitly theoretical undertake a kind of theorizing that does not presume to float above, but rather is immersed within, a particular discursive landscape" (191). See also Haraway's "Situated Knowledges: The Science Question in Feminism and the Privilege of Partial Perspective."

5. I am influenced here by Luce Irigaray's critique of "Western philosophy" in *Speculum of the Other Woman*. Specifically, Irigaray asserts that the Western tradition has created fictitious, essentialized "truths" about male and female subjectivity. Females, who are born into this tradition, are typically perceived as "virgin, dumb," and Irigaray emphasizes that women must resist these totalizing truths (136). Kingsolver's depiction of female subjectivity in *Prodigal Summer* disproves this tradition of Western metaphysical philosophy.

6. See *Animal, Vegetable, Miracle* for an in-depth look at Kingsolver's own experience concerning tobacco farming. Tobacco is an important focus for Kingsolver, and she reveals her own disdain for its economic importance through her depiction of Lusa in *Prodigal Summer*.

7. See Kingsolver, *Animal, Vegetable, Miracle* (75).

8. For a more detailed explanation of Kingsolver's experiences and her dedication to small, organic farming practices, see *Animal, Vegetable, Miracle*.

9. This is an important aspect of *Prodigal Summer* because it shows Kingsolver's commitment to environmental preservation. Nannie's adamant refusal to use pesticides echoes the principles that are conveyed in Rachel Carson's groundbreaking 1962 work *Silent Spring*, a text that has undoubtedly influenced Kingsolver's bioethical philosophy.

10. See also Wendell Berry's essay "A Native Hill" from *The Art of the Commonplace*, in which he writes of "Kentucky's central upland known as The Bluegrass" (3). Berry is committed to "the welfare of the earth, the problems of its health and preservation, the care of its life," and emphasizes that we must change how we relate to the land (5).

11. See Peter S. Wenz's article "Leopold's Novel: The Land Ethic in Barbara Kingsolver's *Prodigal Summer*," in which he insists that although *Prodigal Summer* may be "feminist" it is not "ecofeminist": "A major contention of ecofeminism is that sexism and anthropocentrism are mutually reinforcing. People associate women with nature and reinforce their denigration of women by associating women with already denigrated nature. In turn, they reinforce their anthropocentrism through associating nature with already denigrated women" (119). I argue that this is a misreading of ecofeminism and diminishes its resistant potential. As I mentioned earlier, ecofeminism is a

philosophical perspective that allows us to perceive the artificial chasm patriarchy has created between culture and women/nature. Women, therefore, have a critical ledge from which to subvert such totalizing narratives and can reassert their subjectivity in a way that has not been mapped out for them. *Prodigal Summer* reveals that women can utilize their relationships with the land to undermine these narratives.

Works Cited

Alaimo, Stacy. *Undomesticated Ground: Recasting Nature as Feminist Space.* Ithaca, NY: Cornell UP, 2000.

Berry, Wendell. *The Art of the Commonplace: The Agrarian Essays of Wendell Berry.* Ed. Norman Wirzba. Washington, DC: Shoemaker & Hoard, 2002.

Carson, Rachel. *Silent Spring.* Boston: Mariner, 1962.

Eaton, Heather, and Lois Ann Lorentzen. *Ecofeminism and Globalization: Exploring Culture, Context, and Religion.* Lanham, MD: Rowman & Littlefield, 2003.

Finkel, Mike. "The Ultimate Survivor." *Audubon Magazine* May-June 1999: 52-59.

Haraway, Donna. "Situated Knowledges: The Science Question in Feminism and the Privilege of Partial Perspective." *Simians, Cyborgs, and Women: The Reinvention of Nature.* New York: Routledge, 1991.

Irigaray, Luce. *Speculum of the Other Woman.* Trans. Gillian C. Gill. Ithaca, NY: Cornell UP, 1974.

Jones, Suzanne W. "The Southern Family as Endangered Species: Possibilities for Survival in Barbara Kingsolver's *Prodigal Summer*." *Poverty and Progress in the U.S. South Since 1920.* Ed. Suzanne W. Jones and Mark Newman. Amsterdam: VU UP, 2006.

Kingsolver, Barbara. *Animal, Vegetable, Miracle: A Year of Food Life.* New York: HarperCollins, 2007.

_____. *Prodigal Summer.* New York: HarperPerennial, 2000.

_____. *Small Wonder.* New York: HarperPerennial, 2002.

Murphy, Patrick D. "Nature Nurturing Fathers in a World Beyond Our Control." *Eco-Man: New Perspectives on Masculinity and Nature.* Ed. Mark Allister. Charlottesville: UP of Virginia, 2004.

Warren, Karen J. *Ecofeminist Philosophy: A Western Perspective on What It Is and Why It Matters.* Lanham, MD: Rowman & Littlefield, 2000.

Wenz, Peter S. "Leopold's Novel: The Land Ethic in Barbara Kingsolver's *Prodigal Summer. Ethics and the Environment* 8.2 (2003): 106-25.

Wirzba, Norman. *The Essential Agrarian Reader: The Future of Culture, Community, and the Land.* Lexington: UP of Kentucky, 2003.

Zimmerman, Michael. *Contesting Earth's Future: Radical Ecology and Postmodernity.* Berkeley: U of California P, 1997.

The Gothic and the Ethnic in Barbara Kingsolver's *The Bean Trees*_____

Matthew J. Bolton

Matthew J. Bolton offers an engaging reading of *The Bean Trees*, Kingsolver's first and probably still best-known novel, as a clever adaptation of the literary conventions of the gothic novel. Together *Wuthering Heights* and *Jane Eyre*, among the most widely read English novels, feature gothic tropes: the foundling child of uncertain ethnic origin, the supposedly mad woman of non-English ancestry who is hidden on an upstairs floor, and the woman protagonist who falls in love with a married man but decides not to pursue her affection. Bolton explains in detail how Kingsolver employs these tropes but subverts and adapts them to her late-twentieth-century setting. In the process, Kingsolver is able to redefine the notion of ethnicity: what nineteenth-century English readers perceived as a threat in the novels of the Brontë sisters, Taylor Greer sees as an opportunity. Her encounter with the strange and the unfamiliar is characterized by care and concern and, ultimately, a principled decision. — T.A.

Barbara Kingsolver's 1988 novel *The Bean Trees* follows its narrator Taylor Greer as she travels from her native Kentucky to Tucson, Arizona, in search of a better life. Along the way, she picks up not only her new name—Taylor is a trade-up from her given name of Marietta—but also a toddler, foisted upon her by a desperate woman on the edge of a Cherokee Indian reservation. Once in Tucson, Taylor must create a new life for herself and for the child, whom she calls Turtle. Gradually, she gathers about her a circle of friends who will serve as a surrogate family for Turtle: her roommate, Lou Ann; her employer, Mattie; and Estevan and Esperanza, two of the illegal immigrants whom Mattie shelters. When the state challenges her custody of Turtle, however, Taylor must risk all this by returning to the Cherokee Nation to secure her rights to be Turtle's mother.

On one level, Kingsolver's novel is representative of its own time and place: the American Southwest of the 1980s. Its depiction of Tucson is as vivid as its exploration of class, race, and gender in American life is insightful. Yet on a deeper, structural level, *The Bean Trees* draws on the long tradition of the gothic novel. While Taylor's narrative voice is distinctly American and distinctly modern, her story itself is rooted in the great English gothic novels, and in particular the masterpieces of the Brontë sisters, Emily's *Wuthering Heights* and Charlotte's *Jane Eyre*, both published in 1847. Kingsolver structures her novel around three tropes that are familiar to readers of the Brontës: the adoption of a foundling child of uncertain ethnicity and parentage, the discovery that someone lives hidden in the upper stories of an old house, and a heroine's struggle to overcome the obstacles that stand between her and the man she hopes to marry. These gothic elements are the machinery of the novel, the engine that propels Taylor's narrative forward. Yet Taylor, who made it across the country in a car she had to push to get started and who works at Mattie's garage patching and rotating tires, knows something about engines. She may be driven by the events around her, but she is also a driving force. By refusing to accept the gothic formulation by which people of other races and ethnicities are equated with the strange, the dangerous, and the cursed, she creates for herself and for her loved ones a future that is beyond what Catherine, Heathcliff, Jane, or Rochester could have envisioned.

The stories of both *Wuthering Heights* and *The Bean Trees* are set in motion with the discovery and de facto adoption of a foundling child. In Emily Brontë's novel, Mr. Earnshaw finds a child

> starving, and houseless, and as good as dumb in the streets of Liverpool, where he picked it up and inquired for its owner. Not a soul knew to whom it belonged . . . and his money and time being both limited, he thought it better to take it home with him at once. (30)

Earnshaw introduces the child, whom he has named Heathcliff, to the rest of his family with the admonition: "you must e'en take it as a gift of God, though it's as dark almost as if it came from the devil" (29). Heathcliff's skin color and his language—unidentified, but certainly not English—immediately mark him as being different from the Earnshaw children. Mrs. Dean, the Earnshaws' housekeeper, was herself a child at the time that Heathcliff arrived, and recalls her initial impression of him:

> We crowded round, and, over Miss Cathy's head, I had a peep at a dirty, ragged, black-haired child; big enough both to walk and talk . . . yet when it was set on its feet, it only stared round, and repeated over and over again some gibberish that nobody could understand. (29)

One can only speculate as to what this "gibberish" might be: perhaps it is Spanish, or Italian, or the Romanian dialect of the Gypsy, or Roma, people, or even an African language.

The child soon loses this unidentified first language, but his dark hair and complexion will continue to mark him as being different from the Earnshaw children. Catherine and Hindley are English, white, fair-haired, and therefore "normal"; Heathcliff is an ethnic *other*, and his complexion is a marker not only of his unknown parentage but also of his inscrutable moral qualities. In the world of *Wuthering Heights*, ethnicity is a terrifying cipher: Heathcliff could be anything. Many readers have speculated that the boy Mr. Earnshaw claims to have found is actually his illicit son. This reading would explain the patriarch's tenderness toward Heathcliff as well as his puzzling decision to bring the child home in the first place. Yet Heathcliff is consistently described in terms that associate him with hell and damnation, as if Mr. Earnshaw's first introduction—"it's as dark almost as if it came from the devil"— were more true than he could have known. Heathcliff's transformation from a helpless foundling child to Catherine's unrequited lover, to an avenging force who metes out retribution to the Earnshaw line, positions him as an incubus, a devil who draws sustenance from a human family only to wreak havoc on it. Heathcliff's ethnic otherness makes him a destructive force that will ultimately spell doom for the Earnshaw family.

Like Mr. Earnshaw, Taylor Greer unexpectedly finds herself in possession of a strange child. If the industrial city is a site of desolation in the world of *Wuthering Heights*, a lonely rest stop on the edge of the Cherokee Nation serves a similar role in *The Bean Trees*. Here, Taylor eats in a diner where two rough customers are drinking at the bar, men she recognizes as having "a mean streak" (21). At a booth, a woman wrapped in a pink blanket watches the men warily; Taylor recalls, "The way she looked at them made me feel like if I had better sense I'd be scared" (22). As she climbs back into her car to continue her journey west, Taylor is accosted by the woman from the diner, who thrusts a baby into the passenger seat of Taylor's car. "Take this baby . . . ," she says, "There isn't nobody knows it's alive, or cares" (24). Taylor says of the child: "It wasn't a baby, exactly. It was probably old enough to walk, though not so big that it couldn't be easily carried. Somewhere between a baby and a person" (23). Turtle is about the same age as Heathcliff, who is small enough to be carried under Mr. Earnshaw's coat but "big enough to walk" (29). Whereas Heathcliff speaks the "gibberish" that is his first language, Turtle does not yet speak—although developmentally she ought to by now.

Taylor faces a choiceless choice: she does not want the child, but she understands that some worse fate would await it—and perhaps Taylor herself—were she to go back into the diner to relinquish it. The child's history is inscribed on her little body: giving Turtle a bath at a motel later that night, Taylor sees scars and bruises left by physical and sexual abuse. This abuse no doubt accounts for the child's muteness and her other developmental delays. A doctor in Tucson will later say that the child is about a year older than she appears, pointing to signs of healed compound fractures on the child's X rays and explaining that "sometimes in an environment of physical or emotional deprivation a child will simply stop growing" (166). Taylor therefore is an unwitting agent of rescue as she takes Turtle from an environment in which she would in all likehood have died.

Heathcliff and Turtle enter their respective novels in similar ways: as foundling children who carry with them mysterious, troubled pasts. Yet the receptions they receive, and the influence they exert on their adoptive families, are strikingly different. Heathcliff finds himself an object of the Earnshaw children's anger and abuse. Catherine and Hindley were expecting their father to bring them presents from Liverpool, but instead he presents them with a rival. Resentful of Heathcliff, the children subject him to insults and beatings. The consummate rejection comes years later, when Hindley, having inherited Wuthering Heights, disowns and exiles Heathcliff. The "dirty, ragged, black-haired child" may have grown to be a man, but he has never been accepted into the Earnshaw family. Twice rejected—both as a surrogate brother and as a suitor to Catherine—Heathcliff seeks revenge on the family. The Earnshaws are therefore responsible for their own downfall, whether one locates the blame in their treatment of the foundling child or in their adopting him in the first place. One cannot know whether the environment out of which Heathcliff was plucked was as abusive as that experienced by Turtle, but the new environment of the Earnshaw household *is* a fundamentally abusive one. The Earnshaw children's assumptions about Heathcliff's otherness become a self-fulfilling prophecy by which they make him into the monster they suspected him to be.

Turtle, fortunately, finds herself in a loving home with a surrogate mother who does not see her as an "other." Taylor is primed to accept the child in part because she herself had a Cherokee great-grandfather. Living in Kentucky, far from any site of Indian culture, Taylor and her mother have long joked about holding in reserve their Cherokee Nation "head rights." This may seem like a tenuous connection—after all, Taylor is only one-eighth Cherokee—but it is meaningful to her. And before one dismisses the validity of being one-eighth anything, it is worth remembering that such minute calculations of parentage and heredity were central to America's understanding of race for several centuries. In New Orleans, for example, African Americans were classified according to the fraction of "black" blood in their ancestry: a quadroon had one black grandparent; an octoroon, one black great-grandparent. The state of Louisiana long defined as "colored" anyone who had "a trace of black ancestry." In 1970, a challenge to this statute caused the state to clarify its definition: a person was deemed "colored" if he or she was at least one thirty-second of African descent (Daniel 20). In other words, anyone who had a single African American great-great-great-grandparent was considered to be African American. Amazingly, this statute was challenged and overturned only in 1983. Such taxonomies point to the obsessive quality of eighteenth-, nineteenth-, and twentieth-century perspectives on race; the assumption seems to be that whiteness is a sort of pure medium that can be "colored" by even the smallest trace of nonwhite blood. Living in the latter half of the twentieth century, Taylor takes a radically different view. Her own Cherokee heritage begins as a curiosity and then becomes a justification for keeping Turtle as her own. It is an aspect of her history on which Taylor can draw but not one that defines her. In her perception of herself and of Turtle, Cherokee ancestry is neither a detriment nor a determinant.

Turtle comes to Taylor in circumstances that are reminiscent of a gothic novel. Yet by treating Turtle as her own rather than as an "other," Taylor creates an environment in which the child will thrive. Whereas Heathcliff goes from one kind of deprivation and abuse to another, Turtle finds in her new home a sanctuary. In her treatment of the child and in the unbiased expectation she holds for her future, Taylor takes Turtle out of the gothic genre in which she found her. It is as if Kingsolver—and, by extension, Taylor herself—are reworking the conventions of the gothic trope of the foundling child as dangerous and doomed.

The issues of whiteness and ethnicity that swirl around Heathcliff are also central to Charlotte Brontë's *Jane Eyre* and, in particular, to the secret hidden in the attic of Rochester's estate. Jane, who has come to Thornfield Hall to be the governess of Rochester's ward, Adele, has long suspected that a person is hidden in the upper levels of the house. She eventually learns that the inhabitant is Bertha Mason, Rochester's mad wife, whom he married while living in Jamaica. Rochester confesses of the union: "I found her a fine woman . . . tall, dark, and majestic. Her family wished to secure me because I was of a good race; and so did she" (202). Rochester's "good race" is desirable, presumably, because it may help produce children who look more European than African. Rochester continues:

> My bride's mother, I had never seen: I understood she was dead. The honeymoon over, I learned my mistake; she was only mad, and shut up in a lunatic asylum. There was a younger brother, too, a complete dumb idiot. (203)

Madness runs in the family, according to Rochester, and, having married Bertha, he soon begins to see her own streak of insanity. She is "coarse and trite, perverse and imbecile" (203). After four years, "the doctors now discovered that my wife was mad—her excesses had prematurely developed the germs of insanity" (203). Rochester returns to England, with Bertha in tow, and has her confined to the attic under the watchful eye of Grace Poole.

Bertha's race or ethnicity is never far from Rochester's mind. He refers to Bertha as "the Creole" and as "Indian" (206), and he seems to associate the qualities of her character with her ethnic background. Bertha is inherently limited, in Rochester's estimation: "Her cast of mind [is] common, low, narrow, and singularly incapable of being led to anything higher, expanded to anything larger" (203). In the world of *Jane Eyre*, ethnicity, immorality, and madness are closely correlated. Bertha has passed for something she is not—white and sane—and Rochester argues he would have been able to intuit her true character had he only been able to meet more of her family. Yet madness here feels like a code word for blackness, a stand-in for the ethnic identity that Bertha and her father have concealed from Rochester. Appalled at Rochester's "vindictive antipathy" toward Bertha, Jane says, "It is cruel—she cannot help being mad." Rochester replies, "It is not because she is mad that I hate her" (200). If it is not Bertha's madness that inspires Rochester's hate, then what is it? Rochester might argue that it is "the treachery of concealment" by which she hid her mad mother from him, but behind this is the concealment of racial identity on which the marriage was founded. Bertha has been "passing" not as sane but as white. Borrowing a page from Mr. Earnshaw's book, Rochester associates blackness with the devil, calling his wife "a monster" (205) and his marriage an "infernal union" (202). Rochester seems to share in the logic of the one-thirty-second statute, whereby a person who has even a fraction of non-European heritage is wholly not-white. The secret in Thornfield's attic—and, by extension, the one that looms over *Jane Eyre* as a whole—is a racially and ethnically charged one.

Kingsolver reworks Charlotte Brontë's trope of the dangerous ethnic figure hidden in the attic. Mattie, Taylor's employer at Jesus Is Lord Used Tires, operates a safe house for illegal immigrants from Central and South America. The upper story of her house is a haven for refugees who were persecuted in their own country and who face deportation if caught in the United States. In a style that is reminiscent of *Jane Eyre* and other gothic novels, Kingsolver seeds the first half of the book with clues about what really goes on at Mattie's shop. In their first encounter, for example, Mattie gives Turtle some juice in a baby's cup, and Taylor says, "You must have grandbabies around." Mattie replies "Mmm-hmmm. Something like that." Taylor wonders "what, exactly, could be 'something like' grandbabies" (60). A young priest comes by looking for Mattie but will not tell Taylor the purpose of his visit. There is an air of mystery surrounding Mattie and the upper rooms of her house. Much as Jane Eyre began to catch glimpses of Bertha in her employer's house, so does Taylor become aware of Mattie's residents: "People came and went quietly. And stayed quietly . . . there was an upstairs window that looked out over the park. I saw faces there, sometimes Esperanza's and sometimes others, staring across the open space" (159). Yet whereas Bertha is an ominous figure, the strangers in Mattie's upstairs rooms fill Taylor and the reader with sadness rather than dread:

> A woman stood at the window. Her hair was threaded with white and fell loose around her shoulders, and she was folding a pair of men's trousers. She moved the flats of her hands slowly down each crease, as if folding these trousers were the only task ahead of her in life, and everything depended on getting it right. (161)

Bertha Mason embodies otherness and abnormality. This unidentified woman, on the other hand, is performing the most normal and domestic of tasks. Circumstances have forced her to live a fugitive existence, but the attention she gives to folding the trousers speaks to her true nature. She would far rather be living a quiet life at home than hiding in Mattie's house. Her absorption in the task shows both her longing for a normal life and her sadness at the constrained circumstances in which she has been forced to live. If Bertha represents ethnicity or racial identity as a marker of difference and abnormality, the people Mattie shelters are marked first and foremost by what they have in common with Taylor and the other residents of Tucson.

The attic therefore serves different purposes in *Jane Eyre* and *The Bean Trees*: in the former, it is a prison and an asylum; in the latter, a safe house and a sanctuary. Bertha Mason is herself a danger and has been confined and guarded so that she will not hurt herself or others. Her eventual destruction of Thornfield Hall confirms that she has, in fact, been a threat all along. The illegal immigrants living in Mattie's house, on the other hand, are threatened rather than threatening. They face deportation should they be caught, and on their return to their home countries they could be tortured and executed. Mattie keeps these political refugees hidden to protect them from larger social forces. Some of Mattie's fellow Americans may view these immigrants through the lens of racism and xenophobia, but the novel and its narrator do not. Whereas the conclusion of *Jane Eyre* confirms that the ethnic immigrant is inherently dangerous and should be guarded against, *The Bean Trees* suggests the opposite. At the end of the novel, Estevan and Esperanza, two of the refugees whom Mattie and Taylor have sheltered, become themselves Taylor's saviors.

It is through her friendship with Estevan and Esperanza that Taylor comes to embrace Mattie's mission. An English teacher in his home country of Guatemala, Estevan is able to move freely about Tucson. Taylor and Lou Ann insist that he "spoke better English than the two of us combined" (122). Esperanza, his wife, does not speak the language fluently but joins Estevan on his outings, relying on his English to serve for both of them. As a result, the couple are freer than most of the refugees in Mattie's sanctuary. Their past, however, is as terrible as that of any of their countrymen. Because Estevan was in a teachers' union at home, he and his family were the targets of government reprisals. Esperanza was arrested and tortured, members of their extended family were killed, and their child was taken from them, presumably to be raised by a childless military family. Estevan and Esperanza carry with them the great weight of this secret history. Once again, the hidden life of the ethnic other is figured differently in *Jane Eyre* and *The Bean Trees*. Bertha's history is bound up with the mental illness that runs in her family; she is subject to psychological rather than political forces. Estevan and Esperanza have their own demons, but those demons arise from what was done to them rather than from who and what they are.

The trauma of torture and the suffering caused by the loss of her child are so great that Esperanza eventually tries to kill herself. Taylor, not yet knowing what Esperanza has experienced, sees the act as a self-ish one. She says to Estevan: "Esperanza had somebody. Has somebody. How could she want to leave you? It's not fair" (180). For a moment, before Estevan tells her what his wife has been through, Taylor may see Esperanza as a figure not unlike Bertha Mason: unstable, ungrateful, and dangerous. She may think that Esperanza is as much a fetter to Estevan as Bertha is to Rochester—and the fact that Taylor has fallen in love with the married Estevan makes her a second Jane Eyre. Learning of Esperanza's history, however, and understanding that she is the victim of political oppression rather than of some inherent moodiness or madness, changes Taylor's view of her and of all of Mattie's refugees. If her friendship with Estevan in the present makes her sympathetic to the plight of the refugees, her knowledge of the torture and oppression from which the refugees have fled moves Taylor from passive sympathy to action.

There is a moment midway through Kingsolver's novel, when Esperanza lies in the hospital after her failed suicide attempt and Estevan and Taylor sit on Taylor's couch, talking and drinking beer, at which the reader—like Taylor herself—may see the glimmer of a storybook ending. Esperanza, it seems, has removed herself as an obstacle between our narrator and the man she loves. Readers can be ruthless in their sympathies: we are unabashedly rooting for Taylor. As the novel's narrator, she is our point of access to the world that she inhabits. Everything we know about the places, events, and other characters of *The Bean Trees* is filtered through Taylor's eyes and voice. While we do not want to see Taylor win at any cost, we may begin to feel that Esperanza's life is not *too* great a cost if it ensures Taylor's happiness. After all, most readers accept this same logic in *Jane Eyre*. Jane rejects Rochester once she knows that he is still married to Bertha. It is a principled decision, and most readers see it as Jane's assertion of both her own moral probity and her own self-respect; she will not be a second wife to Rochester, no matter how much she may love him. Yet when Bertha dies while burning down Thornfield Hall, she frees Rochester and Jane. In attempting to save Bertha—and in losing his vision and a hand in the process—Rochester both atones for some measure of his guilty past and shows that he is not complicit in his wife's death. It is not exactly a deus ex machina ending, for the novel has long prepared us for Bertha's destructive act, but it is nevertheless one that allows the novel's protagonists to have their cake and eat it too. They make principled choices, and yet the plot of the novel subsequently delivers to them the happy ending they denied themselves.

Esperanza, like Bertha before her, seems to have acted on her own self-destructive impulses and, hence, to have removed herself as an obstacle to the protagonist's happiness. Estevan's explanation of Esperanza's past changes her status in the novel, however, and thereby the range of possibilities open to Taylor. Esperanza herself has been mostly silent, but her personal and political history speak for her. Having learned what drove Esperanza to attempt suicide, Taylor can no longer think of herself as a rival for Estevan's affections:

> The schoolgirl nerves that had possessed me half an hour ago seemed ridiculous now; this was like having a crush on some guy only to find out that he's been dating your mother or your math teacher. This man was way beyond me. (181)

Yet Estevan seems to be making himself available to Taylor: hurt, vulnerable, and lonely, he has sought out a young woman who he must know feels attracted to him. Late in the evening, Taylor and Estevan fall asleep on the couch, and she wakes to find that they are in a position that is something other than innocent:

> Later I woke up again. . . . Estevan and I were curled like spoons on the sofa, his knees against the back of my knees and his left hand on my ribs, just under my breast. When I put my hand on top of his I could feel my heart beating under his fingers.
>
> I thought of Esperanza, her braids on her shoulders. Esperanza staring at the ceiling. She would be lying on a cot somewhere, sweating the poison out of her system. (188)

Thinking of Estevan's wife, rather than of her own happiness, Taylor makes her own principled decision: "All of Esperanza's hurts flamed up in my mind. . . . I lifted Estevan's hand from my ribcage and kissed his palm. It felt warm. Then I slid off the sofa and went to my own bed" (189). Like Jane, Taylor denies herself the man she loves because she acknowledges that he already belongs to another. Yet the machinery of her own novel will not end up delivering this man back to her. Taylor's decision is an irreversible one.

The Bean Trees therefore subverts a third gothic trope by having its marriageable narrator not ultimately marry the man she loves. The heroine not only respects the claims of the first wife, as Jane Eyre did, but by novel's end will also actually help to ensure the couple's future happiness. Taylor's own coming-of-age will not be as a wife but as a mother, and the novel ends with an adoption rather than a wedding.

The final events of *The Bean Trees* represent Taylor's quite brilliant negotiation with race and ethnicity in America, but they also represent her active redrawing of the conventional gothic plotlines that seem to be available to her. On a road trip back to Oklahoma with Turtle, Estevan, and Esperanza, Taylor creates a happy ending that is grounded in a set of assumptions about parentage, ethnicity, marriage, and motherhood that are quite different from those of Jane Eyre or other gothic heroines. It is her willingness to subvert the conventional plotlines available to a single woman—as well as her deep understanding of the conventional attitudes regarding race and ethnicity that so many of the people around her hold—that allows Taylor to create a better future for herself and her friends.

Taylor's trip to Oklahoma has a twofold purpose. First, she must find Turtle's parents and obtain their permission to adopt the child formally. Having resolved to make this trip, Taylor has realized that she could use it as an opportunity to deliver Estevan and Esperanza to a part of the country that is further from the Mexican border and, hence, where they could live under less scrutiny. Both missions are risky. She will lose Turtle to the state if she cannot procure a formal adoption, and she faces a stiff prison sentence—while her friends face deportation— if she is caught harboring and transporting illegal immigrants. Taylor's eventual success on both fronts is grounded in her understanding that race and ethnicity are to a very real extent social constructs. Clothing, for example, goes a long way toward establishing an individual's identity. Mattie and Taylor pay particular attention to what their friends wear on the journey: "Esperanza and Estevan were dressed about as American as you could get without looking plain obnoxious: he had on jeans and an alligator shirt" (254). When stopped at an immigration checkpoint, Taylor says, "This is my brother Steve, and my sister-in-law" (255). With new clothes, a new name, and his flawless English, Estevan can pass for Taylor's brother. This raises a fascinating series of questions about what race and ethnicity really constitute. Taylor, the reader has assumed, is white, while Estevan is from an Indian tribe in Guatemala. If they can pass for siblings, however, then the whole notion of "whiteness" is less monolithic than one might have thought.

If at the checkpoint Estevan passes for Taylor's brother, in the Cherokee Nation he and Esperanza can pass for Cherokee. After seeing an Indian police officer, Taylor reflects: "It must have been a very long time since Esperanza and Estevan had been in a place where they looked just like everybody else, including cops. The relief showed in their bodies" (274). Taylor realizes why this will be a better place for her friends to live:

> We began to understand that Oklahoma had been a good choice: Estevan and Esperanza could blend in here. Practically half the people we saw were Indians.
> "Do Cherokees look like Mayans?" I asked Estevan.
> "No," he said.
> "Would a white person know that?"
> "No." (265)

Because ethnicity is a social construct rather than an inherent set of traits and attributes, Estevan and Esperanza will be able to pass for Cherokee—and hence for Americans. Most white people do not make fine distinctions among Indians because they subscribe to a dichotomy whereby people are either white or nonwhite. To them, the Cherokee and the Mayan are, for all intents and purposes, indistinguishable. Taylor's ingenious plan for securing her rights to Turtle grows out of her awareness that most white people use broad categories to classify those around them. Estevan and Esperanza, dressed in their most threadbare clothes, pose as Turtle's parents and accompany Taylor to the adoption agency to give her the child formally. The plan works because it draws on so many stereotypes and preconceptions regarding race, ethnicity, class, and wealth. The state officials see a poor Indian couple giving their child to a white woman who will better be able to care for her. Because Taylor knows what most white people think about Indians, she is able to create a situation that affirms their worldview and gets her the legal imprimatur that she needs to keep her child.

Taylor's stratagem at the adoption agency not only secures her rights to Turtle but also strengthens Estevan and Esperanza's marriage. Turtle may not be their child, but their giving her to Taylor nevertheless serves as a cathartic experience for a couple whose actual child has disappeared. Kingsolver thus cleverly subverts the gothic marriage plot, for Taylor becomes a mother rather than a wife.

Again and again in her journey west, Taylor finds herself facing situations that are the stuff of a Brontë novel: she has a foundling child thrust upon her, she becomes aware of people who are being hidden away from society, and she falls in love with an unavailable, married man. Yet she reshapes each of these plotlines to create options for herself and the people around her that do not seem to be available to her gothic counterparts. Taylor's happy ending constitutes not only the reinvention of herself but also the reinvention of a genre.

Works Cited

Brontë, Charlotte. *Jane Eyre*. 1847. Ed. Richard J. Dunn. New York: W. W. Norton, 1971.

Brontë, Emily. *Wuthering Heights*. 1847. Ed. Richard J. Dunn. New York: W. W. Norton, 1963.

Daniel, G. Reginald. *More than Black? Multiracial Identity and the New Racial Order*. Philadelphia: Temple UP, 2002.

Kingsolver, Barbara. *The Bean Trees*. New York: HarperCollins, 1988.

CRITICAL
READINGS

Gardens of Auto Parts:
Kingsolver's Merger of American Western Myth and Native American Myth in *The Bean Trees*_____
Catherine Himmelwright

Catherine Himmelwright bases her essay on Kingsolver's adaptations and modifications of familiar myths about the American West, which traditionally involve male adventurers setting out to conquer a place or a people. Women's participation in the westering movement has often been limited to gardening and other domestic occupations. Himmelwright sees the vegetable garden in *The Bean Trees* blossoming right in the junkyard. As if to invert the familiar paradigm of "the machine in the garden," familiar from Leo Marx's groundbreaking study and invoked, in various forms, by critics from Henry Nash Smith to Jane Tompkins, Kingsolver places the garden into the machine age to suggest a fusion of male and female images. Through the plotline of *The Bean Trees*, Kingsolver, according to Himmelwright, challenges "an American mythology of conquest and control." Her protagonist, Taylor Greer, enacts a western flight and creates a new community, but with a feminine twist: her move will result in an integration, not a confrontation. By adopting the Cherokee child handed to her, Taylor takes responsibility for nurturing and privileges matrilineal thinking. Himmelwright's argument is built on the importance she attributes to Kingsolver's manner of allowing Native American spiritual and nurturing traditions to influence her alteration of the limited, male-centered American Western myth.   — T.A.

Outside was a bright, wild wonderland of flowers and vegetables and auto parts. Heads of cabbage and lettuce sprouted out of old tires. An entire rusted out Thunderbird, minus the wheels, had nasturtiums blooming out the windows like Mama's hen-and-chicks pot on the front porch at home. A kind of teepee frame made of CB antennas was all overgrown with cherry-tomato vines. (Kingsolver 45)

Junkyards and gardens: how could two such diametrically opposed worlds flourish together? Seemingly, one would preclude the possibility of the other. Abandoned wrecks would jeopardize new tomatoes, while spilled oil would poison the fertile ground, debilitating the delicate burgeoning of a squash blossom. How can anyone tend a garden in the midst of rusted auto parts? How can growth occur in the midst of abandonment?

In the mythology that surrounds the American West, one of the primary expressions of the western experience has been the male's desire to move. Whether by horse, wagon, raft, or even later by car, action typifies the male western hero, who feels a powerful desire to hit the open road. Action and adventure are tied tightly with the need to be mobile. Adventures do not happen at home; you have to go find them. In contrast, women have been connected rather loosely to the male western archetype despite their presence on the frontier. Rather than a symbol of movement, the female experience has been firmly rooted in the image of the garden. Annette Kolodny has perhaps furthered this construction the most by exploring women's idealization of the garden on the frontier. She states in *The Land Before Her* that women gained access to the U.S. West by connecting themselves both literarily and figuratively with the garden. Embodying both the characteristics of the natural and procreative, gardens evolved into symbols of the home. Cultivating a garden in the West provided women a claim or admittance into a masculine world, if only to a portion of the experience. As a garden must have constant attention, movement is difficult for those who garden. Women, therefore, gained access to the frontier, yet were excluded from the adventure that men sought.

Despite the obvious oppositions, Barbara Kingsolver finds a way to unite the possibilities of a garden with the opportunities of adventure in *The Bean Trees*, her novel about a woman's migration from the American South to the American West. Merging these characteristics, the desire for movement and the desire to tend a home, Kingsolver is able to express a female voice that has heretofore been lost or subsumed by the white male experience. In many ways, Kingsolver creates a character who becomes that individual Kolodny speaks of at the end of *The Land Before Her*, for Kingsolver's main character becomes both "adventurer and domesticator" (Kolodny 240). By combining these two figures, Kingsolver fashions a new American mythology that unites both male and female imaginative constructions. The attempt is not an easy one, as access to the West has almost always been achieved, whether the individual is male or female, through performing white masculine constructions. In *West of Everything*, Jane Tompkins points out the difficulty women have had in gaining admittance to this masculine world, especially access to the role of the hero. Her findings reveal female desire for this access through women's own attempts to "imagine" themselves within the western landscape and culture. Tompkins notes that some women found imagining inclusion impossible, but for those who could, awkward manipulations would take place in order to create a place for the female within this world:

> One friend said she loved "Bonanza" so much that she had to invent a female character so that she could participate as a woman. . . . Another friend told me she could identify with male heroes but only the nonwhite, non-WASP ones, Tonto and Zorro. (16)

Clearly, the struggle to find inclusion in this myth of adventure is difficult; still the passage proves the desire of women to claim in some "real" sense the ideology represented in our imaginative constructions of the American West. Yet how do you write about a female's experience in the West? The West has become so "masculinized" in connotation that the very word evokes images of the male. Thus, finding negotiated space from which to express the female experience in the West is difficult. Although attempts have been made which include the female presence, traditionally these representations privilege a male voice.

Historically, a woman's presence in the "frontier experience" occurs *hysterically*, as she is seen bemoaning the fact that her husband or father has forced her to leave everyone and everything she loves to "go west." Rarely is she seen as a willing participant in her removal to the wide-open spaces. Lillian Schlissel states in *Women's Diaries of the Westward Journey* that "The overland journey wrenched women from the domestic circle that had encased much of their lives in stable communities" (28). Schlissel provides many examples that emphasize this devastating separation. Often the separation from a domestic community proved to be one of the most difficult challenges. As Melody Graulich states, "Adventure, independence, and freedom belong to male characters, while women 'endure,' as does the long-suffering pioneer helpmate who tries to re-create 'home' in the West, memorialized as the Madonna of the plains" (187). Janis Stout in *Through the Window, Out the Door* writes that "narrative conventions and assumptions (of journeys and departures) are so deeply rooted in masculine paradigms that reshaping them to serve a woman's own desire is an enormous challenge" (4). As for some of the women described by Tompkins, active participation seems difficult to imagine within the historical accounts of western experience.[1]

Rejecting the limited representations of women on the frontier that are given by history and literature, many contemporary writers have tried their hand at the "anti-Western." Michael Johnson in *New Westers* defines the "anti-Western" as "going against the grain in pretty direct fashion." The anti-Western emerges as a vehicle to manipulate the literary construction or archetype that has been fashioned within the American imagination. Johnson says that "They portrayed the underside and . . . suggested that the idealist assumptions of the traditional Western formula were naïve and masked the racism, violence, and greed of the historical conquest of the West" (215). Most who have chosen to write the anti-Western have remained within the parameters of a masculine world. In writing about the female experience, they have simply written about a woman who, when faced with the challenges that normally face male protagonists, reacts in a similar way. Such narratives still privilege the masculine experience and undermine how the female experience might be separate from this archetype. In essence, the female figure simply becomes a man, or at least a more androgynous figure who can adopt masculine characteristics in order to experience the West.

Kingsolver does adopt the approach of the anti-Western; however, she brings a new twist to her approach. Envisioning a new western archetype, she is able to leave behind the standard forms of male adventure by finding access to an alternate mythology. Like Tompkins' friends who find access through the alter-hero, "the nonwhite, non-WASP ones, Tonto and Zorro," Kingsolver uses a similarly alternative perspective by evoking a nonwhite mythology which will allow for the participation of the female. By choosing the "ultimate anti-Western," Kingsolver is able to explore a world which gives voice to the female through the Native American experience. Gaining access to a world and mythology which pre-exists the white male construction of adventure, she is able to navigate a space in which the female story has not yet been defined by the masculine voice.

Kingsolver begins her novel by following the male archetype of western myth, the only difference being that her main character is female. Kingsolver creates a strong-minded, independent woman in search of a better life. Turning away from Kentucky, Missy Greer, at twenty-three, heads west with the hope of finding a life that will provide new opportunities. Popular western heroes such as Daniel Boone, Huck Finn, and Natty Bumppo are all brought to mind in Kingsolver's initial description of Missy. She is strong and independent, and appears fully capable of clearing her path in order to achieve her own desires, but most importantly she, like them, desires to leave civilization and "light out for the territory" (Twain 283). Similar to Leslie Fiedler's depictions of westering men in *The Return of the Vanishing American*, Kingsolver creates a protagonist who yearns for escape. Many male literary figures "together constitute the image of the runaway from home and civilization whom we long to be when we are our most authentic selves"; their female counterparts "add up to the image of his dearest enemy, spokesman for the culture and the European inheritance he flees" (118). Men leave their homes in order to flee women; women represent opposition to the fulfillment of their identities. Building on this tradition, Kingsolver inverts the usual pattern in order to explore the female's search for identity.

Important to note as well is the fact that *The Bean Trees* is a southern novel, or certainly a novel that begins in the South. Taking place initially in Kentucky, it is replete with rural images and the vivid dialogue of the South. However, Missy's southern origins take up very little of this novel. Giving the reader only a glimpse, Kingsolver shows us the impetus for Missy's search and an explanation for the western novel that *The Bean Trees* becomes. The nasturtiums might bloom like "Mama's hen-and-chicks pot on the front porch at home," but by the end of the novel, Missy is not in Kentucky anymore. And in leaving Kentucky, Missy and *The Bean Trees* leave the South behind in an attempt to head west and craft a western adventure. How can a southern novel be a western novel? Robert Brinkmeyer explores this question in *Remapping Southern Literature*. He notes the proliferation of western novels written by southerners and their interests in exploring notions of southern place and western space. In *The Bean Trees*, Brinkmeyer sees the main character as forming a place in the West, finding some type of regeneration that comes through "reintegration—reintegration into family and community that closes . . . *The Bean Trees*" (101). While the novel might certainly be read in this way, it neglects to consider the lack of community described in this southern locale. Missy Greer may find something typically considered "southern" in Arizona, but the remarkable thing is she doesn't find this "typically southern" place in Kentucky. For this reason, a "reintegration" does not seem possible; instead she crafts a new place, her own place, out of the space she seeks. Much of what sparks the events of *The Bean Trees* proves a dramatic reaction against the main character's southern upbringing.

Unlike the societal pressures depicted in traditional western novels, *The Bean Trees* reverses the paradigm in which the demands of society are represented by women. In contrast to the depictions of men seeking freedom away from the demands of women, Kingsolver suggests a world in which women and children feel limited by the demands of the father. Although Kingsolver creates no father figure for Missy (her father leaves long before she is born), she does paint a vivid picture of another family in Pittman County: Newt Harbine's. Missy sees many likenesses between herself and Newt. "If you were to look at the two of us . . . you could have pegged us for brother and sister" (2). Due to these similarities, Kingsolver suggests that the events that occur in Newt's family are at least partially responsible for Missy's flight. Missy relates the story of watching Newt Harbine's father propelled "over the top of the Standard Oil sign" due to his inability to fill a tire correctly. Despite the comedy provided for the reader, this experience leaves a lasting impression on Missy. "I had this feeling about what Newt's whole life was going to amount to, and I felt sorry for him. Before that exact moment I don't believe I had given much thought to the future" (1). And it is later, after Newt Harbine shoots his wife and kills himself, that Missy saves her money in an attempt to leave Pittman County. Jolene, Newt's wife, tells Missy that Newt's father was responsible for everything. She claims that: "he [Newt's father] beat him up, beat her up, and even . . . hit the baby with a coal scuttle" (9). As similarities have already been drawn between Newt and Missy, it is difficult not to see the feelings of being trapped and lost to all opportunity for Newt as well. Escaping "daddy" is seen as a difficult feat, as in Newt's eventual demise, as well as Jolene's challenges of escaping her own father's abuse. Learning Jolene's past, Missy feels she may have been lucky: "I told her I didn't know, because I didn't have a daddy. That I was lucky that way. She said yeah" (9).

In addition to this pressure, Missy is also desperate to escape the pressures to conform to the woman's role in Pittman County, Kentucky. Most of the women at Missy's high school have become pregnant before their senior year: "Believe me in those days the girls were dropping by the wayside like seeds off a poppyseed bun and you learned to look at every day as a prize" (3). Graduating from high school, Missy describes herself as incredibly lucky to have been given a job at the local hospital. In fact, she says that her science teacher who helped her get the job "changed my life, there is no doubt" (3). In an environment where most young girls become pregnant and marry, Missy describes a place where opportunities for a different kind of life are limited or non-existent. Her mother cleans homes for people in town, and before the hospital, Missy's only options for gaining money are helping her mother with other people's laundry, babysitting, or picking bugs off farmers' beans. Missy prizes the job at the hospital, as it contrasts dramatically with the dead end jobs she has had before. She states: "But this was a real job at the Pittman County Hospital, which was one of the most important and cleanest places for about a hundred miles" (4). Missy pursues a life that deviates from the ones around her: "Mama always said barefoot and pregnant was not my style. She knew" (3). Escaping pregnancy, Missy feels she has the opportunity to flee Pittman County and the dim future it represents for her.

Perhaps more telling than the lack of opportunity is the lack of community in Pittman County, Kentucky. Nowhere does Kingsolver describe this southern community in a positive way. Unlike other southern novels rife with the close, sometimes smothering bonds of family and community, Kingsolver describes no close friends or caring extended family in Missy's life. The only positive forces are her mother, who always acted as if her daughter "hung [the moon] up in the sky and plugged in all the stars," and her teacher who is "from out of state, from some city college up north" (3). They are the only ones described who are able to envision a life larger than Pittman County. Telling, too, is the fact that Missy's teacher is not even from the South. He seems easily able to imagine a larger, more expansive world, due to his outsider's perspective. That a southern community might be found stifling is not necessarily surprising or strange; southern literature abounds with such descriptions. What is considerably more notable is that this small southern county is completely devoid of any representation of community. Perhaps Missy is denied admittance; yet she never mentions a positive view of community for anyone, including her mother or her school friends. Certainly if she were able to accept life in Pittman County on its own terms, she might find herself with a larger body of friends; however, even those who seem to acquiesce seem devoid of any support. Regardless of this larger absence found within Pittman County, the focus remains on Missy's lack of community. Take out Missy's mother and her northern teacher, and she has no one. Within this environment, Missy Greer is well-fostered to become a self-sufficient and independent individual. She has no real choice. Missy's society prescribes a role that she does not desire and denies her a sense of community. For these reasons, the dream of freedom that has always loomed large for the westering man is now sought by the woman in her equally powerful desire to escape. Southern society threatens her vision of personal identity. Flight is essential.

Missy will be like the fish she finds in the "old mud-bottomed ponds" of Kentucky—"The ones nobody was ever going to hook, slipping away under the water like dark-brown dreams" (3). She will not be the "hooked bass" that remains. After working at the hospital for more than five years, she makes enough money to buy a modern-day horse, a "55 Volkswagen bug with no windows to speak of, and no back seat and no starter" (10). She leaves Kentucky unaided and relying on her own abilities: "I would drive west until my car stopped running, and there I would stay" (12).

Soon after she leaves, Missy decides she will change her name. "I wasn't crazy about anything I had been called up to this point in life, and this seemed like the time to make a clean break. I didn't have any special name in mind, but just wanted a change" (11). The name change certainly marks Missy's desire to "re-create" herself, or at least her attempts toward that re-creation, but it also marks Missy's recognition of her own success at leaving Pittman County, and, similar to other western figures, her ability to claim her own autonomy due to her escape. R. W. B. Lewis notes in *The American Adam* this pivotal moment in Cooper's *Deerslayer*. Once "the trial is successfully passed—the trial of honor, courage and self-reliance—Deerslayer earns his symbolic reward of a new name" (104). Missy's name change is equally pivotal. She decides to name herself for the nearest town in which her car runs out of gas. Although she claims to desire leaving this decision to the fates, she proves she has control over what her destiny will be. "I came pretty close to being named after Homer, Illinois, but kept pushing it. I kept my fingers crossed through Sidney, Sadorus, Cerro Gordo, Decatur, and Blue Mound, and coasted into Taylorsville on the fumes" (12). She chooses the name Taylor. She has fashioned her own name, which denotes not only western movement but also someone empowered and able to adapt or create. This change further marks Taylor as a creative participant in her new identity.

Taylor's adventure west continues to follow this male pattern at the beginning of the novel. Just as she leaves the South behind and begins to create her own identity, she crosses the path of the Native American. As Fiedler states: "The heart of the Western is not the confrontation with the alien landscape . . . but the encounter with the Indian" (21). Much has been written concerning the white male's relationship with the Indian. Smith writes in *Virgin Land*: "As the literary Western hero moves beyond the Mississippi he is becoming more and more fully assimilated into the mores of the Indian. At the same time, he is conceived as more and more completely autonomous, isolated, and self-contained" (91). Regardless of the result, which has often been dramatic, the exchange between whites and Native Americans usually has taken place between men.[2]

Kingsolver's *The Bean Trees* places equal importance on this confrontation, but its approach differs dramatically from earlier literary representations. Just as Taylor begins to feel she has left Pittman County behind, she is surprised by a Cherokee woman who emerges out of the night to leave a small child with her as she is leaving a diner. Taylor is confused and muddled about what she should do. A child is not part of her plan, and she quickly feels the promise of her new life threatened: "If I wanted a baby I would have stayed in Kentucky . . . I could have had babies coming out of my ears by now" (18). Yet Taylor does not leave the child, and she continues on her journey with baby in tow. Once she realizes that the child has been abused, Taylor becomes more convinced that she really has no choice: "I thought I knew about every ugly thing that one person does to another, but I had never even thought about such things being done to a baby girl" (23). Finding "bruises and worse" on the child's body, Taylor confronts the dark shadows of abuse which have tormented the child's young life.

Important to note, as well, is the fact that Kingsolver has chosen that the Native American child should be Cherokee. Through this choice, Kingsolver evokes the forced removal of Native Americans from the southeastern part of the United States, including Cherokee, along the Trail of Tears (1813-1855). Allusions to this historical event intensify Kingsolver's questioning of an American mythology of conquest and control. Arriving in Oklahoma, Taylor states, "It was not a place you'd ever go to live without some kind of lethal weapon aimed at your hind end. It was clear to me that the whole intention of bringing the Cherokees here was to get them to lie down and die without a fight" (13). Sympathizing with the Native American plight, Taylor is perhaps further moved due to her own belief that she is one-eighth Cherokee. Raised by her mother, Taylor has been brought up to believe that if times grew tough she could always claim her "head rights." On arriving in Oklahoma, Taylor realizes that these "rights" promise very little. When she writes home she informs her mother: "No offense, but the Cherokee Nation is crap. Headed west" (15). Kingsolver emphasizes the despair Taylor finds at the Oklahoma reservation. "I sat in the parking lot looking out over that godless stretch of nothing and came the closest I have ever come to cashing in and plowing under" (13). What her mother has imagined as possible freedom, Taylor discovers to be stagnation and ultimate despair. Claiming the child, however, ties Taylor to this heritage, regardless of her rejection of reservation life.

The acquisition of the child is pivotal in Kingsolver's novel, for at

---

this point Kingsolver breaks from the archetypal male construction. Although the confrontation with the Native American is comparable in importance, Taylor's experience no longer mirrors that of the masculine. Choosing to adapt a Cherokee creation myth, Kingsolver severs her previous connection to a white masculine perspective and investigates the female experience through Cherokee mythology. Traditionally in American literature, the white male experience has been closely defined through his relation to the Native American. Much of the white male interaction has relied heavily on the physical component of that relationship. The white male gains from his experience with the Native American by modeling many of his physical abilities. Learning the ways of the woods, the white male learns how to navigate through the frontier landscape through the guidance and expertise of the Native American.[3] However, although these behaviors are often successfully modeled, males tend to stray from the spiritual nature of their "borrowed" behavior. The inner workings of Native American mythology have no place in the white world and in many ways frighten white males in their search to gain access and control of a mysterious wilderness.

Fiedler comments on the threat of Indian mythology in *The Return of the Vanishing American*:

> The really disturbing threat of the Indian, technologically backward and eternally surprised at the white man's treachery, was never military—nor even, despite the unexpectedness of the pox venereal—but mythological, which is to say, based not on what he did, only on what he was. (39)

Kingsolver explores levels of Native American mythology and Native American spirituality which have been traditionally avoided in white literary representations. Even as her character follows the male pattern of confrontation with the Native American, the encounter, and the ramifications of that encounter, will differ vastly from the male approach. Rather than confronting and adopting the *physical* attributes of a Native American world, Kingsolver creates a character who explores the *spiritual* or mythological ways of Native Americans.[4] Despite the radical differences in the contact, a growing sense of identity still emerges from this experience.

Important to note as well is the fact that the specific myth that Kingsolver incorporates is based on female deities. By looking to the Cherokee world, Kingsolver's story further gains strength by employing a myth derived from a society in which women are empowered. Historically, Cherokee society was matrilineal. The influence of the woman in Cherokee culture is seen through the power demonstrated by females in the area of kinship. "The only permanent members of a household were women. Husbands were outsiders; that is they were not kinsmen. When a man married, he moved from the household of his mother to that of his wife" (Perdue 43). Empowerment of women in areas of kinship is equally represented in the mythology that surrounds Cherokee thought. Some critics state that "the existence of an important female deity indicates the acceptance of female rights, privileges, and even power" (Perdue 40). Many of the deities that exist in the Cherokee world reflect the essential role of the woman in Cherokee society. Two examples include the deity of corn and the deity of creation.[5] Commanding a role in the Native American's main source of food, as well as in the act of creation, exemplifies the unequivocal importance of the female within Cherokee society.

Kingsolver's choice of myth not only describes the female experience but also glorifies the power of the woman and her ability to create. The central figure of the Cherokee myth of creation is Star Woman; she creates not only gardens but also new worlds. In the ancient Cherokee myth, Star Woman is responsible for the creation of the natural world and for bringing consciousness to those around her:

Many people say it was Star Woman who was the primal cause. One story says she was in her father's garden, that is in Galunlati, when she heard drumming under a tree and dug a hole to see what was going on. Star

Woman fell through the hole and spun toward the earth. At that time the earth was under the primeval flood, and earth creatures lacked the spark of deep consciousness or understanding. They did have feelings, however.

The father watched his daughter fall and called on the winds to get the earth creatures to help her. Turtle suggested that his back become a landing place for her, so the animals dove into the depths to find something soft to place on Turtle's back.

Now the earth on Turtle's back grew. . . . All was ready for Star Woman, who landed on Turtle's back and immediately produced corn, beans, other plants, and rivers from her body. Most of all, she brought the spark of consciousness, symbolized by the Cherokee's sacred fire, which is always kept alive for the ceremonies. (Leeming 47)

Kingsolver's knowledge of this myth is revealed on a variety of levels due to the emphasis placed on certain themes. The myth details the empowerment of the female, which is central to the human connection to a natural world, as well as the importance of community. In choosing and adapting this myth to her novel, Kingsolver dramatically opposes traditional themes of the western archetypal tradition.

In both the myth and the novel, women leave the world they have previously known for another. Star Woman falls through a hole from her father's world, while Taylor leaves a patriarchal southern world that restricts her. After their departure, their journeys are radically changed through their meeting with (the) Turtle. Star Woman is saved from the destructive "primeval flood," where no land mass exists, through the concerted efforts of the natural world to find a means for her survival. She enters a world in which the human and natural world come together in a communal effort.

In Kingsolver's novel, Taylor has a similar experience. Soon after receiving the Cherokee child, Taylor names her Turtle due to her powerful grip:

The most amazing thing was the way that child held on. From the first moment I picked it up out of its nest of wet blanket, it attached itself to me by its little hands like roots sucking on dry dirt. I think it would have been easier to separate me from my hair. . . . You're like a mud turtle. If a mud turtle bites you, it won't let go till it thunders. (22)

Difficult to ignore is the similarity that emerges between the relationship between the two pairs (Star Woman and the turtle, and Taylor and Turtle). Both lives are dramatically changed due to the productivity that arises through their meeting.

Although Kingsolver focuses on the relationships that occur in the human world, she describes these relationships in terms that reflect the natural world. By doing so, Kingsolver compares the connections between people with the relationships essential in the plant and animal world, as seen in Taylor's description of Turtle's holding on. Despite the fact that the dirt is "dry," there is still the powerfully natural connection between soil and plant and the creative act that occurs between the two. Whether between people and plants or between soil and animals, productivity only occurs through relationship. Unlike mythic adventures of the male, creation is the goal, rather than acquisition or destruction.

In many ways Kingsolver enacts the Indian belief of the Sacred Hoop through her choice of creation myth. The myth and thus the novel function as reminders that the individual belongs to a larger body. As Paula Gunn Allen states in *The Sacred Hoop*:

At base, every story, every song, every ceremony tells the Indian that each creature is part of a living whole and that all parts of that whole are related to one another by virtue of their participation in the whole of being. . . . Beauty is wholeness. . . . The circle of being is not physical, but it is dynamic and alive. It is what lives and moves and knows, and all the life forms we recognize—animals, plants, rocks, winds—partake of this greater life. (241)

Therefore the natural world and the human world often reflect and combine to emphasize the vital interconnectedness of a larger, spiritual world.

Kingsolver continually mixes and merges images of nature with people. Often the very act of nature described is the spark for bringing the characters together. One such powerful instance occurs when the drought in Tucson finally ends. "Around 4 o'clock we heard thunder. Mattie turned over the 'closed' sign in the window and said 'Come on. I want you to smell this'" (160). Hustling everyone to come along, Mattie brings Taylor, Lou Anne, Esperanza and Estevan to witness the Indian New Year. Mattie explains to Taylor that "They celebrated it on whatever day the summer's first rain fell" (161). Taylor's small community is again drawn together by nature's instigation. Knocking on her door late at night, Virgie Mae, her older neighbor, comes to announce the appearance of her night-blooming cereus.[6] Gathering up the children, Taylor and Lou Ann walk over to Virgie Mae and Edna's to witness the amazingly rare natural occurrence. "The petals stood out in starry rays, and in the center of each flower there was a complicated construction of silvery threads shaped like a pair of cupped hands catching moonlight. A fairy boat, ready to be launched into the darkness" (186). Lou Ann states that "it's a sign . . . [of] something good" (186). Occurring in the midst of personal challenges, the cereus unites community and proves the existence of beauty, even in the darkness.

Taylor's relationships are strengthened due to their communal participation in nature, but it is also important to realize that the community which exists around her arises through Taylor's own relationship with Turtle. Just as vegetative productivity is the result of the connection between Star Woman and Turtle, so is communal productivity the result of the connection between Taylor and Turtle. Kingsolver challenges Taylor by confronting her directly with the problems of motherhood as well as her growing comprehension of the difficulties in the world around her. Although these difficulties surround

Taylor, she is strengthened by the group that encompasses her due to Turtle's presence. When Taylor has questions about mothering or needs a babysitter, she soon finds support through the women around her.

On their first meeting at Jesus Is Lord Used Tires, Taylor and Mattie develop a bond when discussing the care of Turtle. Mattie quickly informs Taylor, as she gives more juice to the baby, that "It's so dry out here kids will dehydrate real fast. . . . You have to watch out for that" (44). Taylor slowly begins to realize the enormous responsibility she has assumed: "I wondered how many other things were lurking around waiting to take a child's life when you weren't paying attention. I was useless" (45). Fortunately for Taylor, she is surrounded by a group of strong women. Although Taylor's mother is also depicted as a strong woman, community is not described as a source of support in Kentucky. In Tucson, Taylor finds a world where women aid and help those around them. Quickly meeting Lou Ann when she moves to Tucson, Taylor shares rent with her in order for the two women to afford raising small children as single parents. Child-care and meals are often shared, and the burden seems lighter due to the bond that grows between these two strangers. Lou Ann and Taylor soon meet others who are invited to share meals and discuss their lives and personal struggles. Estevan tells a story one evening which epitomizes Kingsolver's growing point concerning the bonds and need of community.

If you go to visit hell, you will see a room like this kitchen. There is a pot of delicious stew on the table, with the most delicate aroma you can imagine. All around, people sit, like us. Only they are dying of starvation. . . . They are starving because they only have spoons with very long handles. . . . With these ridiculous, terrible spoons, the people in hell can reach into the pot but they cannot put the food in their mouths. Oh, how hungry they are . . . you can visit heaven. . . . You see a room just like the first one, the same table, the same pot of stew, the same spoons as long as a sponge mop. But these people are all happy and fat. . . . Why do you think?

He pinched up a chunk of pineapple in his chopsticks, neat as you please, and reached all the way across the table to offer it to Turtle. She took it like a newborn bird. (108)

Struggles still surround, yet the community members are able to make their way with each other's help. Amid these powerful women is Mattie, the matriarchal leader who runs the used tire shop. Although Mattie runs her own business, she also uses her store as a sanctuary for illegal aliens. Providing food and care for those who need it, Mattie's home and business thrive as a means of support for those who find themselves hiding from the law. Mattie's ability to repair and sell tires emerges as a fitting metaphor symbolizing the importance of action. This is seen most clearly through Mattie's ability to "control" tires. This power scares Taylor initially, as she is haunted by Newt Harbine's father's inability to control them. However, Mattie is able to rid Taylor of her fears, and ultimately teach her the importance and need for the power tires possess, if one only knows how to control them.

Much of the male western myth has been founded on the desire to explore adventure on the edges of a shifting frontier. As men gain and cultivate, the frontier moves outward, while civilization slowly follows. Male characters must travel farther and farther away from civilization in order to confront those explosive areas which exist on the ever-moving frontier. Kingsolver also explores this occurrence; however, she finds a movement which shifts inward as opposed to one that continues outward. The dangers come from areas close to home, those areas which have already been settled and defined as safe. For Taylor, adventures emerge in the challenge to survive within the domestic frontier. Although in Taylor's "adventure" the landscape no longer presents an overt threat, the landscape does hide would-be molesters who jeopardize the physical as well as the spiritual growth of children. Escaping one danger that occurs within her biological family, Turtle is further abused by an unknown assailant's attack. While Taylor is at work, Edna, an older blind neighbor, takes Turtle to the park. During their day there, Edna hears that Turtle is being attacked, yet even with her blindness she is able to strike the attacker with her cane and drive him away. Those places which appear to be the safest may hide dark elements of violence and destruction.

Taylor's adventures multiply as she gains a greater understanding of the challenges of those individuals who live around her. Her naiveté quickly explodes when she learns of the plight of illegal aliens like Estevan, who tells Taylor one evening what happened to him and his wife in Guatemala. After the police killed Estevan's brother and two of his friends, they looked to Esperanza and Estevan for the names of the remaining members of a teacher's union to which they belonged. They refused to release the seventeen names, and Estevan and Esperanza's child was taken from them as a leveraging tool. Without proof of the malevolent treatment which awaits their return to Central America, Estevan and Esperanza become fugitives who must hide from an American government which refuses them aid. Threatened with removal, the illegal aliens depend upon Taylor's ability to guide them to a sanctuary hidden from the law. Opening her eyes to the world around her, Taylor vents her frustration with those who question the safety of such an expedition: "Just stop it okay? . . . I can't see why I shouldn't do this. If I saw somebody was going to get hit by a truck I'd push them out of the way. Wouldn't anybody? It's a sad day for us all if I'm being a hero here" (188). Taylor is confronted with the fact that she must finally grow up and face the real world, which is often dangerous and cruel. There seems no need to look very far for adventure. Dangers and threats circle and impinge on life for the individual and the community, even in the perceived safety of society.

Some critics believe that Kingsolver's story appears too "politically correct" in its approach.[7] Occasionally the tension or conflict is rather too easily resolved, given a world which is often more messy than neat. Some also argue that her easy incorporation of multi-cultural communities exists primarily to provide images rather than to attempt to confront realistic representations of these integrations. However, to be blinded by these shortcomings would certainly be a loss. For Kingsolver has found a way to give voice to that experience which has yet to be explored. By re-writing the western experience through the female mythology of the Cherokee, Kingsolver has gained access to that part of our American experience which has been lamentably absent in our imaginative constructions of the American West.

Many critics have noted the importance of the Native American in the development of our American identity, yet few have fully explored that legacy. Through *The Bean Trees*, Kingsolver launches our pursuit of that complete voice by providing the voice of the female as well as the spiritual legacy of the Native American. Despite Taylor's re-creation of self, her metamorphosis is radically different from the creation of self found in stories of western male adventure. Rather than relying on the power of the individual and the individual's ability to conquer challenges on his own, Kingsolver creates a female character who is empowered and able to transform herself and others through the act of creation through community. As Allen states in *The Sacred Hoop*, motherhood brings that power:

> A strong attitude integrally connects the power of Original Thinking or Creation Thinking to the power of mothering. That power is not so much the power to give birth, as we have noted, but the power to make, to create, to transform. Ritual, as noted elsewhere, means transforming something from one state or condition to another, and that ability is inherent in the action of mothering. . . . And as the cultures that are woman-centered and Mother-ritual based are also cultures that value peacefulness, harmony, cooperation, health, and general prosperity, they are systems of thought and practice that would bear deeper study in our troubled, conflict-ridden time. (29)

And it is through this experience that Taylor is empowered. Facing a role she initially tried so doggedly to avoid, Taylor has been initiated in the role of mother. Through this acceptance of responsibility she has dramatically transformed a small, abused, silent little girl into a growing child who is able to play, sing, and dance. Yet Turtle's life is not the only life to be transformed; Taylor has also created a new identity for herself by becoming a mother. She has turned her back on an individualistic approach for one of nurturing help and assistance through community. As the traditional male approach depicts the need of males to explore their own individual desires and powers, it also depicts a turning away from social responsibility. Desiring freedom from the demands that such a responsibility entails, men have exemplified an individualistic search. Although Kingsolver describes a similar desire to explore individual pursuits, she does not depict a woman who is able to turn her back on responsibility. Through this acceptance, Taylor gains the powers of motherhood, as well as the essential powers of community.

This delicate natural system is described by Taylor to Turtle when she attempts to define their family. Similar to the Cherokee creation myth, ideas of community and the natural world are again combined. Taylor explains all these connections to Turtle when she questions her about their family:

> But this is the most interesting part: wisteria vines, like other legumes, often thrive in poor soil, the book said. Their secret is something called rhizobia. These are microscopic bugs that live underground in little knots on the roots. They suck nitrogen gas right out of the soil and turn it into fertilizer for the plant.
>
> . . . "It's like this . . . There's a whole invisible system for helping out the plant that you'd never guess is there." I loved this idea. "It's just the same as with people. The way Edna has Virgie, and Virgie has Edna, and Sandi has Kid Central Station, and everybody has Mattie. And on and on." This wisteria vines on their own would just barely get by, is how I explained it to Turtle, but put them together with rhizobia and they make miracles. (227-228)

Kingsolver ends the novel in much the same way as the ending of the Cherokee myth. Both end with the production that arises through relationship. Star Woman is surrounded by the "corn, beans, other plants, and rivers from her body," while Taylor is amazed by the profundity of friends, family, and a larger body of community that surrounds her. Kingsolver formulates the idea of regeneration through communal productivity. As the organic relationship serves to symbolize the power of community in Taylor's life, it also seems to speak to the larger messages of a changing mythology which exists throughout.

The relation between the wisteria and rhizobia represents Maggie's garden as described at the beginning of the novel. Wisteria "thrives in poor soil" just as Maggie's vegetables grow within auto parts. Both plants are surrounded by elements which would seem to impede their growth. However, something "invisible" exists which nourishes and enables their productivity. In much the same way, Kingsolver addresses the American mythology of the West. By turning from the male archetype, Kingsolver claims a new mythology which proves in her novel to be a productive means of experience. On their own, the American myths of the West are weakened by their inability to produce a viable future, yet by adapting Native American myth, the rhizobia, to the American experience, balance is possible.

As Star Woman brings consciousness to the natural world, Kingsolver's archetype is created with the same hope. In this way, Taylor becomes like Star Woman, bringing the world consciousness, and, perhaps more importantly, balance. And by expressing that hope, Kingsolver has succeeded in creating an archetype that melds the two myths together. By attempting a "new" archetype, she has initiated the process of finding a new mythic model from which to view the American experience. Although Taylor's initial story seems to be her attempt to escape her southern past, her story grows into a much larger vision. Taylor's move enlarges her scope and understanding of herself in relation to the world as a whole. Her story is certainly an escape from the South, but Kingsolver uses this regional move to express the need to escape any type of limited vision. A vision of wholeness in relation to America and the world as a whole is needed in order to gain understanding. Through her creation of Taylor, she molds an individual who empowers the American experience by stitching together two mythologies, the male western narrative of individualism and the female-centered Native American myth of connectivity, in order to reveal the need for balance within our American mythology. By doing so, Kingsolver provides a vision of the feminine as well as the masculine. The hero is both adventurer and domesticator. The power of creation and motherhood, as well as the need for action and adventure, is essential for growth and productivity. The garden no longer symbolizes that space relegated as a safe portion outside the male experience, nor does it symbolize a limited place in which women are empowered to create. Adventures and dangers abound in the communal garden.

Rusted Thunderbirds and CB antennae for tomato vines imply that the movement these auto parts once represented has been dismantled. Motion has subsided in order to provide support. Whether for nasturtiums, cabbage or tomatoes, all come together to aid in the growth of the garden. This image certainly strengthens the image of the garden as a place of power and support, yet it is important to keep in mind that this garden exists directly outside of a car shop. There may be a lot of cars that have been dismantled into parts, yet these parts still provide the potential to go when needed. This garden is prepared for action when the need arises, which is exemplified by Taylor's departure to help Estevan and Esperanza. When those within the community are in danger, action must be taken. However, action takes place on behalf of the community, as opposed to an individual's departure in search of adventure. And with that hope, Kingsolver has developed a new western archetype, a hero who is both mother and adventurer.

From *Southern Literary Journal* 39, no. 2 (2007): 119-139. Copyright © 2007 by the University of North Carolina Press. Reprinted by permission.

Notes

1. There were times when westering women found some liberation through their experience. Sandra Myers and to a lesser degree Lillian Schlissel reveal some examples of women "who greeted the adventure of the western frontier with zeal and independent spirit" (Schlissel 155). However, these occurrences are not the norm.

2. Women certainly experienced meetings with the Indian, yet this introduction rarely resulted in any dramatic change in female behavior. As men are described as becoming more assimilated to Indian behaviors, women's encounters more often reflect a reaction that reflects their own white femininity. Often they are shown as becoming frightened, or in contrast they become more sympathetic to the Indian. Rarely, however, do they become more like the Indian—unless of course they are captured and forced into assimilation. This lack of self-willed assimilation shows a marked difference in this encounter.

3. Richard Slotkin notes in *Regeneration Through Violence* these behavioral techniques by relating to Colonel Smith's published account of life with the Native Americans. By offering a description of Indian discipline and tactics, he hopes to enable his countrymen to share the benefits of his experience (329).

4. Slotkin exemplifies the contrasting *physical* version. In learning the physical prowess of the Indian, the male also learns the ways of the wilderness. Learning the ways of the Indian, the male then turns his new-found knowledge against the Indian. He claims that this kinship is justified in that it makes the hunter more effective as the destroyer of the Indian, as the exorcist of the wilderness's darkness. "He comes to know the Indian only in the act of destroying him" (563).

5. In the Cherokee myth of Corn Mother, told by Joseph Bruchac, there is the story of a grandmother who is mysteriously able to provide corn for her family by rubbing her sides. Once her secret is found out, she must leave, but she makes her grandson promise to clear the land and bury her body in the cultivated field, and "wherever a drop of blood fell, a small plant grew up" (97). In this act, she promised to always be with her people. This myth exemplifies the importance of the female in that a female deity provides for her community through her act of giving.

6. Cereus is also known as the "Queen of the Night." Kingsolver positions this natural occurrence the night before Taylor is to attempt to take Estevan and Esperanza to safer sanctuary, in the midst of their personal and political turmoil. The natural image works well in showing light amid the darkness. The Latin root of *cereus* is candle. The common name also works well in this scene, evoking the power of women to handle and persevere in difficulties.

7. For example, see Ryan, 77-82.

Works Cited

Allen, Paula Gunn. *Off the Reservation*. Boston: Beacon, 1998.

_____. *The Sacred Hoop*. Boston: Beacon, 1986.

Brinkmeyer, Robert. *Remapping Southern Literature*. Athens: U of Georgia P, 2000.

Bruchac, Joseph. *Native American Stories*. Golden, CO: Fulcrum, 1991.

Fiedler, Leslie A. *The Return of the Vanishing American*. New York: Stein and Day, 1971.

Graulich, Melody. "O Beautiful for Spacious Guys." *The Frontier Experience and the American Dream*. College Station: Texas A&M UP, 1989. 186-201.

Johnson, Michael. *New Westers*. Lawrence: UP of Kansas, 1996.

Kingsolver, Barbara. *The Bean Trees*. New York: HarperCollins, 1988.

Kolodny, Annette. *The Land Before Her*. Chapel Hill: U of North Carolina P, 1984.

Leeming, David. *Creation Myths*. New York: Oxford UP, 1994.

Lewis, R. W. B. *The American Adam*. Chicago: U of Chicago P, 1955.

Perdue, Theda. *Cherokee Women*. Lincoln: U of Nebraska P, 1998.

Ryan, Maureen. "Barbara Kingsolver's Lowfat Fiction." *Journal of American Culture* 18 (1995): 77-82.

Schlissel, Lillian. *Women's Diaries of the Westward Journey*. New York: Schocken Books, 1982.

Slotkin, Richard. *Gunfighter Nation*. Norman: U of Oklahoma P, 1992.

_____. *Regeneration Through Violence*. New York: HarperCollins, 1973.

Smith, Henry Nash. *Virgin Land*. New York: Vintage Books, 1950.

Stout, Janis. *Through the Window, Out the Door*. Tuscaloosa: UP of Alabama, 1998.

Tompkins, Jane. *West of Everything*. Oxford: Oxford UP, 1992.

Twain, Mark. *Adventures of Huckleberry Finn*. 1885. New York: Harper and Row, 1987.

The Loner and the Matriarchal Community in Barbara Kingsolver's *The Bean Trees* and *Pigs in Heaven*_____

Loretta Martin Murrey

Focusing on Kingsolver's earlier novels *The Bean Trees* and *Pigs in Heaven*, Loretta Martin Murrey combines a character study with an investigation of matriarchy as a principle of social organization. Taylor Greer, the protagonist of *The Bean Trees*, whose life story shares some parallels with Kingsolver's biography, finds that she cannot remain the loner she intended to be. Instead, she joins matriarchal communities in a number of differing cultural settings and, through her experiences in Tucson and on a Cherokee reservation, develops a deeper consciousness of the interconnectedness of human lives across geographical, racial, and cultural boundaries. Murrey tracks Taylor's roles both as mother (to Turtle) and as daughter whose own mother takes a hand in resolving the plotline. Unlike many male loners in western American fiction, Murrey contends, female loners tend to return to healthy and thriving communities. In shaping Taylor Greer, Kingsolver thus builds upon and also responds to stereotypes of the American West that are deeply embedded in American culture. — T.A.

From the Old Testament wanderer to the Ancient Mariner, the loner has long been a staple in Western thinking, and much has been written about this individual in literature. The loner is described positively as *solitary* and negatively as *lonely*. Literary critics in some cultures have seen loners as characters who begin *outside* the community and, as time passes, make their way *inside* the community. In contrast, loners in American literature—which also has its share, in spite of the stereotype of the gregarious American—often begin *inside* the community and end up *outside* the community. At the conclusion of *Huck Finn*, for example, Huck is leaving for the territories without Jim, Aunt Sally, or anyone else. Sometimes, as in *Winesburg, Ohio*, the people of the town are proud that someone has been able to break away. In the introduction to *American Women Writing Fiction: Memory, Identity, Family, Space*, Mickey Pearlman explains the solitary character in American literature in this way:

> It is a commonplace in criticism to define American literature, in short story or novel form, as the chronicle of the solitary hero, of man alone, man against society, man as individual, endlessly testing his strength and durability against his own resources on a mythic, adventurous journey to epiphany and knowledge. (1)

Loners can also be seen in the works of American women writers: Emily Dickinson's poems reflect her life of separateness; Louisa Mae Alcott married off Jo only at her editor's insistence; Sylvia Plath's work reveals her need for aloneness; Carson McCullers's female protagonist in *The Member of the Wedding* ends up skeptical toward society, though not openly rebellious. Yet loners in the works of American women writers are somewhat different from those in the works of American men writers. Like the male loners, female loners begin by breaking their ties and establishing their independence, yet while male loners in American literature may succeed in disassociating themselves from the community—though they may not necessarily be happy in that lot—many female loners in American literature cannot or do not completely escape the community. "Most American women do not write of open spaces and open roads, rife with potential and possibilities, or of successful escapes from multiple and various enemies," Pearlman continues. "They write . . . of the usually imprisoning psychological and actual spaces of American women, of being trapped, submerged, overwhelmed, of the 'suffocation of family life,' and of the 'suffering of living'" (5).

Female characters in American literature often move away from and back to the community and, to a larger extent than male characters, seem to be linked to previous or future families. Barbara Kingsolver's female characters are no exception. Kingsolver—the author of three novels, *Bean Trees, Pigs in Heaven*, and *Animal Dreams*; *Homeland*, a collection of short stories; *Another America*, a book of poetry; *Holding the Line*, a nonfiction book dealing with striking women copper miners in Arizona; and *High Tide in Tucson*, a collection of essays—is taking her place in American literature as one who writes about the female character's place in the community. Two of Kingsolver's novels, *The Bean Trees* and *Pigs in Heaven*, chronicle the movement of the loner Taylor Greer away from and back to various matriarchal communities.[1] In many ways like Kingsolver herself, Taylor Greer breaks away from the matriarchal community in Kentucky, establishes her independence as a loner, becomes a part of the matriarchal community in Tucson, and finally deals effectively with the matriarchal community of the Cherokee Nation.

Taylor Greer grows up in the home of her mother, Alice Greer, never having seen her father or known his name. She prides herself on having made it through high school and beyond without falling victim to marriage or pregnancy. She says the other girls "were dropping by the wayside like seeds off a poppyseed bun and you learned to look at every day as a prize. You'd made it that far" (*BT* 3). Taylor leaves home some five years after high school because she doesn't want to end up married to Sparky Pike, "who most people considered to be a high-class catch because he had a steady job as a gas-meter man—" (*BT* 10).

Up until this point, Taylor's name has actually been Marietta, which she doesn't like, so the first thing she does as she crosses the Pittman County line in her 1955 Volkswagen is determine to get herself a new name. "[T]his seemed like the time to make a clean break" (11), she thinks, and decides to choose a name based on where she runs out of gas. "I came pretty close to being named after Homer, Illinois, but kept pushing it," she says. "I kept my fingers crossed through Sidney, Sadorus, Cerro Gordo, Decatur, and Blue Mound, and coasted into Taylorville on the fumes" (12). Taking a new name has been used many times in literature to suggest an individual's new identity, and it seems an appropriate step in Taylor Greer's progression as a loner. Interestingly, Taylor Greer takes on both the traditional male role of loner and the traditional male name (or surname) of Taylor. Had Kingsolver wanted a feminine town name, she could have chosen Catlin, which precedes Homer, or Honey Bend, which follows Taylorville; or a few miles on down the road, Mt. Olive or St. Louis could have become Olive or Louise.[2]

The solitary Taylor encounters some obstacles in her journey as a loner. When car trouble in central Oklahoma takes nearly half her money, she considers giving up on her attempt at independence and turning back, but eventually decides her car is repaired and she might as well go on.

Another obstacle, and the strongest example of irony in any of Kingsolver's novels, is motherhood. Having left home to avoid being tied down by motherhood, Taylor becomes a mother when car trouble forces her to stop at a service station and a distraught Cherokee woman from a nearby restaurant thrusts her dead sister's abused and malnourished baby through Taylor's car window, saying, "Take this baby." Taylor innocently responds, "Where do you want me to take it?" only to learn that the Cherokee woman means her to take it on a permanent basis. "If I wanted a baby I would have stayed in Kentucky," Taylor tells her. "I could have had babies coming out my ears by now" (*BT* 18). Nevertheless, Taylor starts driving down the road, hoping her mind will clear, and only some time later realizes the baby is now her responsibility.

By the time Taylor has car trouble again in busy, modern downtown Tucson, she has begun to feel she is in another time and place. It is at this point that she accepts her status as a loner:

It's hard to explain how this felt. I went to high school in the seventies, but you have to understand that in Pittman County it may as well have been the fifties. Pittman was twenty years behind the nation in practically every way you can think of, except the rate of teenage pregnancies. For instance, we were the last place in the country to get the dial system. Up until 1973 you just picked up the receiver and said, Marge, get me my Uncle Roscoe, or whoever. The telephone office was on the third floor of the Courthouse, and the operators could see everything around Main Street square including the bank, the drugstore, and Dr. Finchler's office. She would tell you if his car was there or not.

In Tucson, it was clear that *there was nobody overlooking us all. We would just have to find our own way.* (italics mine) (47)

At this point, Taylor realizes she's on her own.

Nevertheless, Kingsolver, herself a native of rural Kentucky now transplanted to Arizona, describes the now-independent Taylor finding a place for herself and the little girl to live and easily establishing a friendship with the motherly Mattie, the proprietor of Jesus Is Lord Used Tires, which doubles as a shelter for Central American refugees. Dianne Aprile notes that Kingsolver "consistently focuses on people searching for a sense of community and discovering it in the least likely of places" (11), and this is certainly true here.[3]

Eventually Taylor settles into living in Tucson, and her Cherokee daughter—whom she names Turtle because of her turtle-like grip on Taylor's hand—grows into a little girl. When Indian-rights lawyer Annawake Fourkiller comes to tell Taylor of the Cherokee Nation's rights to Turtle, Taylor's maternal instincts take over, causing her to pack the child and a few belongings into the car and flee. But weeks later, as the flight continues, Taylor comes to realize the impossibility of caring for Turtle outside the matriarchal community.[4] Eventually Taylor and Turtle find themselves poor and lonely. Because Taylor cannot afford a babysitter, Turtle must spend her after-school hours roaming the department store where Taylor works. When Taylor's supervisor notices this arrangement, Turtle is relegated to sitting in the locked car in the parking lot.

In the meantime, Taylor's mother, Alice, has taken matters into her own hands. Aware of Taylor's situation, Alice makes a visit to the Cherokee Nation in Oklahoma, home of Annawake Fourkiller, and looks on the Cherokee Dawes Rolls, trying to find the names of both her cousin, the Native American Earth Mother Sugar Hornbuckle, who has married a member of the Cherokee Tribe, and her own grandmother, in order to prove Taylor one-eighth Cherokee.[5]

Finally, exhausted and confused, Taylor makes her way to the Cherokee Nation in Oklahoma, where Alice has located and moved in with her cousin Sugar Hornbuckle and fallen in love with Cash Stillwater, who turns out to be Turtle's grandfather. Eventually an arrangement is worked out with the Cherokee Nation so Turtle will spend summers on the Cherokee Nation with her adoptive grandmother and her biological grandfather, soon to be married, and the rest of the year in Arizona with Taylor. In some ways Taylor's fear of losing Turtle is reminiscent of the bereavement of Demeter/Ceres over the loss of her daughter Persephone/Proserpina, just as the compromise solution with the Cherokee Nation is reminiscent of the solution for Persephone to spend three seasons with her mother and one season in the underworld with Hades/Pluto.

Mother-daughter relationships are significant in Taylor Greer's escape from and return to these matriarchal communities. Asked why Taylor grabbed Turtle and ran, Taylor's friend Jax responds: "For the reason mothers throw themselves in front of traffic or gunfire to save their offspring. It's not an answerable question" (*PH* 155). Kingsolver once explained the difference motherhood made in her own life. She says that, before her own daughter was born, "in the spectrum of love, I had only known blue and ultraviolet. Then suddenly there was this whole rainbow of possibilities of what you could feel for someone" (Aprile 16).

For the most part in *The Bean Trees*, the reader gets to know Taylor's mother, Alice Greer, only through Taylor's thoughts about her, frequent though these thoughts are.[6] Early in the novel, Taylor describes her mother in this way:

There were two things about Mama. One is she always expected the best out of me. And the other is that then no matter what I did, whatever I came home with, she acted like it was the moon I had just hung up in the sky and plugged in all the stars. Like I was that good. (10)

Taylor and Alice have a comfortable, well-defined relationship, almost ideal by today's standards. Their unspoken support of each other provides them with the freedom to make their own decisions, however unconventional.[7] Unlike the mothers who have remained silent throughout much of masculine American literature, Alice is anything but silent in *Pigs in Heaven*.[8] She helps Taylor, both as a traditional grandmother providing occasional child care and as a gutsy woman functioning as the key to the resolution of the conflict between maternal rights and cultural correctness. Like her mother, Taylor is comfortable in the role of a single-parent working mother, and like her mother, she takes pleasure in meeting new people and seeing new places, easily making friends and establishing herself in a matriarchal community in Tucson, a city vastly different from the community in which she grew up.[9] Essentially, Kingsolver suggests that whether they love their mothers or hate them or have any emotion in between, women must come to terms with their mothers because the mother-daughter relationship is fundamental to their concepts of themselves as women.

Though normally the mother-daughter relationship is reinforced and encouraged by society, an unusual situation arises in *Pigs in Heaven*. The mother-daughter relationship that has developed between the caucasian Taylor Greer and her adopted Cherokee daughter, Turtle Greer, is threatened by the Cherokee Nation. Laura Shapiro writes that Kingsolver "pit[s] . . . cultural correctness against the boundless love between a mother and child" (61). Kingsolver's reader feels torn between the cultural correctness of Turtle's being returned to the Cherokee Nation to grow up with a full appreciation of her heritage and the "boundless love" that has developed between Taylor and Turtle. King-

solver, herself part Cherokee, says, "I think readers begin by sympathizing with the mother and Turtle, as I did. I understand the gut-
wrenching attachment and nuclear family relationship that seem to su-
persede all others. But clearly there was another view, and I wanted to
bring readers to sympathize with the tribe, too" (Myszka 20).[10]

In *The Bean Trees* and *Pigs in Heaven*, Taylor Greer sees society,
and particularly the matriarchal community, as the place to rear children. Though Kingsolver herself shares this view, she believes most
people in the United States don't. In "Everybody's Somebody's Baby,"
Kingsolver says that while living in Spain she constantly observed total strangers talking to, flirting with, and smiling at her own daughter.
Kingsolver says the Spanish see children as "the meringues and
eclairs" of their culture (20). The United States, on the other hand,
Kingsolver says, "has a proud history of lone heroes and solo flights,
so perhaps it's no surprise that we think of child-rearing as an individual job, not a collective responsibility" (49). Many Americans regard
children as "a sort of toxic-waste product: a necessary evil, maybe, but
if it's not their own they don't want to see it or hear it or, God help us,
smell it" (20), she continues.

During the course of these two novels, Taylor Greer undergoes a
complete transformation from a young woman loner fleeing motherhood and community membership to a young mother accepting the
matriarchal relationships of the family, community, and tribe as the
best place to raise her daughter, Turtle. Alice observes this change in
Taylor's choice of T-shirt:

> She's wearing a pale pink T-shirt . . . a color Taylor used to make a point of
> hating. She always had to wear outspoken things, red, purple, orange,
> sometimes all at once. Alice realizes something important about her
> daughter at this moment: that she's genuinely a mother. She has changed in
> this way that motherhood changes you, so that you forget you ever had
> time for small things like despising the color pink. (*PH* 138)

Bonnie Jean Cox says this interest in the matriarchal community has led Kingsolver to examine both "the theme of women's ability to empower themselves by forming unique bonds and social organizations" and "the energy that women can gain and share when they join forces in previously unexpected ways" (F6).

In this modern female rite of passage, the free-spirited Taylor Greer breaks away from the matriarchal community in Kentucky, establishes her independence as a loner, becomes a part of the matriarchal community in Tucson, and finally deals effectively with the matriarchal community of the Cherokee Nation. She reconciles the American desire for independence with the human desire for community and children. In *The Bean Trees* and *Pigs in Heaven*, Barbara Kingsolver celebrates both the independence of Taylor Greer and the rich generosity of the matriarchal communities, led by the Kentuckian Alice Greer, the Arizonan Mattie, and the Cherokee Sugar Hornbuckle.

From *Southern Studies* 5, nos. 1 & 2 (1994): 155-164. Copyright © 1994 by The Southern Studies Institute. Reprinted by permission.

Notes

1. Just as *Bean Trees* and *Pigs in Heaven* examine the strong mother-daughter relationship, Barbara Kingsolver's other novel, *Animal Dreams*, examines the void created by the absence of this relationship. Writings about matriarchal communities are not new to the American literary scene. Charlotte Perkins Gilman wrote *Herland* and *With Her In Our Land* in 1915 and 1916, describing an earthly utopia of women in which all social institutions were governed by women and all decisions were based on matriarchal thinking.

2. Maya Angelou in "My Name is Margaret" and Alice Walker in "Everyday Use" also relate the importance of names in the African-American culture.

3. Taylor's friend Jax, whom she "enjoys" but doesn't "love," assumes only a peripheral position in this matriarchal community. Aware of his position as an outsider, Jax wishes for a baby and his own kind of pregnancy: "He and Turtle could take it to the park, where they go to observe duck habits. He would wear one of those corduroy zipper cocoons with the baby wiggling inside, waiting for metamorphosis. He likes the idea of himself as father moth" (*PH* 146). Jax too considers himself a loner. At one point he gives his spin on the conflict between being a loner and being part of a com-

munity: "My natural state is solitary, and for recreation I turn to church or drugs or biting the heads off chickens or wherever one goes to experience sublime communion" (*PH* 155).

4. During her flight, Taylor befriends another female loner, the wandering waitress Barbie, whose makeup "looks as if she's given birth to a child" (*PH* 138).

5. At this point in the novel, a woman's loss of identity when she joins the community through marriage is illustrated. Alice comments, "Isn't that the dumbest thing, how the wife ends up getting filed under the husband? The husband is not the most reliable thing for your friends to try and keep track of" (*PH* 182).

6. Taylor seems to be constantly thinking about her mother, sending her mother a postcard, remembering things her mother told her, or evaluating a situation she encounters by the paradigm set up by her mother.

7. Maggie and Mama have a similar relationship in Alice Walker's "Everyday Use." These supportive relationships are in sharp contrast to those in Amy Tan's *The Joy Luck Club*, another contemporary novel dealing with mothers and daughters. Mothers in Kingsolver's novels don't project their ambitions onto their daughters or feel torn between their artistic yearnings and their daughters, as is the case in several modern novels (DuPlessis 90-94).

8. In *The Mother/Daughter Plot: Narrative, Psychoanalysis, Feminism*, Marianne Hirsch says the female has been inscribed "into the male plot only by . . . silencing one aspect of women's experience and identity—the maternal" (4). To her credit, Alice wants a husband who isn't silent either. She leaves her second husband Harland as he sits glued to the silent television set surrounded by his collection of headlights.

9. In the preface to *High Tide in Tucson: Essays from Now or Never*, Kingsolver gives some insight into her relationship with her own mother: "When I told my mother I was making a book of my essays, many of which had been published previously in magazines, she responded with pure maternal advocacy: 'Oh, good! I think there are some out there that I've missed.' Hurray for Moms, who give us the courage to take up our shelf space on the planet. . . ." (ix).

10. In Elisabeth Beattie's *Conversations with Kentucky Writers*, Kingsolver explains that what is best for the individual Taylor may not be best for the Cherokee community: "It also goes back to the thing I always write about, which is individualism versus community. How to balance community and autonomy" (170).

Works Cited

Aprile, Dianne. "Kinship with Kingsolver: Author's Characters Long to Belong, Something That Touches Readers." *The Courier-Journal* 25 July 1993: I1.

Beattie, L. Elisabeth. *Conversations with Kentucky Writers*. Lexington: UP of Kentucky, 1996: 151-171.

Cox, Bonnie Jean. "The Need in Us All: A Caring Dynamic Connection with Past." *The Lexington Herald-Leader* 16 September 1990: F6.

DuPlessis, Rachel Blau. *Writing Beyond the Ending: Narrative Strategies of Twentieth-Century Women Writers*. Bloomington: Indiana UP, 1985.

Hirsch, Marianne. *The Mother/Daughter Plot: Narrative, Psychoanalysis, Feminism*. Bloomington: Indiana UP, 1989.

Kingsolver, Barbara. "Everybody's Somebody's Baby." *The New York Times Magazine* 9 February 1992: 20, 49.

_____. *High Tide in Tucson: Essays from Now or Never*. New York: HarperCollins, 1995.

Myszka, Jessica. "Barbara Kingsolver: 'Burning a Hole in the Pockets of My Heart.'" *DePauw Magazine* 5.2, Spring 1994: 18-20.

Pearlman, Mickey, Ed. *Introduction to American Women Writing Fiction: Memory, Identity, Family, Space*. Lexington: UP of Kentucky, 1989: 1-7.

Shapiro, Laura. "A Novel Full of Miracles." *Newsweek* 12 July 1993: 61.

Tan, Amy. *The Joy Luck Club*. New York: Ivy, 1989.

Walker, Alice. "Everyday Use." *The Riverside Reader*, 3rd ed. Ed. Joseph F. Trimmer and Maxine Hairston. Boston: Houghton Mifflin, 1990: 209-219.

Trauma and Memory in Kingsolver's *Animal Dreams*

Sheryl Stevenson

The 1990s saw the beginning of a systematic investigation into how traumatic events are represented in literature and what such representation says about literary language. "Trauma studies" is by now a fully developed subspecialty in literary theory that devotes its attention to the study of personal pain, political repression, and other ruptures of "normal" life as they are mirrored in literary texts. Sheryl Stevenson analyzes Kingsolver's 1990 novel *Animal Dreams* as a contribution to trauma studies, since it thematizes questions of repression, memory, and recovery; invokes the U.S. involvement in Nicaraguan political struggles; and chronicles the onset of Alzheimer's disease in the protagonist's father. What Sigmund Freud called a "repetition compulsion" is built right into the structure of the novel, Stevenson finds, both through the novel's modes of storytelling and through the symmetrical arrangement of chapters. Because language can convey meaning through what is *not* said as well as what is said explicitly, Stevenson's essay becomes a meditation on Kingsolver's language and its ability to evoke repressed realities. The depiction of rituals, prominent in the novel, mirrors the way in which the language of fiction tentatively approaches truth.   — T.A.

The twentieth century may well be remembered as a century of historical trauma. As citizens facing the third millennium, we daily confront the unthinkable in news and television reports, in bizarre public trials, and in relentless statistics exposing rape, murder, torture, battering, and child abuse in an increasingly violent society.

—Suzette A. Henke, *Shattered Subjects*

In a 1997 review essay, "Trauma and Literary Theory," James Berger asks why psychological trauma has "become a pivotal subject connecting so many disciplines," from literary studies to historiography (569). Berger's query encompasses the question of value Geoffrey Hartman poses in a 1995 issue of *New Literary History*, focusing on trends and topics in higher education. But where Hartman asks, "What is the relevance of trauma theory for reading, or practical criticism?" (547), Berger probes possible reasons for "such interest in trauma among literary and cultural theorists" (571). One explanation is that saturated exposure to family dysfunction, violence, wars, and global disasters has created widespread awareness of the effects of traumatic events, making it "not surprising that theorists have turned to concepts of trauma as tools of [. . .] analysis" (Berger 572). Furthermore, both Hartman and Berger show that conceptions of trauma dovetail with other critical theories that emphasize problems of representation. As a "discourse of the unrepresentable," trauma theory attempts to deal with "the event [. . .] that destabilizes language" (Berger 573), an event so threatening that it provokes denial, amnesia, delayed memory, and forms of expression that, as Cathy Caruth says, are "always somehow literary"—indirect, coded, and full of gaps that are themselves revealing (*Unclaimed Experience* 5). The theoretical texts that Berger examines—by Caruth, Dominick LaCapra, and Kalí Tal—are part of a larger field of trauma studies, led by burgeoning research in psychology and sociology. But Berger's essay is perhaps most provocative for literary scholars in his suggestion that theory needs to be extended through study of literary representations of trauma (577). Among many works that might be designated the "literature of trauma," Barbara Kingsolver's *Animal Dreams* invites further attention, particularly as an illuminating exploration of complex relationships between trauma and memory.

Published in 1990, a decade after "post-traumatic stress disorder" was added to the American Psychiatric Association's official diagnostic manual, *Animal Dreams* appeared during a great surge of interest, both scholarly and popular, in trauma and its effects on memory. As Judith Lewis Herman observes in her highly influential 1992 study

Trauma and Recovery, since traumatic experiences "overwhelm the ordinary human adaptations to life," the normal reaction to such threats, for individuals and the public at large, "is to banish them from consciousness" (1). Connecting the individual and society in her view of trauma's manifestations, Herman asserts that phenomena like the Truth and Reconciliation Commission in South Africa demonstrate that the needs of "traumatized communities" parallel those of traumatized individuals: "Remembering and telling the truth about terrible events are prerequisites both for the restoration of the social order and for the healing of individual victims."[1] Yet this return to traumatic experiences through memory conflicts with the need for self-protection, thus provoking further denial and forgetting, a catch-22 which Herman calls the "dialectic of trauma" (2). Immense resistance to facing painful, disturbing knowledge can be seen in individuals who block out and then later recall traumatic memories, while acrimonious debates over recovered memories display similarly strong social resistance to dealing with experiences of trauma survivors.[2] But without the effort of remembrance and witnessing, unresolved fear, anger, and grief fester, and the avoidance of memory produces a numbed, constricted self. Kingsolver describes this outcome when explaining the genesis of *Animal Dreams*: "I wanted to write about the way that loss of memory is the loss of self, both for a culture and an individual" ("Serendipity" 3).

Animal Dreams embodies this loss in its central character Cosima Noline (nicknamed Codi), whose story emerges through a split narrative, alternating between her first-person account and third-person narration that presents her father's perspective. Codi returns to her hometown of Grace, Arizona, in the mid-1980s, apparently because her much-loved sister Hallie has left the house they shared in Tucson, going to Nicaragua as an agricultural expert; in addition, their father Homer, still practicing medicine in Grace, is showing signs of Alzheimer's. As Codi gradually reveals her persistent problems with memory, Kingsolver's dual narrative structure reinforces the symbolic doubling of the troubled daughter and her distant, disoriented father.

Characterized by oscillation between numbed inability to remember and sudden overpowering floods of memory and feeling, Codi's sections of the novel constitute a crisis autobiography, uncovering the intensity of her fears and grief as she faces the possible, then actual, loss of Hallie, who is killed by U.S.-supported contras. Yet both Codi's perspective and her father's show that the present crisis elicits memories of unresolved losses in the past—the death of Codi's mother when she was three and that of a child she secretly miscarried when she was fifteen, a daughter she frequently dreams about, even as her father is also haunted by memories of this event. Homer Noline's increasingly disoriented, present-tense narrative, focusing on memories but confusing them with present interactions, has a quality of disconnected impressionism that sharply differs from Codi's retrospective account, which conveys her sense of her life through the story she tells, an order she imposes. Ironically, her father's confused thoughts reveal aspects of Codi's past that she has repressed, yet he loses his ability to bring order to his memories and impressions, and thus loses himself, a condition suggested by his lack of first-person narration. In contrast, Codi moves toward memory regained, a process that involves reconstructing her past, her place within Grace, and her identity.

By concentrating on three aspects of *Animal Dreams*, we can see how Kingsolver's novel sheds light on theories of trauma and discourses of trauma survivors. First, Codi's narrative is one of gaps, evasions, and sudden fissures of erupting emotion—an unstable discourse that resembles those of traumatized people, pulled by conflicting impulses, controlled by the need for safety. Multiple repetitions and returns are another important feature of Codi's narrative, illustrating the human compulsion to return to, and even reenact, disturbing situations. For Codi and other trauma survivors, such returns are crucial spurs to remembering the past, a process inseparable from mourning. Kingsolver's presentation of memory as dialogic emerges through a third set of devices which convey the traumatized person's need for other individuals and for community, for collective remembrance and social action.

These aspects of *Animal Dreams* reflect motifs it shares with many survivor stories—themes of safety, memory and mourning, and the struggle to reconnect with others in spite of debilitating distrust. The novel confirms Judith Herman's view that these motifs describe stages of recovery for trauma survivors (155), but Codi also dramatizes the universal character of these human needs. As a person whose disturbing experiences (unlike those of the Holocaust survivor, war veteran, or victim of incest) may not be seen as traumatic, Kingsolver's protagonist embodies an emerging view of trauma as not unusual but ordinary and frequently unrecognized (Brown 100-03; Hartman 546). *Animal Dreams* also depicts Codi as a representative figure, one whom we might call Citizen Cain, "[a] good citizen of the nation in love with forgetting" (149). Her amnesia becomes a metaphor for the widespread tendency of responsible citizens to "forget" unpleasant social realities, to become desensitized and apathetic, as in Kingsolver's chosen example, America's well-known but widely ignored financing of violence against civilians in Nicaragua. By making Codi's responses to loss and violence seem both ordinary and representative, part of a widely shared process in which memory is crucial, *Animal Dreams* highlights trauma theory's everyday implications along with its power as a tool of social analysis.

The Catch-22 of Safety

Since traumatic experiences are defined by their "power to inspire helplessness and terror," it is apparent that providing people with safety is a first necessity, as is seen in all crisis-intervention and disaster-relief efforts, such as work with survivors of rape, large-scale accidents, and terrorist attacks (Herman 34, 159-62). A more subtle problem then arises, when the need for safety causes survivors to use various psychological means to distance themselves from threatening memories and feelings (Herman 42-47). The opening chapter of Codi's narrative ("Hallie's Bones," the novel's second chapter) reveals how the dialectic of trauma—the deadlocked impulses to remember and to repress—produces an indirect, impeded disclosure. In her first three sentences, Codi defines herself by negation and implies that the real story is happening elsewhere, with Hallie as hero: "I am the sister who didn't go to war. I can only tell you my side of the story. Hallie is the one who went south, with her pickup truck and her crop-disease books and her heart dead set on a new world" (7). Mocking the classic Western whose hero rides into town and takes care of everyone's problems, Codi's first chapter describes the day she returns to Grace after fourteen years, riding into town on a Greyhound, soon to find that the orchards (and thus the economy) are dying, poisoned by the irresponsible mining company that is polluting the town's river. Belying her cowboy nickname, Codi underscores that she's no hero, mentioning that she has been in medical school but has devolved downward, to the point of dispensing remedies in an ironically debased manner: "For the last six months in Tucson I'd worked night shift at a 7-Eleven, selling beer and Alka-Seltzer to people who would have been better off home in bed" (10). Codi's mode of narration reinforces effects of her self-lacerating humor. Following her ironic description of arriving by Greyhound "like some rajah," she questions her memory of a scene she has just presented, tells how she had "lied on the bus" (saying she was "a Canadian tourist"), and abruptly feels "dragged down by emotions" she doesn't explain (8, 12, 13). Codi's self-undermining narrative mirrors those of traumatized people who, as Judith Herman explains, "often tell their stories in a highly emotional, contradictory, and fragmented manner which undermines their credibility and thereby serves the twin imperatives of truth-telling and secrecy" (1).

Kingsolver shows that the trauma survivor's conflicting needs for disclosure and safety are also met through language that is literary, using metaphor, analogy, and flashbacks as means of control. Thus, after describing Hallie as "dead set on a new world," Codi shifts abruptly to another time and place, perhaps in response to the threatening words "dead set":

I stood on a battleground once too, but it was forty years after the fighting was all over: northern France, in 1982, in a field where the farmers' plow blades kept turning up the skeletons of cows. They were the first casualties of the German occupation. In the sudden quiet after the evacuation the cows had died by the thousands in those pastures, slowly, lowing with pain from unmilked udders. But now the farmers who grew sugar beets in those fields were blessed, they said, by the bones. (7)

This passage faces the danger to Hallie with superb indirection, echoing the chapter's title "Hallie's Bones" with a repeated image of bones and bone-fed soil that becomes one of the novel's recurring metaphors. An analogy similarly draws attention to Hallie's danger yet replaces it, shifting from the war she went to join to the vast destruction of life in World War II, affecting not only farmers (similar to Hallie with her "crop-disease books," her version of weapons) but even animals of the most harmless kind, cows whose "unmilked udders" underscore their femaleness and wasted fertility. Codi's next paragraph reveals the fragile sense of safety provided by the deflections of her thinking:

Three years later when my sister talked about leaving Tucson to work in the cotton fields around Chinandega, where farmers were getting ambushed while they walked home with their minds on dinner, all I could think of was France. Those long, flat fields of bonefed green. Somehow we protect ourselves; it's the nearest I could come to imagining Nicaragua. Even though I know the bones in that ground aren't animal bones. (7)

Prominently displayed in the chapter's title, human bones, specifically Hallie's, emerge even under a kind of erasure, through deflection, comparison, and substitution—a perfect example of language that meets the conflicting demands of self-protection and truth-telling that constitute the dialectic of trauma.

Though personal stories of trauma survivors are especially prone to such devices, Mark Freeman's analysis of autobiographical narratives suggests that order and clarity in every life story are imposed retro-spectively, with the following implication: "Perhaps [. . .] we ought to be paying greater attention to 'discontinuities,' 'ruptures,' 'fissures' [. . .]" (47). *Animal Dreams* illustrates how this approach is necessary for understanding the words of traumatized people. The end of Codi's first chapter offers a telling example, as she describes walking to the place she will stay through an orchard whose unnatural rows remind her of a vast military cemetery in northern France, showing how per-sistently her memory brings up what she fears in deflected, substitute images. After noting that the orchards of Grace are "full of peacocks, living more or less wild and at the mercy of coyotes but miraculously surviving in droves" (14), she seems to stumble into a kind of horrify-ing primal scene involving one such bird. Perceiving from a distance that a peacock is being beaten by children elicits the following sudden, fissure-like response from Codi: "I'm not the moral guardian in my family. Nobody, not my father, *no one* had jumped in to help when I was a child getting whacked by life, and on the meanest level of in-stinct I felt I had no favors to return" (15). But, prompted by what she sees as "Hallie's end of my conscience," she does try to intervene, im-mediately uncovering her mistake: she has disrupted a common festiv-ity for children, the opening of a candy-filled piñata (15). Her reaction is extremely telling, but in ways she doesn't intend: "I felt disoriented and disgraced, a trespasser on family rites. [. . .] I wondered in what dim part of Grace I'd left my childhood" (16). Exemplifying the trauma survivor's tendency toward guilt and self-criticism (her "loss of self"), Codi characteristically defines herself by negation—she's "not the moral guardian," not Hallie, but instead is dis-Graced, cut off from the town and the Grace part of herself, her past. But if we focus on dis-continuity or rupture, the eruption of words that seem to escape Codi's control, we might conclude that she has not lost touch with her past. In-stead, this incident has called forth a memory that could be taken from the narratives of many incest survivors: "*no one* had jumped in to help when I was a child." Though these words are half-erased by Codi's shift of attention to her mistake, this passage teaches us that once we start looking at gaps, partial erasures, and sudden eruptions, these places where the narrative gets messy are prime sources for self-disclosure, as Freud long ago showed and Derrida reinforces. But because Codi's linguistic devices allow *her* to ignore the slip, we can also see what many analysts of survivor discourse have noted, that telling or writing the story provides a "safe space" for those who are dealing with overwhelmingly painful memories (Kuribayashi and Tharp 1).

Codi's narrative also illustrates the need of traumatized people for actual places of safety or "sanctuary," to use therapist Sandra Bloom's term, which evokes the American "sanctuary movement." This underground movement of people who provide refuge for illegal aliens escaping Latin American political terror appears prominently in Kingsolver's first novel, *The Bean Trees*, as well as in *Animal Dreams*. Codi describes the time when Hallie began to offer such protection, her action putting an end to a period Codi idealizes: "We'd had one time of perfect togetherness in our adult lives, the year we were both in college in Tucson [. . .]. [Then] Hallie [. . .] befriended some people who ran a safehouse for Central American refugees. After that we'd have strangers in our kitchen every time of night, kids scared senseless, people with all kinds of damage. Our life was never again idyllic" (35). Codi vividly recalls her contacts with traumatized refugees, such as a victim of torture whose "eyes offered out that flatness, like a zoo animal" (93), but she stresses the contrast of her reactions and Hallie's: "where pain seemed to have anesthetized me, it gave Hallie extra nerve endings"; "When Hallie and I lived in Tucson, in the time of the refugees, she would stay up all night rubbing the backs of people's hands and holding their shell-shocked babies. I couldn't. I would cross my arms over my chest and go to bed" (89, 149). Hallie's need to take risks for others is expressed in attempts to provide protection, yet ironically these very efforts destroy Codi's sense of safety. Thus, after Hallie's departure for Nicaragua, the house once shared by the sisters "fell apart"; the plants die along with Codi's relationship with her boyfriend of that time (10).

As *Animal Dreams* begins from moments of departure—Hallie's to Nicaragua and Codi's to Grace—the novel contextualizes Codi's individual search for safety in terms of a political movement, so that the parallel between Codi and Central American refugees highlights specific political issues and the universal need for safety. (This idea is extended with Codi's realization that industrial pollution may destroy the orchard-based economy of Grace, thus forcing longtime residents to move "to Tucson or Phoenix" for jobs, making them "refugees too" [149].) The novel's images of tormented refugees underscore the intense fear connected with place and displacement, the fragility of safety which survivors of traumatic experiences feel and convey to others. But Kingsolver especially reveals how places of safety are inherently symbolic and subjective. Hence it is clear that Codi subjectively constructs the Tucson house; whether it is "safe" or not, "home" or not, is personal for her, not even corresponding to her beloved sister's viewpoint.

In Grace, Codi's "safe house" is provided by her friend Emelina Domingos, who represents an alternative view of safety, a carnivalesque vision in which life and death, safe and unsafe, are accepted as inseparable. The second chapter of Codi's narrative encapsulates this vision. Entitled "Killing Chickens," the chapter is paired with the preceding peacock-piñata scene, as Codi comes upon an actual family rite of bird-killing. Yet this scene is surprisingly positive, introducing Emelina as an affectionate, capable mother of five, supervising the slaughter of roosters, showing her twin sons how to make sure that the animals feel as little pain and fear as possible. A fertile, tough-talking, down-to-earth mother, watching over children "dappled with blood" (30), Emelina brilliantly embodies the carnivalesque worldview which Bakhtin presents through similarly contradictory female figures, the life-giving mother who is also closely tied to death (Bakhtin 25-26). The Domingos' household is thus immediately established as a place in which safety and its opposites (violence, suffering, death) coexist. But Emelina also plays a crucial role in relation to Codi's memory. She brings up Codi's adolescent campaigns against chicken killing, and when Codi claims it was Hallie who was the caring activist, that she and Hallie are opposites ("chalk and cheese"), Emelina disputes one of Codi's basic self-constructions by insisting that her own memory is correct, that Codi was the leader and Hallie "copied [her] like a picture" (29, 31). This challenge to Codi's remembered self is the first of many cases in which her friends and family push her to move past her memory blocks and faulty self-images. As Emelina plays the role of mother and of memory for Codi, she exemplifies an attitude of open acceptance, in touch with reproduction, death, and the past—aspects of life that have long been problematic for Codi.

Furthermore, the place Emelina provides—a tiny, detached "guest-house"—seems to fit Codi's view of herself as an orphan and outsider, while it also suggests what she seeks in her journey: "The bed had a carved headboard, painted with red enamel, and a soft-looking woven spread. It was a fairytale bed. I wished I could fall down and sleep a hundred years in this little house [. . .]" (26). Like an exiled or enchanted princess, having found her small place of protection, Codi lies down on its "fairytale bed," and it is in this childlike space that she first allows herself to really think of Hallie: "It was frightening to speculate on specifics; I'd been rationing my thoughts about her, but now I was exhausted and my mind ran its own course. I thought of Hallie at border crossings. Men in uniforms decorated with the macho jewelry of ammunition. No, not that far. I pulled her back to Tucson, where I'd seen her last and she was still safe" (31). Unable to handle thoughts about the dangers Hallie may be encountering as she crosses literal borders and symbolic barriers of gender, Codi refuses to let her imagination go: "No, not that far" (31). So she uses her memory self-protectively, to bring her sister "back" to the last time she "was safe," to the scene where she left Codi in Tucson. Yet as she remembers this scene—having sought this memory as a safe space for her thoughts—she suddenly confronts her worst fear while remembering how she felt when Hallie was about to drive away: "I was thinking that if anything happened to her I wouldn't survive" (32). With a deflection of her thoughts from this deep fear, Codi overlays the scene of Hallie's departure with yet another memory, as she thinks of the "one time of perfect togetherness in our adult lives," the time before Hallie took in refugees (35). Through Codi's manipulations of her memories, *Animal Dreams* vividly illustrates how memory can be controlled by the need for safety. Though Emelina's "safe house" enables Codi to begin to deal with her fears and her past, at a much later point, more than halfway through her narrative, she writes to Hallie of the stunting effects of her fears: "I feel small and ridiculous and hemmed in on every side by the need to be safe" (200). Codi's narrative is similarly controlled and hemmed in by self-protective uses of language, because she is trapped by the catch-22 of trauma: to heal she must remember, and to remember she must feel safe, but as soon as she begins to remember, she loses her sense of safety as she faces her grief, her need to mourn.

Memory as Mourning

For traumatized people, deliberate efforts to remember are crucial to the necessary process of reconstructing their life stories, even though such memories resemble (or even trigger) involuntary flashbacks and nightmares which reenact terrifying events. Though memory blocks and a constricted, numbed awareness help ward off this painful experience, many survivors are drawn, often unconsciously, to return to the people and places associated with their traumatic past (Herman 39-40). This process of reenactment, described by Freud as the "repetition compulsion" (32), is clearly reflected in *Animal Dreams*, a novel that seems to be structured by the compulsion to return and repeat. Faced with Hallie's dangerous journey and possible loss, Codi doesn't simply make her own journey to the place where she experienced the traumatic losses of her mother and her child. She also returns to her high school (as a biology teacher, for one school year) and eventually to her relationship with Loyd Peregrina, the man who had unknowingly impregnated her when they were high school students. While the latter re-lationship may seem too convenient a coincidence for some readers, Codi's attraction back to Loyd precisely fits the psychology of reenact-ment explained by Herman and others—the need to master a wounding experience of the past (Herman 41). In *Fiction and Repetition*, Hillis Miller suggests another way in which the returns effected through memory and reenactment can be deeply satisfying. Such repetitions can accomplish, as in Virginia Woolf's *Mrs. Dalloway*, a "raising of the dead," the return of beloved people who have been lost (Miller 178). Miller's insights concerning *Mrs. Dalloway* bring out intriguing simi-larities between Kingsolver's novel and Woolf's dual narrative which features a traumatized veteran and explores the presence of the past through memory.[3] But *Fiction and Repetition* also sheds light on King-solver's repeated depictions of All Souls' Day, especially when Miller points out Woolf's allusion to this holiday through Richard Strauss's song "Allerseelen," which includes these lines: "One day in the year is free to the dead,/ Come to my heart that I may have you again,/ As once in May" (190). Even if painful, returns of the past through memory can sometimes be the only way to remain connected with those we have lost, a view expressed by a Vietnam veteran: "I do not want to take drugs for my nightmares, because I must remain a memorial to my dead friends" (qtd. in Caruth, Preface vii). Codi's narrative reveals a similarly com-pelled, emotionally charged adherence to remembering and grieving.

The spurs to released memory and emotion in *Animal Dreams* pre-cisely mirror those listed by Judith Herman, who suggests that re-pressed memories may return through "observance of holidays and special occasions," along with "viewing photographs, constructing a family tree, or visiting the site of childhood experiences" (185).[4] One of the novel's most evocative sequences renders the powerful effect of returning to a place of great pain. After spending her second day in Grace shopping with Emelina, meeting people she doesn't remember, Codi describes her overcharged, blocked off response: "Grace was a memory minefield; just going into the Baptist Grocery with Emelina had charged me with emotions and a hopelessness I couldn't name" (46). That night, dealing with the insomnia characteristic of many traumatized people, Codi goes out after midnight to try to find the road "to Doc Homer's" (47). This dream-like scene renders the dense, obscure nature of her emotions along with a startling gap in her memory, as revealing as any slip of the tongue: "I wasn't ready to go [to Doc Homer's] yet, but I had to make sure I knew the way. I couldn't ask Emelina for directions to my own childhood home; I didn't want her to know how badly dislocated I was. I'd always had trouble recalling certain specifics of childhood, but didn't realize until now that I couldn't even recognize them at point-blank range. [. . .] In fact, I felt like the victim of a head injury" (47). Finally admitting that "Doc Homer's" is her "own childhood home," Codi shows that she has no idea how to find the house where she lived until she was eighteen. And when she seeks this house—secretly, in the middle of the night—she thinks instead of the field where her mother died, recalling the scene in rich, visual detail; including the stretcher "like a fragile, important package," the helicopter "sending out currents of air across the alfalfa field behind the hospital," and the "alfalfa plants show[ing] their silvery undersides in patterns that looked like waves," so that "[t]he field became the ocean I'd seen in storybooks, here in the middle of the desert; like some miracle" (48). Since Codi was "home with a babysitter" when this occurred, she accepts that this vivid memory is actually one of her many "fabrications based on stories I'd heard" (48), suggesting the self-doubts of incest survivors whose memories are denied. Yet remembering her mother's famously strong will, supposedly shown in her tenacious refusal to fly, leads Codi to see how she herself differs from Hallie in having known their mother as a "ferociously loving" presence, something Codi "tried to preserve" and be for Hallie, though feeling she "couldn't get it right" (49). This memory reestablishes a connection between her mother, herself, and Hallie that seems to enable her to find her father's house, perhaps blocked out because it lacked her mother: "I stopped suddenly in the center of the road, in the moon's bright light, with shadow trickling downhill from my heels like the water witcher's wellspring finally struck open. I'd found the right path" (50).

Codi repeatedly associates memories with imagery of water in the desert, suggesting their preciousness and life-sustaining power. Similar to therapeutic techniques for getting past trauma-based amnesia (one technique is called "flooding"), when she opens herself to remembering her father's house and her mother's death, other memories come and with them "the familiar, blunt pressure of old grief" as Codi first fully discloses her traumatic past: "Even the people who knew me well didn't know my years in Grace were peculiarly bracketed by death: I'd lost a mother and I'd lost a child" (50; cf. Herman 181-82, 184). Here, the straightforward, direct syntax and repetitions emphasize Codi's double loss, while the statement's parallelism ("I'd lost a mother and I'd lost a child") resembles two brackets. Codi is able to reach this difficult disclosure through trying to return to and remember the place of each loss, the house where her child was stillborn and the field where her mother died. Just as the river through Gracela Canyon is "Grace's memory of water" in times of no rain (270), so too specific places preserve Codi's past and connect her with feelings that she has defensively "bracketed" off as her "years in Grace" (50).

Like places she returns to, Codi's dreams hold memories of her past, often in a disguised form that discloses yet hides, fitting the self-protective dialectic of trauma. Judith Herman notes, "The traumatic moment becomes encoded in an abnormal form of memory, which breaks spontaneously into consciousness, both as flashbacks during waking states and as traumatic nightmares during sleep" (37). Such "dreams are unlike ordinary dreams" in that they "occur repeatedly" and "include fragments of the traumatic event in exact form [. . .]" (39). Herman's points are confirmed by both Codi's and Homer's narratives. In chapter 6, "The Miracle," describing the circumstances of her secret pregnancy and miscarriage, Codi tells of recurring dreams that have continued to bring her daughter back to her: "In one of the dreams I run along the creek bank looking among the boulders. They are large and white, and the creek is flooded, just roaring, and I know I've left a baby out there" (51). Though at this point Codi apparently doesn't remember the night of her miscarriage, Homer's memories reveal the extent to which her dream includes fragments of memory. In one of his flashbacks, to a time when he was secretly aware that his daughter was about six months pregnant, Homer observes that she locks herself in the bathroom for hours and then leaves the house with a "small bundle in her arms" (140). Mirroring her secrecy, he follows her to the dry riverbed where she buries the child: "Round volcanic boulders flank her, their surfaces glowing like skin in the moonlight. She is going down to the same dry river where they nearly drowned ten years ago, in the flood" (140). Homer's narrative shows that Codi's dreams and even her waking thoughts about finding her baby in water (221) reflect her buried memories of where she left her child. But his memories also suggest a reason for one of her most prominent memory gaps—her inability to recall her childhood attempt, with Hallie, to save a litter of motherless coyote pups, abandoned in a burrow above the river that flooded, nearly drowning the girls along with the similarly orphaned animals. Though Homer, Emelina, and Hallie each recall this incident (19-21, 77, 121), said by Emelina to be "famous" (77), for Codi it remains blocked out until more than halfway through the novel (191), undoubtedly because of the riverbed's association with her lost child. Most strikingly, Codi needs the people who have shared her life, especially her father, in order to recover more of their past and see it differently—to remember the night she lost her child, to understand that Homer tried to help, and to see through Loyd and her father that the baby was not just hers and not just her loss (332). The novel's dialogic narrative structure, separating Homer's memories from Codi's dreams and reflections, vividly conveys how reconstructing the past is a dialogic process, requiring an interplay of incomplete perspectives.

Thoughts of Codi's child keep returning, both to her and to her father, suggesting that traumatic memories indeed have the "frozen," repetitive quality Herman describes, causing them to be repeated until the individual can reconceptualize and thus rewrite the past, seeing it within new frameworks of meaning (Herman 37, 41). *Animal Dreams* shows how this process might occur through place, as new places enable Codi to think about her child within different contexts. This mode of healing can be seen when Loyd takes Codi to Kinishba, an 800-year-old Pueblo structure with "more than two hundred rooms—a village under one roof" that provides a vision of interconnected life, as its stones fit together naturally, looking "like cells under a microscope" (128, 129). When Codi notes the thick walls, Loyd tells her, "The walls are graveyards. When a baby died, they'd mortar its bones into the wall" to keep it "near the family" (128). This attitude of seeing the dead as a natural part of one's daily life is one that Codi moves toward, as she shifts from its opposite, thoughts of the unnatural rows of military graves in distant Europe, to scenes of unique, creatively decorated family graves, lovingly tended on All Souls' Day, as children play among their dead ancestors, so that the families of Grace seem "lush as plants, with bones in the ground for roots" (165). Similar words capture Codi's new sense of life springing up amid death when she and Loyd drive through snowy mountains in December and find "lush plants thriving" near a stream fed by hot springs, reminding Codi of her dreams of finding her child, miraculously alive: "I wondered if perhaps I was, after all, in one of my strange dreams, and whether I would soon be looking under the foliage beside the stream for my lost baby" (221). In these new places, Codi's familiar memories are replaced, as she forms new associations with her dead loved ones.

Among Codi's many comments about memory, one of the most provocative is that "memory runs along deep, fixed channels in the brain" (269), a metaphor she develops by describing the river as "Grace's memory of water" (270). This metaphor is richly suggestive, implying the utter necessity of memory while also pointing toward research which has shown that traumatic memories are deeply imprinted and thus especially fixed (Herman 38-39). Codi's description also resembles Susan Griffin's imagery in *Woman and Nature*: "We say everything comes back. And you cannot divert the river from the riverbed. We say every act has its consequences. That this place has been shaped by the river, and that the shape of this place tells the river where to go" (186). Griffin conveys, as Codi says in *Animal Dreams*, that "the land has a memory," though Codi offers a different example: "The lakes and the rivers are still hanging on to the DDT and every other insult we ever gave them" (255). Griffin's river that cannot be diverted particularly coincides with the view of Grace's older women, who steadfastly oppose the mining company's attempt to divert the river away from the town, a place so "shaped by the river" that it would no longer exist without its water. But although Codi's metaphors evoke key insights, they do not fully describe how memory works, since for both Homer and Codi memories do not stay in fixed channels. In fact, Homer's disordered memories frequently show his mind skipping channels, making poetic, true connections between times and people by mixing them up. Though Codi's memory is not as disordered or creative as her father's, the novel shows that dialogic interactions with others enable Codi to recover previously repressed memories, discard false ideas, and reinterpret her own identity. Hence, for example, once she discovers that her father has lied about their family's not being from Grace, she remembers her past differently, rewriting herself in a more positive way as a child who was watched over by "fifty mothers" (the women of Grace [311, 328]), not a No-line but a Nolina, a Gracela descendant and also, Roberta Rubenstein notes, a hardy desert plant, "capable [. . .] of surviving for years between flowerings" (15). As she revises her identity, from "victim" to "survivor," Codi decidedly confirms narrative therapy's central tenet that neither the past nor one's self is fixed, that "[s]elf is a perpetually rewritten story."[5] But since those around Codi—her father, Emelina, Loyd, and the women of Grace—play an instrumental role in spurring her memories and new self-knowledge, *Animal Dreams* adds this crucial emphasis: that it takes a town to raise a child, to resurrect her memories, to help her grieve and heal.

Only Reconnect

> My heart is moved by all I cannot save:
> so much has been destroyed
>
> I have to cast my lot with those
> who age after age, perversely,
>
> with no extraordinary power,
> reconstitute the world.
>> Adrienne Rich, "Natural Resources"
>> (171-76; qtd. in Welch 153)

Since overwhelming experiences of violence and loss produce feelings of helplessness, distrust, isolation, and despair, relationships with others are both essential and difficult for traumatized people. Recovering "a sense of control, connection, and meaning" is problematic in any case, but is especially so when the trauma is hidden or given little recognition (Herman 33, 188). Too often, the survivor avoids speaking about and grieving for the inevitable loss, whether it is an unborn child or her own innocence and trust. As Codi unfolds her feelings about her secret pregnancy and miscarriage—starting with adolescent shame and fear, later compounded by grief and anger—she exemplifies the pressures that silence those who feel their experience cannot be shared. A society alarmed by the impact of unresolved trauma (seen, for example, in cycles of violence in families) needs to recognize the role of community and culture for those like Codi, overwhelmed by the awareness that "so much has been destroyed" (Rich 172). People surrounding the survivor can help create the sense of security necessary to risk memory and relationship; communities can also offer rituals and gatherings for collective mourning. But further, according to Judith Herman, "the breach between the traumatized person and the community" requires not just "public acknowledgement of the traumatic event," but also "some form of community action" (70), as Rich suggests in the choice to "cast [her] lot with those" joined through generations of struggle. *Animal Dreams* illuminates how communities and cultural influences can enable traumatized people to connect with their past and with other people, thus finding value in their lives however much has been destroyed or lost.

One way the novel presents such influences is through prominent depictions of rituals. Psychiatrist Marten deVries highlights the importance of rituals for individuals and communities affected by traumatic events. He notes that both long-established ceremonies and informal gatherings at a symbolic place—a church, tree, or schoolyard—can help reconnect individuals as a community, reestablishing their sense of being part of the social order and "life cycle."[6] *Animal Dreams* precisely renders this effect of rituals by focusing on Codi's relationships to others during three celebrations of All Souls' Day. As Rubenstein observes (14), these events structure the novel, occurring in chapter 1, chapter 14 (a midpoint), and chapter 28 (the final chapter). Beginning with Homer's memory of the last All Souls' festivities he allowed for his daughters, these three chapters suggest that Codi is deeply drawn to the yearly rite because it expresses ties with community and ancestors which her father has denied and effaced, but which she finally recovers. The novel's last chapter, "Day of All Souls," conveys in its title the inclusiveness of relationships Codi has sought. The chapter depicts November 2, 1989, more than two years after the story's main events, a day that reveals how Codi—pregnant and tending her father's grave among those of the other Nolinas—has become fully reconnected with her community and the cycle of generations (the novel's 28 chapters structurally reinforce the impression that she is part of something larger, a female fertility cycle). But this "particular day in 1989" is also chosen by Codi for her return to her mother's death site, with the woman who took her secretly to witness that departure (339). Thus Codi ends her narrative with a long-denied, long-cherished memory, and her new understanding of it: "This is what I remember: Viola is holding my hand. [. . .] I can see my mother there, a small white bundle with nothing left, and I can see that it isn't a tragedy we're watching, really. Just a finished life" (342). Through the novel's final words, describing how the helicopter, "empty and bright, [. . .] rises like a soul" (342), Kingsolver suggests that Codi's participation with others in rituals of memory and mourning enables her to release her grief for her mother, as though she can finally heed her dream about carrying her fully grown daughter and hearing Hallie say, "Let her go. Let go. She'll rise" (301).

While revealing the power of traditional holidays and customs, *Animal Dreams* shows that unconventional rites are also sometimes necessary for traumatized people, especially for those who have experienced losses which are "invisible" or which "rupture the ordinary sequence of generations" (Herman 188), as is the case with Codi's secret miscarriage and her loss of a 29-year-old sister. Codi also speaks for many whose loved ones have died in ways that make their bodies unrecoverable: "[. . .] I kept coming back to this: we had no body. I wanted to have a funeral for Hallie, but I was at a loss. I knew the remains should not have been important, but in a funeral the body gives the grieving a place to focus their eyes" (324). Like those affected by the Oklahoma City bombing, for whom the "Survivor Tree" became a symbol and gathering place, Codi tries to find a miraculously thriving tree (one that the people of Grace call a "*semilla besada*—the seed that got kissed" [324, 49]) where the community can meet to remember Hallie.[7] Though the informally created memorial rite has many rough edges, other people's mementos of Hallie's childhood enable Codi to experience the powerful grief she feared would be "unbearable" (327; cf. Herman 188, 195). Furthermore, in an unconscious reenactment of the night of her miscarriage, Codi leaves the memorial gathering "alone," to bury the bundle of mementos wrapped in a black wool afghan, which replicates the black sweater (her mother's) she had chosen for her daughter's burial (328, 139). Homer's perspective blends the two times (331), though it is clear that Codi replaces an earlier act of secret hiding with a ritual of mourning that includes her father and allows her to "let go" of both her daughters, an idea reinforced when she tells Homer that they "gave [. . .] Hallie" to the world (333). As Rubenstein points out, this "ritual reburial of her lost child" allows Codi "to lay to rest and to reconnect with—the spirits of others she has lost" (17). The scene ends with Homer's confused perception that both his daughters are present, but in contrast to previous passages in which his strong love for them and for his wife seemed a painful burden that "trapped" them all (98), the final moment of his narrative suggests that Codi's rite of mourning has also made it possible for him to release his grief: "He understands for the first time in his life that love weighs nothing. Oh God, his girls are as light as birds" (335).

Through repeated image patterns, Kingsolver connects Codi with her mother, sister, and daughter: they are like birds but also like seeds; they "rise" but also go back to the earth, a carnivalesque image suggesting the cycle of life inseparable from death (Bakhtin 21, 24-25). Embodied in many forms of culture, including rituals and works of art, a vision of interconnected life is crucial to Codi, her father, and others paralyzed by loss, violence, and despair. Ursula Le Guin sees this sense of "relatedness" as central to *Animal Dreams*—indeed, she holds that the novel "belongs to a new fiction of relationship, aesthetically rich and of great political and spiritual significance and power" (8). Kingsolver develops this vision through several memorable devices. The most striking is use of multiples, as in the networks of women who hold the town together: Codi's "fifty mothers"; the town's founding Gracela sisters, also called "the great-grandmothers"; and the many Grace women (including Codi's mother) named Althea, such as those Codi refers to collectively as "the Altheas," who operate the town's popular restaurant (265). The novel's title and 16 of its 28 chapter titles foreground plural words: "Pictures," "Mistakes," "Endangered Places," "The Souls of Beasts," and so on. *Animal Dreams* also features two sets of twins and two sets of drowned coyote pups, a doubling that underscores the story's basic pairing, that of Codi and Hallie, whom the reader sees are very much alike (as Emelina says) rather than being the opposites Codi projects. In addition, ties between the opening and closing chapter titles create the impression of a circle, with the last chapter title, "Day of All Souls," being a one-word variation of the first, "Night of All Souls"; similarly, the penultimate chapter, "Human Remains," connects with the second, "Hallie's Bones." Numerous repetitions of the novel's beginning, along with images of return, characterize the last four chapters, starting with Codi's return to earth (and Grace) in chapter 25 and culminating with her second pregnancy and signs of plant life returning to Grace's poisoned and badly irrigated lands. Overall, the novel's repetitions form a cyclical structure that encapsulates Codi's many reconnections—with herself and her past, her community and the earth—as she comes to feel the sense of belonging and responsibility that is fundamentally necessary for those who have been isolated and anesthetized by trauma.

Codi reaches this point, in part, through another cultural influence: she has been drawn into collective action as she finds she cannot separate herself from large-scale social conflicts affecting Grace and Nicaragua. Aware that her tax dollars are financing the contras (262), Codi's deeply ingrained sense that she is her sister's keeper conflicts with her Cain-like disavowal of social responsibility. The two major threats that spur her involvement converge as painfully realistic details of the letter-writing campaign to obtain Hallie's release are interwoven with colorful vignettes showing the Stitch and Bitch Club's successful efforts to release Grace from the mining company's hold (270-72, 273-77; cf. 261-67, 313-17). Through this pervasive doubling, *Animal Dreams* links the problems in two sites of struggle, and these mirroring depictions (with their contrasting outcomes) reinforce key ideas about collective action. The most important of these ideas closely resemble what Sharon Welch has called "a feminist ethic of risk," in which "[a]ction begins in the face of overwhelming loss" and "[t]he fundamental risk [. . .] is the decision to care and to act although there are no guarantees of success" (67, 68). Needing to learn "how to live without guarantees, without safety" (298), Codi searches Hallie's letters and is struck by her sister's sense that she is "doing the only thing [she] can live with"; she is "not Saving Nicaragua," and even knowing that her side in the war may fail doesn't matter so much as the "daily work" that does some good (299). The same ethos underpins the Stitch and Bitch Club, Grace's older women who feel they have no other choice than to try to stop the mining company. When union-style demonstrations fail, they turn to their domestic skills, making peacock piñatas that draw attention to Grace's plight, even though they know that "a piñata" probably will not "stop a multinational corporation."[8]

Though at first self-defeated by her crippling sense of failure, Codi is compelled into action by threats to those she cares about—her students, her town, and her family. Before returning to Grace, she has taken after her father, dwelling on personal failures as a healer, just as Homer recalls his helplessness when Codi was pregnant, her resemblance to his wife (who died from complications of childbirth) paralyzing him with the sense of his family as "a web of women dead and alive, with himself at the center like a spider."[9] In contrast, Codi as a teacher is galvanized by her feelings, as pregnancy among her students, like the damage done to the local river, brings out her crusading zeal and gift for vivid explanation, traits she shares with Hallie. Hence, in the aftermath of the novel's crises, after Hallie has been killed and the mining company defeated, Codi, like many trauma survivors, finds that drawing upon what she has witnessed and learned in order to educate others gives her a sense of hope and purpose, a "survivor mission" (Herman 207-11). When she describes her goals for her students—that they will develop "a cultural memory" and "be custodians of the earth" (332)—it is clear that she becomes able to survive her sister's death by fusing her own mission with Hallie's. She thus feels that Hallie lives through her: "Everything we'd been I was now" (328).

Like many survivor discourses, *Animal Dreams* ends with a sense of affirmation, emphasizing resolution, continuity, new life, and the next generation. Especially resembling *The Color Purple* with its controversial "happy ending," Kingsolver's novels have been criticized for their optimism, perceived by some readers as an evasion of difficult issues (see Comer; Ryan). However, such a charge seems to overlook that the small battles for Grace and for Codi's soul are won in the context of a greater war in which thousands of civilians were killed, and Codi's efforts make no discernible difference. Moreover, the violence against Hallie is not forgotten in the novel's conclusion, since Codi is able to speak about what was done to her sister only a few chapters from the end.[10] But *Animal Dreams* does conclude with Codi's growth and recommitment to life, literally embodied in her pregnancy. Why this emphasis on hope? One reason offered by Kingsolver's writings is that the turn toward hope is true to life, as she shows based on her close involvement with a failed mining strike and her personal experiences of violence and loss.[11] Audre Lorde speaks for Kingsolver and many others when she asserts that hope and meaningful action are necessities for survival, just as "despair and isolation are [the] greatest internal enemies" (126; cf. 80). Though a natural defense and a mode of healing, commitment to social action also constitutes, for survivors, a compelling ethical choice. Hence, along with others who have felt the impact of violence or who write about effects of trauma, Kingsolver moves from describing individual recovery to setting forth responsibilities of citizens and communities. If what occurs in Grace is "such an American story" and Codi is a "good citizen" of a numbed, disengaged nation (240, 149), then *Animal Dreams* prescribes what American citizens need—commitment to individual and collective remembrance, to acts of memory that are inseparable from risk, mourning, and social involvement.

From *LIT: Literature Interpretation Theory* 11, no. 4 (2001): 327-350. Copyright © 2001 by Taylor & Francis Ltd. Reprinted by permission.

Notes

Many thanks to my colleague Daryl Palmer, a generous reader whose suggestions promote not only revision but new understanding. I also wish to thank Laura Cameron for invaluable research assistance.

1. Herman 1, 242-43. For other studies which examine parallels between individuals and communities or societies affected by psychological trauma, see Erikson, deVries, and Bloom.

2. Herman 2, 242-47. Among numerous texts dealing with the recovered memory debate, see Armstrong's spirited contribution, Haaken, and two recent collections of scholarly viewpoints, that of Williams and Banyard, and Appelbaum et al.

3. See also DeMeester's analysis of *Mrs. Dalloway* for a provocative and cogent argument presenting connections between modern literature and psychological trauma.

4. Herman 185: For examples of how such activities bring back Codi's repressed memories, see passages depicting All Souls' Day (159-60, 164-65, 342) and her discovery of her father's photographs showing that she and Hallie had the pale eyes of infants descended from the Gracelas (284), knowledge that reconstructs her family tree.

5. In "From Victim to Survivor," Warner and Feltey illuminate the process of identity reconstruction for trauma survivors; Kingsolver similarly writes of the need to move from "casualty to survivor" in "Stone Soup" 139. See Bruner, "The 'Remembered' Self" 53, for the idea that self is "perpetually rewritten." Cf. Bruner's "The Narrative Construction" and also Freedman and Combs 34-35.

6. For deVries's comments on symbolic places, see 410. Along with discussing potentially positive effects of culture for traumatized individuals and groups, deVries also offers equally significant ideas about the growth of "negative social forms" (such as gangs) among the traumatized when traditional culture is weak (407-08).

7. For a description of the "Survivor Tree" as a symbol and a site of informal rituals, see Daugherty (510-11). It is significant that Codi cannot find the specific *semilla besada* that she remembers, which for her symbolizes Hallie; instead she sees that "[e]very tree in the orchard looked blessed" (324), suggesting that she needs to relinquish her tendency to set Hallie apart and thus devalue herself and others.

8. *Animal Dreams* 266. Grace's older women show the union's influence in their clothes (a Steelworkers T-shirt), meetings, and strategies for opposing the mining company; see 175, 179. As Kingsolver notes, *Animal Dreams* in many ways draws upon *Holding the Line*, her nonfiction account of women's roles in the 1983 Arizona mining strike. See Kingsolver's 1996 introduction to *Holding the Line* xiv; also see Swartz 74-75.

9. *Animal Dreams* 98. For a discussion of the "wounded healer" that sheds light on Codi's and Homer's struggles, see Palgi and Dorban, who analyze the vulnerability of doctors, stemming from the necessity of facing inevitable failures to heal.

10. *Animal Dreams* 316-17. At the opposite pole from critics of Kingsolver's optimism, one survivor of child abuse rejected *Animal Dreams* because of the violence it depicts, leading Kingsolver to explain her criteria for "committing an act of violence in the written word"; see "Careful" 255, an essay that speaks to many people's concerns about evaluating representations of violence in culture.

---

11. For the "lesson [of] hope" Kingsolver derived from observing women in the mining strike, see *Holding the Line* xxiii. The first and last essays of *High Tide in Tucson*, providing a conceptual frame for that collection, present hope as a basic impulse of survival; the essays reflect Kingsolver's scientific training as well as her experience of violent assault and miscarriage. Also see her comments on writing as a rape survivor (Interview 163).

Works Cited

American Psychiatric Association. *Diagnostic and Statistical Manual of Mental Disorders*. 3rd ed. Washington, DC: APA, 1980.

Appelbaum, Paul S., Lisa A. Uyehara, and Mark R. Elin, eds. *Trauma and Memory: Clinical and Legal Controversies*. New York: Oxford UP, 1997.

Armstrong, Louise. *Rocking the Cradle of Sexual Politics: What Happened When Women Said Incest*. Reading, MA: Addison-Wesley, 1994.

Bakhtin, Mikhail. *Rabelais and His World*. Trans. Hélène Iswolsky. Bloomington: Indiana UP, 1984.

Berger, James. "Trauma and Literary Theory:" *Contemporary Literature* 38 (1997): 569-82.

Bloom, Sandra L. *Creating Sanctuary: Toward the Evolution of Sane Societies*. New York: Routledge, 1997.

Brown, Laura S. "Not Outside the Range: One Feminist Perspective on Psychic Trauma." Caruth, *Trauma* 100-12.

Bruner, Jerome. "The Narrative Construction of Reality." *Critical Inquiry* 18 (1991): 1-21.

⸻. "The 'Remembered' Self." *The Remembering Self: Construction and Accuracy in the Self-Narrative*. Ed. Ulric Neisser and Robyn Fivush. New York: Cambridge UP, 1994. 41-54.

Caruth, Cathy. Preface. Caruth, *Trauma* vii-ix.

⸻, ed. *Trauma: Explorations in Memory*. Baltimore: Johns Hopkins UP, 1995.

⸻. *Unclaimed Experience: Trauma, Narrative, and History*. Baltimore: Johns Hopkins UP, 1996.

Comer, Krista. "Sidestepping Environmental Justice: 'Natural' Landscapes and the Wilderness Plot." *Breaking Boundaries: New Perspectives on Women's Regional Writing*. Ed. Sherrie A. Inness and Diana Royer. Iowa City: U of Iowa P, 1997. 216-36.

Daugherty, Tracy. "After Murrah: An Essay on Public and Private Pain." *Southwest Review* 83 (1998): 489-511.

DeMeester, Karen. "Trauma and Recovery in Virginia Woolf's *Mrs. Dalloway*." *Modern Fiction Studies* 44 (1998): 649-73.

deVries, Marten W. "Trauma in Cultural Perspective." van der Kolk 398-413.

Erikson, Kai. "Notes on Trauma and Community." Caruth, *Trauma* 183-99.

Freedman, Jill, and Gene Combs. *Narrative Therapy: The Social Construction of Preferred Realities.* New York: Norton, 1996.

Freeman, Mark. *Rewriting the Self: History, Memory, Narrative.* London: Routledge, 1993.

Freud, Sigmund. *Beyond the Pleasure Principle: The Standard Edition of the Complete Psychological Works of Sigmund Freud.* Trans. James Strachey. Vol. 18. London: Hogarth, 1955. 7-64.

Griffin, Susan. *Woman and Nature: The Roaring Inside Her.* New York: Harper & Row, 1978.

Haaken, Janice. *Pillar of Salt: Gender, Memory, and the Perils of Looking Back.* New Brunswick, NJ: Rutgers UP, 1998.

Hartman, Geoffrey H. "On Traumatic Knowledge and Literary Studies." *New Literary History* 26 (1995): 537-63.

Henke, Suzette A. *Shattered Subjects: Trauma and Testimony in Women's Life-Writing.* New York: St. Martin's, 1998.

Herman, Judith Lewis. *Trauma and Recovery.* 1992. Afterword by Herman. New York: Basic, 1997.

Kingsolver, Barbara. *Animal Dreams.* New York: HarperCollins, 1990.

_____. *The Bean Trees: A Novel.* New York: Harper & Row, 1988.

_____. "Careful What You Let in the Door." *High Tide in Tucson* 243-56.

_____. *High Tide in Tucson: Essays from Now or Never.* New York: HarperCollins, 1995.

_____. *Holding the Line: Women in the Great Arizona Mine Strike of 1983.* 1989: introduction by Kingsolver. Ithaca, NY: ILR Press/Cornell UP, 1996.

_____. Interview. *Backtalk: Women Writers Speak Out.* By Donna Perry. New Brunswick, NJ: Rutgers UP, 1993. 143-69.

_____. "Serendipity & the Southwest: A Conversation with Barbara Kingsolver." *The Bloomsbury Review* Nov.-Dec. 1990: 3+.

_____. "Stone Soup." *High Tide in Tucson* 135-45.

Kuribayashi, Tomoko, and Julie Tharp. Introduction. *Creating Safe Space: Violence and Women's Writing.* Albany: State U of New York P, 1998. 1-8.

LaCapra, Dominick. *Representing the Holocaust: History, Theory, Trauma.* Ithaca: Cornell UP, 1994.

Le Guin, Ursula K. "The Fabric of Grace." Rev. of *Animal Dreams*, by Barbara Kingsolver. *The Washington Post* 2 Sept. 1990: Book World 1+.

Lorde, Audre. "A Burst of Light: Living with Cancer." *A Burst of Light.* Ithaca: Firebrand, 1988. 49-134.

Miller, J. Hillis. *Fiction and Repetition: Seven English Novels.* Cambridge: Harvard UP, 1982.

Palgi, Phyllis, and Joshua Dorban. "Reflections on the Self of Homo Hippocraticus and the Quest for Symbolic Immortality." *Trauma and Self.* Ed. Charles B. Strozier and Michael Flynn. Lanham, MD: Rowman & Littlefield, 1996. 221-30.

Rich, Adrienne. "Natural Resources." *The Dream of a Common Language: Poems 1974-77.* New York: Norton, 1978. 60-67.

Rubenstein, Roberta. "*Homer*ic Resonances: Longing and Belonging in Barbara Kingsolver's *Animal Dreams*." *Homemaking: Women Writers and the Politics and Poetics of Home*. Ed. Catherine Wiley and Fiona R. Barnes. New York: Garland, 1996. 5-22.

Ryan, Maureen. "Barbara Kingsolver's Lowfat Fiction." *Journal of American Culture* 18.4 (1995): 77-82.

Swartz, Patti Capel. "'Saving Grace': Political and Environmental Issues and the Role of Connections in Barbara Kingsolver's *Animal Dreams*." *ISLE* 1.1 (1993): 65-80.

Tal, Kalí. *Worlds of Hurt: Reading the Literatures of Trauma*. Cambridge: Cambridge UP, 1996.

van der Kolk, Bessel A., Alexander C. McFarlane, and Lars Weisaeth, eds. *Traumatic Stress: The Effects of Overwhelming Experience on Mind, Body, and Society*. New York: Guilford, 1996.

Warner, Susan, and Kathryn M. Feltey. "From Victim to Survivor: Recovered Memories and Identity Transformation." Williams and Banyard 161-72.

Welch, Sharon D. *A Feminist Ethic of Risk*. Minneapolis: Fortress, 1990.

Williams, Linda M., and Victoria L. Banyard, eds. *Trauma & Memory*. Thousand Oaks, CA: Sage, 1999.

Exploring the Matrix of Identity in
Barbara Kingsolver's *Animal Dreams*_____

Lee Ann De Reus

From the professional perspective of a family researcher, Lee Ann De Reus draws on several theories of the family and the self in this essay devoted to the concept of female identity development. Employing the developmental theories of Erik Erikson but also considering contemporary challenges to Erikson, especially those of psychologist Sally Archer, De Reus seeks to understand more fully the development of Codi, the protagonist of *Animal Dreams*. Through a variety of approaches, De Reus analyzes the stages of Codi's self-finding insofar as the plot of *Animal Dreams* allows readers to reconstruct them. De Reus identifies both material and cognitive ingredients of Codi's identity development. By ending her emotional codependency with her political-activist sister, Codi develops an authentic sense of self as a strong androgynous female.   — T.A.

Strange that some of us, with quick alternative vision, see beyond our infatuations, and even while we rave on the heights, behold the wide plain where our persistent self pauses and awaits us.

—George Eliot, *Middlemarch*

In Barbara Kingsolver's critically acclaimed novel *Animal Dreams* (1990), we accompany the protagonist, Codi Noline, in her quest for acceptance, love, and identity as she journeys home to Grace, Arizona, to confront her past and her dying, distant father. Weaving Native American folklore, flashbacks, and dreams, Kingsolver tells the tale of a young woman's search for meaning in life. It is this quest for a renewed sense of self that lends itself well to the study of identity development in Kingsolver's novel.

While Kingsolver's fiction has enjoyed high praise—including numerous literary awards, such as the 1990 Edward Abbey Award for

Ecofiction and the 1991 PEN Center USA West Literary Award for Fiction—there is a paucity of Kingsolver criticism, including only one book-length, academic literary analysis in existence to date, Mary Jean DeMarr's *Barbara Kingsolver: A Critical Companion* (1999), which offers merely a rudimentary introduction to Kingsolver's works. Further, attention by critics has focused primarily on her themes of ecology, feminism, political activism, and concern for Native American and African peoples and culture. Although all of her novels contain strong female characters, the specific examination of an individual female's identity development in conjunction with a family systems analysis is absent in the criticism devoted to Kingsolver. In a 1994 interview with Jennifer Fleischner, author of *A Reader's Guide to the Fiction of Barbara Kingsolver*, Kingsolver states that *Animal Dreams* was predicated on the following questions, "Why do some people engage with the world and its problems, while others turn their backs on it?" and "Why is it that these two sorts of people often occur even in the same family?"[1] By their very construction, Kingsolver's questions implore us to consider the nature of individual identity development in the context of family relationships.

In this essay, I will identify the process by which Codi begins to establish her sense of self in the world. Drawing on the intellectual traditions of several eminent scholars as well as their critics, this paper will utilize Erik Erikson's theory of psychosocial development, James Marcia's identity statuses, and Family Systems Therapy as a means for illuminating and marking Codi's level of identity development. To better understand the complexities of the identity formation process, however, consideration will also be given to identity researcher Sally Archer's feminist criticisms of Erikson and Marcia, as well as to several individual cognitive and sociocontextual factors, such as the family, which are known to influence the creation of self.

No single individual has influenced our understanding of identity development more than Erik Erikson. Considered the premiere theorist of identity, he is credited for bringing this vital element of our existence to the forefront of popular and scientific attention.[2] While multiple frameworks for understanding identity exist, Erikson's understanding of identity is embedded in an eight-stage psychosocial theory of development from infancy to old age.[3] This life-span developmental approach is a particular strength of this model, as it provides an understanding of development over time. Unlike any other identity theory, Erikson's model also integrates the historical, biological, psychological, and sociocultural forces that shape individual development. As Erikson himself observes, "The whole interplay between the psychosocial and the social, the developmental and the historical, for which identity formation is of prototypal significance, could be conceptualized only as a kind of psychosocial relativity."[4] So influential is Erikson's work that traces of this theory are found in most, if not all, other stage theories of adulthood and identity theory.[5] For example, Erikson's key identity concepts of identity crisis, foreclosure, and moratorium are virtually inherent in all discussions of adolescent development and for the purposes of this paper, lend themselves well to an analysis of Kingsolver's *Animal Dreams*. Until a new grand theory is tested and established, Erikson's theory will maintain its central position and value for understanding identity formation.[6]

According to Erikson's eight-stage life cycle scheme of development, identity formation is the primary task of adolescence. Labeled as Identity versus Role Confusion, this fifth developmental stage builds on the resolution of preceding stages and serves as a foundation for adulthood.[7] The outcome of Identity versus Role Confusion sets the stage for the subsequent psychosocial stages of Intimacy versus Isolation, Generativity versus Stagnation, and Integrity versus Despair to be found during the years of young, middle, and later adulthood, respectively.[8] A positive resolution of this identity crisis prepares the adolescent for adulthood while irresolution of this stage results in a sense of confusion about one's identity or role in life. Further, the sense of identity established during late adolescence determines to a great degree an individual's success in intimate relationships. Similarly, whether or not an individual experiences positive or negative resolution of the Identity versus Role Confusion stage is associated with one's ability to be generative or make a meaningful contribution to one's children or community. Finally, identity outcomes have bearing on one's last psychosocial task of finding meaning in life before it ends.[9]

It must be noted, however, that Erikson's theory is not without limitations. Identity researchers fault this model for its lack of attention to intrapsychic developmental structures.[10] While structural stage models such as those proposed by Jane Loevinger and Robert Kegan attend specifically to the intrapsychically defined stages of meaning construction, they do so at the expense of contextual factors influencing development. Psychosocial models such as Erikson's, however, are thought to reflect an intermediate position between structural stage and sociocultural approaches, viewing identity in terms of the interaction between internal structural characteristics and social tasks demanded by a particular society or social reference group.[11] Thus, due to the historical significance, timelessness, and comprehensiveness of Erikson's psychosocial theory of identity development as well as its ease of "fit" with the storyline, his model will serve as the framework for the present analysis of Codi's experiences in *Animal Dreams*.

Other critics of Erikson's work include feminists who have negatively judged his theories for portraying a primarily Eurocentric male model of normality with an emphasis on the stereotypical male characteristics of will, autonomy, competence, industry, initiative, personal agency, and individuation.[12] Based on this reading of Erikson, it has been argued that this theory reflects the values of a capitalistic, patriarchal society as opposed to recognizing the importance of attachments, intimacy, and relationships in people's, especially women's, lives.[13] Further, Erikson has been criticized for viewing women's reproductive and mothering capabilities as the single most important determinants of their adult identity while men can achieve identity through intellectual, occupational, and other public endeavors.[14] The unfortunate consequence of this conceptualization, according to Archer, is an artificially constructed dichotomy that portrays identity in narrow terms.[15] Historically, identity researchers have perpetuated this dichotomy by analyzing the intrapersonal identity variables of vocation, religious, and political ideologies for men while women's identity was determined by interpersonal variables related to sexuality and family roles (as though males are not sexual, or husbands or fathers). By dichotomizing identity versus intimacy, one set of characteristics precludes the expression of the other.[16] In response, identity researcher Sally Archer calls for a feminist approach to identity that is orthogonal in nature and therefore recognizes androgynous characteristics of both males and females. The dichotomy of identity versus intimacy, according to Archer, "prevents us from getting on with an understanding of human development. Very few people live without community, and very few people are comfortable having no inner sense of self."[17]

So why use Erikson? As Archer notes, "It is a subjective preference to choose to either ignore Erikson's theory or select components of it as a foundation or as a framework for one's understanding of the concept." However, she continues, "Rather than expend energy arguing over whose position is most true . . . it would appear far more fruitful to draw upon this bounty and enthusiastically embrace learning about identity formation from multiple perspectives."[18] For the purposes of this essay, Erikson's psychosocial theory of development provides a framework for analysis that, when combined with various feminist critiques, creates a particularly resonant and revelatory tool for a largely inaugural reading of Kingsolver's *Animal Dreams*.

Identity is often characterized as "a consistent definition of one's self as a unique individual, in terms of roles, attitudes, beliefs, and aspirations."[19] As the key developmental task of adolescence, identity formation is best understood as an evolutionary "process." The complexities of this process involve the interaction of an individual's biology, psychology, and societal contexts which result in themes of stability and change, psychological autonomy and connection, and intrapsychic and contextual components across adulthood.[20] James

Marcia, a seminal scholar in this area, describes the identity formation process as involving "a synthesis of childhood skills, beliefs, and identifications into a more or less coherent, unique whole that provides the young adult with both a sense of continuity with the past and a direction for the future."[21] Identity formation, then, creates a paradox of separating oneself from one's past and environment while finding new connections to the separated self.[22] It is this simultaneous experience of both belongingness and separateness, according to Kegan, that is necessary for the continued development of the individual.[23] Optimal identity development, according to Erikson, is the discovery and establishment of one's niche or place in the larger community. However, it is important to note that once discovered, an individual's identity does not remain fixed but is dynamic as shifting needs and circumstances necessitate change in an individual's sense of self.[24] From the Family Systems Therapy perspective, according to John V. Knapp, "one of the biggest jobs for the family is to provide support both for integration into a solid and enduring family unit and differentiation into relatively separate selves—being able to think, act, and feel for one's self."[25]

Building on Erikson's identity work, James Marcia has moved the empirical research in this area forward with his creation of four distinct identity statuses into which persons can be categorized. According to Marcia, these statuses are the outcomes of an identity formation process that can be divided into two discrete steps of exploration (questioning, experimentation) and commitment (resolving questions, deciding on a role or niche). These statuses, which range from lower to higher levels of ego maturity, include diffusion, foreclosure, moratorium, and identity achievement. A diffused individual exhibits no signs of exploration, nor does he or she endeavor to make occupational or ideological commitments. An individual who is foreclosed in identity has foregone exploration and accepted parental values and advice without question or the examination of alternatives. An individual is considered to be in a state of moratorium if he or she is actively searching for an identity, while an identity achieved person has made self-defined occupational and ideological commitments following a period of questioning and searching.

Similar to her criticisms of Erikson, Archer has taken Marcia to task for the reductive methodology imposed by his four identity statuses. It is her contention that such taxonomies inadvertently discount the context and motivations surrounding identity development. Thus, Archer proposes that "social facts" such as teenage pregnancy, sexual abuse, and the feminization of poverty, for example, must be considered as determinants of female identity formation given that "the identity process for the female adolescent can easily be described as potentially confusing and complex."[26]

Like Archer, Carol Markstrom-Adams has also given consideration to intervening factors thought to influence adolescent identity formation. From her synthesis of a broad body of theoretical and empirical literature, much of which is embedded in Marcia's identity status model, several social-contextual and individual cognitive factors were ascertained as pertinent to the creation of a sense of self. For the purposes of this essay, the contextual factors of family relationships and ethnic and racial group membership, the cognitive factors of assimilation and accommodation, differentiation and integration, and continuity of self, as well as relevant social facts, will be discussed.

In *Animal Dreams*, Codi Noline is in the developmental period of early adulthood (twenty-three to thirty-nine years of age)—which is characterized by Erikson's psychosocial crisis of Intimacy versus Isolation and Generativity versus Stagnation—at the time of her move back to her hometown of Grace, Arizona, to care for her ailing father. However, Codi appears to be rather delayed in her development as her struggles in the novel revolve around her search for an identity. With no sense of purpose in life, she moves from job to job, lover to lover, unable to make commitments: "I tended to drift, like a well-meaning visitor to this planet awaiting instructions."[27] And upon arriving in Grace, Codi says that "I was *here*, after all, with no more mission in life than I'd been born with years ago."[28]

The untimely death of Codi's mother at the tender age of three, her emotionally unavailable father, and her own miscarriage at the age of fifteen culminate in a lost young woman in her early thirties with little sense of identity. At this point in the novel, Codi exhibits a diffuse identity status (the least developmentally advanced) by her lack of commitment to values or goals, lack of identity exploration, and expressed feelings of dissatisfaction and emptiness: "I spent my whole childhood as an outsider to Grace. . . . I'd sell my soul and all my travelling shoes to *belong* some place."[29]

As stated previously, identity formation does not occur in a vacuum and must be understood in context as social facts and the social environment exert great influence on all developmental processes. The social facts that transpire upon her return to Grace and prove consequential to Codi's identity development include her position as a biology teacher at the local high school, her reconnection with Loyd Peregrina, the father of her miscarried baby, the environmental catastrophe about to befall Grace, and the kidnapping and murder of her younger sister Hallie by Nicaraguan rebels. The social-contextual factors identified in relation to identity and to be discussed here in conjunction with these social facts include family relationships and ethnic and racial group membership.

Creating a sense of self is clearly linked with particular styles of family interaction and communication. A family system that balances closeness with encouragement toward autonomy and individuation is considered an optimal family environment for facilitation of identity development. Research has shown that adolescents in these families engage in more identity exploration and make more stable identity commitments. Conversely, families characterized by little parent-child closeness and connectedness have been associated repeatedly with difficulties in resolving the adolescent identity crisis with diffused youth reporting the least emotional attachments to parents.[30] Further, diffusion is related to adolescent perceptions of maternal and paternal rejection coupled with a perceived affection-lacking relationship with the mother. Thus, it is not surprising that diffusion is associated with strained and distant relationships between adolescents and their parents.[31] According to Knapp, "fear and anxiety usually force members to create a pseudo-self, so that one's inner feelings and outer behavior are not congruent, since one's thoughts must be carefully monitored to avoid intensifying anxiety and fear through exposure to others of whom one is afraid."[32]

The death of Codi's mother, due to complications following the birth of Hallie, was for Codi a vague memory that resulted in the negative resolution of the first developmental crisis, trust versus mistrust. Feeling abandoned and relegated to the negligent care of their father, Codi and her sister were subjected to the desperate, awkward attempts of Doc Homer to raise daughters acceptable to a community that had previously rejected him. For example, Doc Homer's insistence that the girls wear specially ordered orthopedic shoes to prevent irreparable harm to their bodies created by impractical footwear was the cause of much humiliation inflicted by their peers during their school years. Although conceived out of love for his daughters, many of Doc Homer's parenting techniques were interpreted by the girls as uncaring, strict codes of conduct whose violation met with harsh punishments. Codi's resulting relationship with Doc Homer is quite characteristic of the distant parent-child relationship associated with diffused adolescents. This is evident when she described her father as "being like no one else, being alone, was the central ethic of his life."[33] As Codi contemplates this remoteness, she recalls that "from Doc Homer you didn't expect hugs and kisses. He was legendary in this regard. Hallie and I used to play a game we called 'orphans' when we were with him in a crowd: 'Who in this room is our true father or mother? Which is the one grownup here that loves us.'" Waiting for a sign of affection or recognition from any adult in the room, Codi learns at a young age that "that person would never be Doc Homer," validating her perception that her father did not love her or Hallie.[34] This acuity of a distant father persisted into adulthood when upon her return to Grace Codi lamented that conversing with her father while he developed pictures in his darkroom "was the nearest I'd ever come to feeling like I had a dad."[35] The emotional unavailability of Doc Homer, combined with the distressing loss of Codi's mother at age three, leaves her without the loving, supportive attachments and the nurturant socialization characteristic of most parent/child relationships, contributing to her diffuse identity formation. Says Codi, "Nobody, not my father, *no one* had jumped in to help when I was a child getting whacked by life."[36] Without a secure family base, Codi has no solid foundation from which to conduct her identity exploration.

Codi's isolation while "getting whacked by life" is nowhere more apparent in the novel than when she endures a tragic miscarriage at the age of fifteen. Too ashamed and fearful to confide in Hallie, Doc Homer, or Loyd Peregrina, the baby's father, Codi miscarries the six-month-old fetus at home and buries it immediately in the backyard. Doc Homer, who is quite aware of Codi's pregnancy, observes the burial and later protects and marks the grave with stones; yet ironically, the only parental comfort he can muster is to offer her medication to alleviate the post-delivery symptoms. As Doc Homer laments, "This is the full measure of love he is qualified to dispense."[37] For Codi, the miscarriage is a turning point in her life, which she describes as dividing her from the people she knows:

As Hallie had bluntly pointed out in her letter, I'd marked myself early on as a bad risk, undeserving of love and incapable of benevolence. It wasn't because of a bad grade on a report card, as she'd supposed. It ran deeper than that. I'd lost what there was to lose: first my mother and then my baby. Nothing you love will stay. Hallie could call that attitude a crutch, but she didn't know, she hadn't loved and lost so deeply . . . she'd never been born—not into life as I knew it. Hallie could still risk everything.[38]

Unable to trust others and take risks, Codi copes with her painful past and negotiates her teen years by repressing her childhood memories and creating obdurate boundaries between herself and life. As Codi keenly surmises about herself from this point forward: "I wasn't keeping to any road, I was running, forgetting what lay behind and always looking ahead for the perfect home, where trains never wrecked and hearts never broke, where no one you loved ever died."[39] The combined social facts and context of the death of Codi's mother, Doc Homer's conflicted parenting, and Codi's miscarriage at age fifteen propel her identity on a developmental trajectory toward diffusion.[40]

Another social-contextual factor related to identity formation is that of ethnic and racial group membership. At issue is the necessity for racial and ethnic minorities to reconcile the cultural values of their own minority group with those of the mainstream culture. Further, ethnic and racial prejudice may limit opportunities for identity exploration.[41] For Codi, however, the intervening factor is not her particular membership in a racial group, but rather her lack of identification with any ethnicity. Out of shame for his family history and heritage in Grace, Doc Homer has not provided his daughters with a complete family record, exacerbating Codi's uninformed sense of self. Underpinning her deficient knowledge of family history, Kingsolver artfully contrasts Codi's misinformation with Loyd's keen sense of his own Native American heritage. In one poignant scene, when Loyd inquires about Codi's ethnicity by asking, "What are you?" Codi replies, "I have no idea. My mother came from someplace in Illinois, and Doc Homer won't own up to being from anywhere. I can't remember half of what happened to me before I was fifteen. I guess I'm nothing. The Nothing Tribe."[42] A paucity of information regarding family history proves to be another barrier to Codi's self-discovery.

The second category of intervening factors related to identity formation includes individual cognitive aspects such as cognitive assimilation and accommodation, cognitive complexity, and the ability to conceptualize continuity of self.[43] Cognitive or identity assimilation gives the individual positive information about the self, even if this information is inaccurate. Forms of identity assimilation include self-justification, identity projection, defensive rigidity, and lack of insight. If not in balance with accommodation, individuals may resist change and have limited self-awareness, possibly resulting in a foreclosed identity. In comparison, identity accommodation is the creation of a realistic appraisal of the self in relation to experiences, which may result in the change of identity. Positive changes in identity, self-doubts, considering alternatives, and responding to external influences are all mechanisms of identity accommodation. In extreme cases, individuals may have an underdefined identity and a reliance on external factors as opposed to individual factors in decision-making, possibly resulting in identity diffusion or a prolonged moratoria.[44]

Codi utilizes negative assimilation and accommodation strategies early in the novel as methods for protecting herself against positive self-attributions and for avoiding the difficult process of self-discovery and creation. Negative assimilation is accomplished by Codi's subconscious suppression of all memories prior to the age of fifteen. Without the knowledge and life meaning of several significant events such as the death of her mother and the details surrounding her miscarriage, Codi is left with an identity void that only the interpretation of these events could fill. Negative accommodation is evidenced initially by Codi's reliance on external factors to determine her life course. "I was suddenly disgusted with what I was doing. I'd go anywhere Carlo wanted, I'd be a sport for my students in Grace, I'd even tried to be a doctor for Doc Homer. . . . If I kept trying to be what everybody wanted, I'd soon be insipid enough to fit in everywhere."[45] Further, in order to avoid resolving her own identity crisis, Codi chooses to live vicariously through, and in the shadow of, her younger sister Hallie, whom she idolizes. In reference to Hallie, she remarks, "Every man I'd ever loved had loved Hallie best and settled for me. It didn't bother me as much as you might think; I could understand it. I loved her too."[46] This judgement of herself as inferior to Hallie provides Codi with a convenient excuse for life's failures and for self-sabotaging her own identity resolution.

Cognitive complexity, or the ability to use more sophisticated and efficient modes of cognitive functioning, is characterized by differentiation and integration. Differentiation requires the adolescent to examine various complexities of the personality and psyche as a means for determining likes and dislikes, interests, values, motives, and so on. The inability to introspect to this degree may result in a premature foreclosure of identity or an opting out of the identity search process altogether as in the case of diffusion. An inability to integrate the complexities of personality and psyche may result in ongoing states of moratoria where the individual is able to differentiate but not integrate by making a commitment to an identity.[47] Initially, Codi is unable to differentiate as she lives her life according to those around her.

This is evident in her choice to attend medical school, not for herself, but rather to garner approval from her father who was also a physician: "It's true that I tried myself to go into medicine, which is considered a helping profession, but I did it for the lowest of motives. I did it to win love, and to prove myself capable."[48] Codi's desire to win her father's love and overcome the space between them is predictable behavior from a diffused adolescent who perceives parental rejection.

Codi's lack of differentiation, however, is most discernible in her dependent relationship with her sister Hallie. Codi describes her attachment to Hallie as being "like keenly mismatched Siamese twins conjoined at the back of the mind."[49] For Codi, Hallie represents all things virtuous: stability, autonomy, a sense of direction and purpose, optimism, strength, and hope. She is Codi's anchor and a shield against her own insecurities. Thus, with Hallie in her life, Codi is able to substitute dependency for the difficult process of self-creation.

The first turning point for Codi in her identity development is when she—literally and figuratively—returns to Grace. With Hallie's departure to fight for peasant farmers in Nicaragua, Codi is slowly weaned of her codependence and pushed toward autonomy. Previously diffused in her identity, Codi shifts to the status of moratorium and begins to forge a new identity after this relocation and her ensuing life experiences. It is during Hallie's absence that Codi reconnects with long-lost friends, her father, and Loyd Peregrina. As a result, Codi begins to explore her occupational, interpersonal, and ideological options and begins to move beyond the psychosocial stage of Identity versus Role Confusion to Intimacy versus Isolation and Generativity versus Stagnation. Codi is unwittingly engaged, for example, in a process of introspection and self-definition due to an environmental crisis that occurs in Grace. As Codi's biology expertise is called upon by the townspeople to avert ecological disaster created by a local mining company, she begins to feel needed and discovers in herself a degree of passion about the environment that rivals her sister's enthusiasm—an aspect of Hallie's persona that Codi envies. Unable to contain her newly developed desire for environmental justice, Codi carries her activism into the classroom, where she delivers a fervent plea to the students to be responsible stewards of the world around them. Of her classroom rant, she says, "I felt strangely high. Furious and articulate."[50] From this experience, Codi is drawn closer to her authentic self as she experiences brief glimpses of what life could be like for her in the future.

As Codi's work roles and ideological commitments become defined, her relationship with Loyd evolves simultaneously. The combination of his patience and loving support for Codi fosters her ability to accept his wise counsel that "for everybody that's gone away, there's somebody that's come to you." Hence, "You can trust that you're not going to run out of people to love."[51] This line of reasoning represents a major paradigm shift for a woman whose entire life was previously predicated on a personal philosophy of scarcity and fear. Codi's acceptance of Loyd's advice likewise serves as the catalyst for her resolution of Intimacy versus Isolation.

The validation that Codi receives from her successful leadership of the local community against the Black Mountain Mining Company and her award as teacher of the year empower her to confront Doc Homer at last about her dearth of family history. Doc Homer's worsening dementia impedes this process, however, preventing absolute resolution of the relationship for either the father or daughter. As Codi observes, "We were comically out of synchrony—a family vaudeville routine. Whatever one of us found, the other lost."[52] Yet with a new-found determination, Codi is not deterred from piecing together her past. Information from women in the community and family relics in the attic provide Codi with the necessary clues to discover her family's historical connection to Grace. In addition, these revelations afford Codi with new insights about her father: "He was doing exactly the opposite of setting himself apart. He was proving we belonged here, were as pure as anybody in Grace."[53] The orthopedic shoes and the strict parenting methods were his loving attempts to prove that his daughters *belonged* in the community of Grace, despite his own previous rejection. Realizing that she had misjudged his actions, Codi is able to forgive Doc Homer and let go of her previous perception of paternal rejection.

From this point in the novel, Codi's identity formation process is catapulted forward from moratorium to identity achievement due to Hallie's untimely death. This event forces Codi to at last differentiate from her sister and reconcile her past with her present and her future, the result of which is the conceptualization of the continuity of self—the third and final intervening factor in identity formation. This important component of identity formation is the ability to conceptualize the self as the product of existence over time. This process provides an integration and understanding of the continuities between the self in the past, present, and the person whom one will become in the future.[54] Failure to do so may result in feelings of aimlessness and meaninglessness, the likely causes of a diffuse identity.[55] As Codi's past is unveiled, negative assimilation is overcome and meaning is created out of her assorted life events. Codi's realizations are exemplified when she says, "I was getting a dim comprehension of the difference between Hallie and me. It wasn't a matter of courage or dreams, but something a whole lot simpler. A pilot would call it ground orientation. I'd spent a long time circling above the clouds, looking for life, while Hallie was living it."[56]

No longer afraid of love or dependent on Hallie to protect her from confronting her self, Codi finally achieves her own "ground orientation."

In *Animal Dreams*, Kingsolver provides us with the portrayal of a woman's life that goes beyond the archetypal tale of a woman's courtship leading to marriage. Unlike *Cinderella* or *Anna Karenina*, Codi discovers the empowering possibilities of self-determination—not through a man or suicide, but via an empowerment that is derived en route to her own identity.[57] In Codi, Kingsolver successfully achieves Archer's androgynous female who exhibits the stereotypical male attributes of will, autonomy, competence, industry, initiative, personal agency, and individuation *in the context* of her intimate relationships, thereby defying the traditional and limiting dichotomy of inter- *and* intrapersonal characteristics of identity. In the end, with her current and past psychosocial crises resolved and her present sense of identity achieved, Codi emerges as a self-possessed young woman capable of genuine commitments both to herself and to others.

From *Reading the Family Dance: Family Systems Therapy and Literary Study*, ed. John V. Knapp and Kenneth Womack (Monmouth Junction, NJ: Rosemont Publishing and Printing Corp, 2003): 93-101. Copyright © 2003 by Rosemont Publishing and Printing Corp. Reprinted by permission.

Notes

1. See Fleischner, *Reader's Guide to the Fiction of Barbara Kingsolver.*

2. See Josselson, *Revising Herself*, 6, 27; see also Kroger, *Identity Development*, 8.

3. See Kroger, *Identity Development*, for a summary of five different theoretical approaches to identity. Identity is currently studied among social scientists via one of five general theoretical frameworks. In brief, these frameworks can be described as follows: 1) the historical approach addresses conditions that precede the contemporary concern with identity; 2) the structural stage approach examines the changing internal structures of ego development through which an individual gives meaning to life experiences; 3) the sociological approach focuses on the role society plays in influencing identity development over time; 4) the narrative approach uses people's stories about their lives in an attempt to assemble many varied life factors into an integrated whole that reflects some sense of sameness or continuity to these experiences; 5) the psycho-

social approach which attempts to integrate the roles played by society and individual's psychology and biology in developing an identity. See xi.

4. Erikson, *Childhood and Society*, 23.

5. See Kroger, *Identity Development*, 14; see also Bee, *Journey of Adulthood*, 35.

6. Berger, *Developing Person Through the Lifespan*, 65.

7. In infancy, the central issue of development is trust versus mistrust. Positive resolution of this stage will result in feelings of trust from environmental support while a negative resolution is equated with a fear of others. This stage is followed by autonomy versus shame and doubt in early childhood during which time a toddler will develop a sense of self-sufficiency if exploration is encouraged. If discouraged, the child will develop self-doubts and dependence. During the play years, the developmental issue is initiative versus guilt. If resolved positively, the young child will discover self-initiative and ways to manipulate his or her environment as opposed to guilt imposed by adults due to the child's actions or thoughts. The final stage of childhood occurring during the school age years is industry versus inferiority. At this time, children will develop a sense of competence if successful at their endeavors such as schoolwork or sports. Conversely, feelings of inferiority will ensue if the child experiences no sense of mastery. See Berger, *Developing Person Through the Lifespan*, 40; see also Kroger, *Identity Development*, 10-11.

8. Kroger, *Identity Development*, 10.

9. Ibid., 11.

10. Ibid., 26.

11. Ibid., 15.

12. Knowledge about women's development in general is minimal. Many scholars of adult development in particular agree that the empirical study of development is devoid of women's experiences. See Archer, "Feminist's Approach to Identity Research," 29; Baber and Allen, *Women and Families*, 18; Franz and Stewart, *Women Creating Lives*, 5; Gergen, "Finished at 40," 472; Josselson, *Revising Herself*, 9; Lytle, Bakken, and Romig, "Adolescent Female Identity Development," 175; Patterson, Sochting, and Marcia, "Inner Space and Beyond," 12. Most of what is known about adult development has been formulated on studies of men and used for the interpretation of women's lives. In addition to Erikson, prominent theorists such as Levinson, Vaillant, and Kohlberg have also been criticized by feminist scholars for their male conceptualizations of adult development. As Gergen observes, "To judge from the major studies of life-span development at middle adulthood, one would think only men survived the third decade of life" ("Finished at 40," 475).

It should be noted, however, that in later life, even Erikson himself questioned the usefulness of his theory for women and reconsidered its implications. See Ryff and Migdal, "Intimacy and Generativity," 471. For example, Erikson noted that his theory did not yet take into account the many changes that have occurred in society; see Hall, "Conversation with Erik Erikson," 24. Rapid social change with respect to women's roles during Erikson's life is no doubt one of the reasons for contemporary feminists' dissatisfaction with the accuracy of his theory for women's lives.

13. Berzoff, "From Separation to Connection," 51.

14. Gergen, "Finished at 40," 476. In Erikson's defense, he was the first social sci-

entist to advocate a human development model that included an ethic of "care" as the hallmark of midlife. See Snarey, *How Fathers Care for the Next Generation*, 16. Further, the model includes issues of trust, intimacy, and generativity which are typically associated with women's, not men's lives.

15. Archer, "Feminist's Approach to Identity Research," 27.

16. Ibid., 43.

17. Ibid., 30. Archer's own research in this area has demonstrated that "females have approached identity formation either comparable to or in a more sophisticated manner than that of males" (43). In the intrapersonal male domains of identity, females and males approach the task of identity formation similarly. With respect to the interpersonal female domains of connection, females have exhibited either comparable or more sophisticated processes of identity development. In addition to Archer's findings, minimal sex differences have been documented in numerous other studies (e.g., Lytle, Bakken, and Romig, "Adolescent Female Identity Development," 182; Kroger, *Identity Development*, 106), yet these findings are rarely included in textbooks, perpetuating the belief that the sense of self and the desire for connection are incompatible as opposed to intertwined.

18. Ibid., 31.

19. Kroger, *Identity Development*, 3.

20. Ibid., 9.

21. Marcia, "Ego Identity Status Approach to Ego Identity," 3.

22. McAdams, *Power, Intimacy, and the Life Story*, 29.

23. See Kegan, *Evolving Self*, 81-85; see also Kegan, *In Over Our Heads*, 340-41.

24. Kroger, *Identity Development*, 12.

25. Knapp, *Striking at the Joints*, 65.

26. Archer, "Feminist's Approach to Identity Research," 45.

27. Kingsolver, *Animal Dreams*, 10.

28. Ibid., 28.

29. Ibid., 30.

30. Fullinwider-Bush and Jacobvitz, "Transition to Young Adulthood," 88; Kroger, *Identity Development*, 108.

31. Markstrom-Adams, "Consideration of Intervening Factors in Adolescent Identity Formation," 175.

32. Knapp, *Striking at the Joints*, 65.

33. Kingsolver, *Animal Dreams*, 69.

34. Ibid., 72.

35. Ibid., 73.

36. Ibid., 15.

37. Ibid., 142.

38. Ibid., 233.

39. Ibid., 236.

40. Ruthellen Josselson, another noteworthy identity researcher, suggests that a third dimension of connectedness be added to the dimensions of exploration and commitment when determining identity status for women. In particular, women in diffusion not only lack commitments and directed exploration but are also isolated. Distant

from their parents, they have not found a long-term, stable, healthy relationship to function in their stead. Their position in relation to their parents can be characterized as "I don't know where I stand, but you stand far away from me." For most of the novel, this is particularly true for Codi's relationship with her father. Women in foreclosure sustain strong commitments to their parents: "Here I stand, loyally at your side." In moratorium, women are caught in the struggle between autonomy and loyalty to their parents: "If I stand here, will you still be there for me?" In Codi's case, there is some resolution of the distant relationship with Doc Homer; however, confronted with the reality of his progressive decline in health, Codi must face her father's continued emotional absence. In identity achievement, women state, "Here I stand," because they possess a secure family base from which to conduct their explorations. In the absence of her parents, Codi has recognized and accepted Loyd and the doting women of Grace, whom she affectionately refers to as her "fifty mothers," as her family by the end of the novel.

41. Markstrom-Adams, "Consideration of Intervening Factors in Adolescent Identity Formation," 176.

42. Kingsolver, *Animal Dreams*, 213.

43. Markstrom-Adams, "Consideration of Intervening Factors in Adolescent Identity Formation," 179.

44. Kroger, *Identity Development*, 65; Whitbourne, *The Me I Know*, 34.

45. Kingsolver, *Animal Dreams*, 201.

46. Ibid., 10.

47. Markstrom-Adams, "Consideration of Intervening Factors in Adolescent Identity Formation," 185.

48. Kingsolver, *Animal Dreams*, 36.

49. Ibid., 8.

50. Ibid., 255.

51. Ibid., 297.

52. Ibid., 289.

53. Ibid., 284.

54. Akhtar, "Syndrome of Identity Diffusion," 1382; Baumeister, *Identity*, 12; Erikson, *Childhood and Society*, 22.

55. Markstrom-Adams, "Consideration of Intervening Factors in Adolescent Identity Formation," 186.

56. Kingsolver, *Animal Dreams*, 225.

57. Josselson, *Revising Herself*, 7.

Works Cited

Akhtar, Salman. "The Syndrome of Identity Diffusion." *American Journal of Psychiatry* 141 (1984): 1381-85.

Archer, Sally. "A Feminist's Approach to Identity Research." In *Adolescent Identity Formation*, edited by Gerald R. Adams, Thomas P. Gullotta, and Raymond Montemayor, 25-49. Newbury Park, CA: Sage, 1992.

Baber, Kristine, and Katherine Allen. *Women and Families: Feminist Reconstructions*. New York: Guilford, 1992.

Baumeister, Roy F. *Identity: Cultural Change and the Struggle for Self*. New York: Oxford University Press, 1986.

Bee, Helen. *The Journey of Adulthood*. 4th ed. Englewood Cliffs, NJ: Prentice Hall, 2000.

Berger, Kathleen Stassen. *The Developing Person Through the Lifespan*. 5th ed. New York: Worth Publishers, 2001.

Berzoff, Joan. "From Separation to Connection: Shifts in Understanding Women's Development." *Affilia* 4 (1989): 45-58.

DeMarr, Mary Jean. *Barbara Kingsolver: A Critical Companion*. Westport, CT: Greenwood, 1999.

Erikson, Erik H. *Childhood and Society*. 2nd ed. New York: Norton, 1963.

Fleischner, Jennifer. *A Reader's Guide to the Fiction of Barbara Kingsolver*. New York: HarperPerennial, 1994.

Franz, Carol, and Abigail Stewart. *Women Creating Lives: Identities, Resilience, and Resistance*. Boulder, CO: Westview, 1994.

Fullinwider-Bush, Nell, and Deborah B. Jacobvitz. "The Transition to Young Adulthood: Generational Boundary Dissolution and Female Identity Development." *Family Process* 32 (1993): 87-103.

Gergen, Mary. "Finished at 40: Women's Development within the Patriarchy." *Psychology of Women Quarterly* 14 (1990): 471-93.

Hall, Elizabeth. "A Conversation with Erik Erikson." *Psychology Today* 17 (1983): 22-30.

Josselson, Ruthellen. *Revising Herself: The Story of Women's Identity from College to Midlife*. New York: Oxford University Press, 1996.

Kegan, Robert. *The Evolving Self: Problem and Process in Human Development*. Cambridge: Harvard University Press, 1982.

_____. *In Over Our Heads: The Mental Demands of Modern Life*. Cambridge: Harvard University Press, 1994.

Kingsolver, Barbara. *Animal Dreams*. New York: HarperCollins, 1990.

Knapp, John V. *Striking at the Joints: Contemporary Psychology and Literary Criticism*. Lanham, MD: University Press of America, 1996.

Kroger, Jane. *Identity Development: Adolescence through Adulthood*. Thousand Oaks, CA: Sage, 2000.

Lytle, Jean L., Linda Bakken, and Charles Romig. "Adolescent Female Identity Development." *Sex Roles* 37 (1997): 175-85.

Marcia, James E. "The Ego Identity Status Approach to Ego Identity." In *Ego Iden-*

tity: A Handbook for Psychosocial Research, edited by James E. Marcia, Alan S. Waterman, Daniel R. Matteson, Sally L. Archer, and Jacob L. Orlofsky, 3-21. New York: Springer-Verlag, 1993.

Markstrom-Adams, Carol. "A Consideration of Intervening Factors in Adolescent Identity Formation." In *Adolescent Identity Formation*, edited by Gerald R. Adams, Thomas P. Gullota, and Raymond Montemayor, 173-92. Newbury Park, CA: Sage, 1992.

McAdams, Dan P. *Power, Intimacy, and the Life Story: Personological Inquiries into Identity*. New York: Guilford, 1988.

Patterson, Serena J., Ingrid Sochting, and James E. Marcia. "The Inner Space and Beyond: Women and Identity." In *Adolescent Identity Formation*, edited by Gerald R. Adams, Thomas P. Gullotta, and Raymond Montemayor, 9-24. Newbury Park, CA: Sage, 1992.

Ryff, Carol, and Susan Migdal. "Intimacy and Generativity: Self-Perceived Transitions." *Signs* 9 (1984): 470-81.

Snarey, John. *How Fathers Care for the Next Generation*. Cambridge: Harvard University Press, 1993.

Whitbourne, Susan K. *The Me I Know: A Study of Adult Identity*. New York: Springer-Verlag, 1986.

Luna Moths, Coyotes, Sugar Skulls:
The Fiction of Barbara Kingsolver_____

Amanda Cockrell

Kingsolver's evocations of animals and the varied landscapes of her novels are the focus of this wide-ranging essay. Amanda Cockrell sees both development and continuity in the novelist's work, manifested in its various connections with the natural world, whether animal, geographical, or astronomical. She argues that Kingsolver's protagonists are shaped through the biological stimuli of their worlds, yet the writer often contrasts human "animal" instincts with the impulses of the human heart. Even though the novels' plots may turn out to be "messy," in Cockrell's words, Kingsolver's characters live out their social consciences in a world that knows honesty and solidarity primarily among those with whom one has established relationships of trust. Cockrell invites readers to join Kingsolver in recognizing and celebrating the biological rootedness of all life.   — T.A.

El Día de los Muertos—the Day of the Dead, November 2, All Souls Day—is a gaudily macabre holiday in Mexico and parts of the American southwest. Everyone turns out for it, bearing armloads of cleaning supplies, fresh paint, and chrysanthemums, gladioli, marigolds, and silk roses. Ancestors' graves are swept; fences and tombs are freshly painted. The graveyard is decorated and decked with flowers. Children play with skeleton toys: skeleton cowboys, skeleton ladies in big flowered hats, skeleton mariachi bands. They dance between the graves, munching on sugar skulls. It is a family party that lasts all day, and all are gathered in. Codi Noline, the narrator of *Animal Dreams*, the second of Barbara Kingsolver's five novels, yearns for that connection: "More than anything else I wished I belonged to one of those living, celebrated families, lush as plants, with bones in the ground for roots. I wanted pollen on my cheeks and one of those calcium ancestors to decorate as my own." On the Day of All Souls, the borders between the worlds are thin, and messages may be exchanged. It is the search for the connection, through death as well as birth, to place and family that drives Kingsolver's fiction.

In the title piece of her book of essays *High Tide in Tucson*, she describes coming home from the Bahamas with an unexpected companion, a hermit crab who crawls from her shell collection as she is displaying it for her daughter. The crab isn't happy about it. "Who would blame this creature? It had fallen asleep to the sound of the Caribbean tide and awakened on a coffee table in Tucson, Arizona, where the nearest standing water source of any real account was the municipal sewage-treatment plant."

Kingsolver and her daughter adopt Buster the crab, since they can't send him back, and supply him with an aquarium and the rest of the shell collection. He proves an entertaining pet, but they notice with interest that he appears to be manic-depressive—alternating periods of burrowing into the sand, apparently dead, with bouts of gravel-rattling hyperactivity. It takes her a while, but Kingsolver is a biologist and a student of animal behavior. It comes to her finally: Buster's activity is linked to the tides. Or the tides that would occur in Tucson if Tucson had tides. "This," says Kingsolver, "is the lesson of Buster, the poetry that camps outside the halls of science."

Kingsolver's fictional characters share a good deal with Buster the crab. They find themselves transported in various ways from their home waters and forced to adapt to strange new clocks. They undergo culture shock (while providing their adopted lands with a bit of their own), learn new tongues and new dialects, and shed and acquire family like Buster trying on shells. In all of it they are moved by the landscape into which they have fallen, as well as by that of the moon, which is to say, by sex. As Kingsolver says:

[H]uman females in their natural state—which is to say, sleeping outdoors—arrive at menses in synchrony and ovulate with the full moon. My imagination remains captive to that primordial village: the comradely grumpiness of new-moon days, when the entire world at once would go on PMS alert. And the compensation that would turn up two weeks later on a wild wind, under that great round headlamp, driving both men and women to distraction with the overt prospect of conception. The surface of the land literally rises and falls—as much as fifty centimeters!—as the moon passes over, and we clay-footed mortals fall like dominoes before the swell. It's no surprise at all if a full moon inspires lyricists to corny love songs, or inmates to slamming themselves against barred windows.

Her first novel, *The Bean Trees*, follows the journey of Taylor Greer, whose first goal is to get through high school without getting pregnant, and whose next is to get out of Pittman County, Kentucky, as fast as possible. On the road, however, she is given a child (literally) when a Cherokee woman puts an abused baby in her car and drives away. Taylor's journey to wherever she is going (it turns out to be Tucson) becomes a journey to motherhood and selfhood simultaneously. In her remaking of herself, she even acquires a new name—she begins in Pittman County as Marietta and takes Taylor from the first town where she runs out of gas.

Like Buster, the landscape has much to do with her transformation. Kingsolver, who herself grew up in Kentucky and settled in Tucson, knows the subtle ways that landscape marks us. She is adept at drawing her reader into that place. Who would not want to swim in a canyon pool where "White rocks sloped up out of the water like giant, friendly hippo butts"? We see the ways that geography scars hearts in the chapter called "Into the Terrible Night": "The sloped desert plain that lay between us and the city was like a palm stretched out for a fortuneteller to read, with its mounds and hillocks, its life lines and heart lines of dry stream beds." And the look and power of desert rain comes to us in the homely image: "A storm was coming up from the south, moving slowly. It looked something like a huge blue-gray shower curtain being drawn along by the hand of God."

In *The Bean Trees*, as in all of Kingsolver's stories, her characters undergo their transformations connected to each other as well as the land, and in a web knit of politics as well as heartstrings. Taylor's love for the abandoned child Turtle and for two illegal refugees from Guatemala, Estevan and Esperanza (whose name means *hope*), is the microcosm of Kingsolver's concern with what we as a country are doing to the land and to its other inhabitants. Her second book, *Holding the Line: Women in the Great Arizona Mine Strike of 1983*, was published in 1989, but researched during the days of the actual strike. In the introduction to the 1996 edition, she says that in the writing of it, "I was forced, almost against my will, to become a smarter, more sympathetic human being. I saw rights I'd taken for granted denied to people I'd learned to care about. I came away with a heart deeply cautioned against the great American tradition of condemning the accused." Vicki Morales, the heroine of "Why I Am a Danger to the Public," the final story in Kingsolver's collection *Homeland*, says, "I was raised up to believe in God and the union, but listen, if it comes to pushing or shoving, I know which one of the two is going to keep tires on the car."

All of Kingsolver's books deal in one way or another with her own government's blind determination to run roughshod over the needs and political inclinations of other peoples. But the political here is personal. These are not poster children. Taylor Greer's empathy for the lost ones, the displaced, the hopeless, stems from her encounters with a woman desperate enough to simply give a baby away, and with Esperanza, whose child has been stolen in a raid by the Guatemalan military, leaving her so damaged that Taylor says of her, "I had this notion that at one time in her life she'd been larger, but that someone had split her in two like one of those hollow wooden dolls, finding this smaller version inside. She took up almost no space." It is Esperanza's story that prompts the realization that, as Taylor says, "my whole life had been running along on dumb luck and I hadn't even noticed." That understanding is complicated by the fact that Taylor is falling in love with Estevan, Esperanza's husband. Nothing is tidy and individual good will may accomplish nothing. Nevertheless, Kingsolver tells us, it is ultimately all we have: hope and children. Taylor, in the doctor's office where she discovers that Turtle is a year older than she had thought, and has been even more badly abused, sees a bird feeding her young outside the window:

> There was a cactus with bushy arms and a coat of yellow spines as thick as fur. A bird had built her nest in it. In and out she flew among the horrible spiny branches, never once hesitating. You just couldn't imagine how she'd made a home in there.

Kingsolver's books are about the ways we make a home in cactus. And for a writer with a social conscience, even book plots may be messy. *The Bean Trees* ends with Taylor conniving an adoption that is on the shady side of legal, in order to keep Turtle from being taken away by the local social services department. Its sequel, *Pigs in Heaven*, Kingsolver's third novel, grew from an increasing awareness of the number of Native American children adopted outside their tribes. The media and the prevailing white culture, Kingsolver said in an interview, "view the basic unit of good as what is best for the child; the tribe sees it as what is best for the group. These are two very different value systems with no point of intersection. . . . I had the option and the obligation to deal with the issue because the moral question was completely ignored in the first book."

In *Pigs in Heaven*, Kingsolver's re-examination of that dilemma, Turtle is brought to national attention and a spot on *Oprah* when she sees a retarded man fall into the spillway of the Hoover Dam and insists on it long enough for someone to go and look for him. Annawake Fourkiller, a Cherokee lawyer, sees the show and recognizes Turtle as one of their lost ones. The issue of motherhood and family, and of the strange patched-together families that fate and circumstance award us, is central to *Pigs in Heaven*. Everyone has lost someone, been torn in some way. Taylor and Turtle go on the run to keep Annawake from finding them. Annawake herself is driven by the loss of her twin, her brother Gabe, who was adopted into a white family when they were ten, and in his misery and isolation drank and fought his way into prison by fifteen. Cash Stillwater, Turtle's grandfather, has lost his wife to cancer, one daughter to a car crash and the other to alcohol. Taylor's mother, Alice, walks away from her husband, whose only occupation is watching television, because she can't stand not having anyone to talk to. All of them are or have been poor: like Alice, people who "grew up with hungry hearts, feeling sure that one day they would run out of everything again." It is the territory of the heart as much as that of the Cherokee Nation that is the landscape of *Pigs in Heaven*.

Taylor and Turtle have an eccentric stone cottage outside of Tucson, and an apricot tree, Turtle's favorite fruit. They share them with Jax, a musician, who regards Taylor as the heart of his world: "the Statue of Liberty and Abbey Road and the best burrito of your life." When Annawake Fourkiller comes sniffing around, Taylor packs Turtle's clothes and a carful of green apricots and flees. On the run, she is driven by the fear of losing Turtle, and terrified into a kind of desperate adulthood where one by one unimportant things drop out of sight and the next things in line lose their importance in turn.

> She's wearing a pale pink T-shirt, Mice notes—a color Taylor used to make a point of hating. She always had to wear outspoken things, red, purple, orange, sometimes all at once. Alice realizes something important about her daughter at this moment: that she's genuinely a mother. She has changed in this way that motherhood changes you, so that you forget that you ever had time for small things like despising the color pink.

Jax is miserable enough at her absence to sleep with the landlady, but knows from the start that he will have to tell Taylor: the power of knowledge that one person possesses and the other does not is too great. Unspoken, it leaves the one guiltily knowledgeable and the other a fool. At first he blames Annawake Fourkiller for arriving with her own unwelcome knowledge. He ponders that while he watches a coyote, belly heavy with puppies, leap into a tree and bring down a dove's nest.

> The coyote crouches at the base of the tree and consumes the eggs in ugly, snapping gulps. She stands a moment, licking her mouth, then creeps away.
>
> Jax is crying. He feels deeply confused about whom he should blame for his losses. The predator seems to be doing only what she has to do. In natural systems there is no guilt or virtue, only success or failure, measured by survival and nothing more. Time is the judge. If you manage to pass on what you have to the next generation, then what you did was right.

This is a theme that recurs in Kingsolver's work, the juxtaposition of the animal drives of the human body with the yearnings of its heart. The coyote, which Loyd Peregrina in *Animal Dreams* calls "God's dog," often stands for that juncture, appearing most often as a female, snapping up one creature's young to feed her own.

In *Pigs in Heaven*, however, it is small-town matchmaking that settles matters in the end. "It's a public service, what those women do," Annawake says to Alice. "Sometimes people have communication problems with their own hearts." All the same, Alice doesn't settle down with Cash until he takes his television into the backyard and shoots a hole in it with his rifle. Nothing is left neatly arranged. Alice marries Cash and Turtle will visit them on the reservation every summer. But Taylor understands that she's lost something she won't get back: "the absolute power of motherhood—that force that makes everyone else step back." In exchange she has got something she didn't ask for, a horde of possible crazy Cherokee relatives and the realization that she needs to marry Jax. It is in the same fashion that Alice comes to terms with Cash Stillwater:

The woods go unnaturally still. All the birds take note of the round black bullet wound in the TV screen, a little right of center but still fatal.

Alice's heart performs its duties strangely inside her chest, and she understands that her life sentence of household silence has been commuted. The family of women is about to open its doors to men.

Women, and children, particularly twins, are the core of Kingsolver's families. Father and brothers die, run off, get drunk and land in jail. Women pick things up and carry on, with their babies, or whatever other impedimenta their lives have accrued, riding on their hips. When they meet the right man he is hard to recognize, but the lost twin, like Annawake's Gabe, is always with them.

Codi and Hallie Noline, the sisters of *Animal Dreams*, are not actual twins, but metaphorical ones, "like keenly mismatched Siamese twins conjoined at the back of the mind," and raised by Doc Homer, their widowed, emotionally damaged father. Hallie goes to Nicaragua, "with her pickup truck and her crop-disease books and her heart set on a new world," at the same time that Codi goes home to Grace, Arizona, to see what is becoming of Doc Homer, recently self-diagnosed with Alzheimer's disease. Grace has its origins in the Arizona mines and the seven blue-eyed Gracela sisters who came from Spain to marry miners, bringing pet peacocks whose descendants now run wild in Gracela Canyon. The Gracela sisters' descendants are a tight-knit group, and Doc Homer has made it clear to his girls that they are not a part of it; they are better, and come from elsewhere. Because of this, Codi has spent her life looking for the place where she does belong. Returned to Grace, she stands in the grocery store,

> looking helplessly at the cans of vegetables and soup that all carried some secret mission. The grocery shelves seemed to have been stocked for the people of Grace with the care of a family fallout shelter. I was an outsider to this nurturing. When the cashier asked, "Do you need anything else?" I almost cried. I wanted to say, "I need everything you have."

It is not Grace that has robbed Codi of belonging, but her father, grimly determined to set himself apart. Returned, she is shattered both by memories of herself, pregnant at 15, miscarrying a baby and burying it by the riverbed, and by the news that Hallie has been kidnapped by the U.S.-funded contras. Doc Homer steps in and out of the present while Codi finds herself with a foot in the past. Loyd Peregrina, the Pueblo boy who unknowingly got her pregnant, is an engineer for the railroad now, not a wild boy any more but a would-be family man with a half-coyote dog named Jack. Like Codi, Loyd is mourning his own lost twin, dead at fifteen in a knife fight outside a bar. But Loyd belongs to Grace now, in a way that Codi has never managed. He knows who he is. Everyone in Grace knows who they are, descendants of those "calcium ancestors," but that identity too is in danger: the local mine has shut down and is poisoning the fruit and nut trees that are Grace's remaining livelihood, with a leaching operation that pours sulfuric acid into the river. Threatened by the EPA, they plan not to clean the river up, but to divert it away from human habitation. If they do, Gracela Canyon will die.

Entwined with Codi's search for her lost child and her own belonging place is the town's search for a way to survive, to make themselves noticed and fight back. Both find what they need in the graveyard, resting place of the seven Gracela sisters and their black-haired, blue-eyed descendants. Amid the buckets of marigolds and bundles of silk flowers and the families sweeping graves on *El Día de Los Muertos*, Codi finds the Nolinas, the reason Doc Homer claimed no kin to them, and, like Jax, the power of secrets to work good or ill.

Reflecting a macabre mirror image to the sugar skulls and flowery remembrances of the Day of the Dead are the reports from Nicaragua, and the fading hope for Hallie. Kingsolver's fury at America's politics of expediency comes through in Hallie's letters:

Sometimes I still have American dreams. I mean literally. I see microwave ovens and exercise machines and grocery-store shelves with thirty brands of shampoo, and I look at these things oddly, in my dream. I stand and think, "What is all this for? What is the hunger that drives this need?"

Kingsolver uses her books to put before us things she wants us to think about, her stories driven not by the political cause she has chosen but by the people caught up in it. Her gifts are voice and description.

A tomcat is "all muscle and slide."

Loneliness is "feeling the cold seep through her like cave air, turning her breasts to limestone from the inside out."

Annawake Fourkiller's "black hair is cropped so close to the nap it stands up like an exotic pelt, and her broad mouth has the complicated curves of a foreign punctuation mark."

A refugee woman stands at a window: "[S]he was folding a pair of men's trousers. She moved the flats of her hands slowly down each crease, as if folding these trousers was the only task ahead of her in life, and everything depended on getting it right."

Loyd Peregrina explains to Codi what a rain dance is for:

". . . The spirits have been good enough to let us live here and use the utilities, and we're saying: We know how nice you're being. We appreciate the rain, we appreciate the sun, we appreciate the deer we took. Sorry if we messed up anything. You've gone to a lot of trouble, and we'll try to be good guests."

"Like a note you'd send to somebody after you'd stayed in their house?"

"Exactly like that. 'Thanks for letting me sleep on your couch. I took some beer out of the refrigerator, and I broke a coffee cup. Sorry, I hope it wasn't your favorite one.'"

. . . "It's a good idea," I said. "Especially since we're still here sleeping on God's couch. We're permanent houseguests."

"Yep, we are. Better remember how to put everything back how we found it."

. . . "The way they tell it to us Anglos, God put the earth here for us to use, westward-ho. Like a special little playground."

Loyd said, "Well, that explains a lot."

We are like the baby in Kingsolver's poem "Babyblues" (part of her single volume of poetry, *Another America*, which includes Spanish translations by Rebeca Cartes): "When I push the bear through the bars,/ why is it gone? I want that bear/ I want/ . . . I shall want/ with the pure blue force/ of a howling wind I want . . . ."

Her fourth novel, *The Poisonwood Bible*, is about wanting. The personal wants of the increasingly deranged missionary Nathan Price mirror the political wants of the West, obsessed with controlling the uncontrollable and indecipherable territory of the Congo. Nathan Price brings his wife and four daughters to the Congo in 1959, determined to bring the people of Kilanga village to Jesus, despite any wishes to the contrary on their part, and completely oblivious to the fact that they have a society, a religion, and a way of doing things that has sustained them for centuries. It is the outsiders, both Nathan Price and the governments of the west, particularly that of the U.S., that bring disaster to the Congo. Nathan Price is a fanatic, and a bully to his family—so dreadful a man that Kingsolver, who spent time in the Congo during her childhood, makes it clear in her Author's Note that he in no way resembles her medical and public-health worker parents, who "brought me to a place of wonders, taught me to pay attention, and set me early on the path of exploring the great, shifting territory between righteousness and what's right."

The book is narrated in turns by Nathan's wife, Orleanna, and his daughters, Rachel, the twins Leah and Adah, and the youngest, Ruth May. Never by Nathan, who has only certainty in his head, and lacks the imagination to wonder about things. He is determined to baptize the children of Kilanga in the river, a notion to which he clings stubbornly until it is his downfall. The parents of Kilanga know what he does not—that the river is full of crocodiles. Nor can he hear the subtleties of their language. *Bangala*, beloved, sounds to him no different than *bängala*, the Poisonwood tree, capable of stripping flesh from body in pus-filled welts. "Tata Jesus is bängala!" he proclaims, with prophetic effect.

The mother, Orleanna's story is told to appease a dead child, the "little beast" who stayed behind in the Congo as the conscience of the forest, "the eyes in the trees," the whisper of the green mamba with sky-blue mouth, the incarnation of might-have-been. Like Codi Noline, every time Orleanna thinks of her lost child, her mind works out how old she would be now. The four girls tell the tale as it happens, while Orleanna speaks only in retrospect.

Leah, the heroine of the story, if one had to choose one, for the simple reason that she is the easiest with whom to identify, the surrogate voice of the author, is the child who makes her peace with Africa, eventually marrying Anatole Ngemba, a Congolese English teacher with a ritually scarred face, and becoming so Congolese that American grocery stores affect her the way they do Hallie Noline.

Adah, her broken twin, born second, is the victim of hemiplegia, leaving her with only half a working brain. Adah limps on her right side, and speaks rarely, but she can work complicated mathematics in her head, and reads backward as well as forward. She thinks in palindromes. *Evil, all its sin is still alive! A, he rose, ye eyesore, ha!* And *Oh, God/God's love! Evol's dog: Dog ho!* Adah refers to Nathan, not lovingly, as Our Father.

Rachel, the eldest, with an eye perpetually on the main chance, pays attention to any conversation that may affect her comfort, but rarely reads, leaving her given to glorious, galloping malapropisms. Arriving in Africa with hymnals, claw hammers and pinking shears concealed beneath three layers of clothes (because the airline weighs the baggage but not the passengers), the Price family steps off the plane into another world. Rachel: "Already I was heavy-hearted in my soul for the flush commodes and machine-washed clothes and other simple things in life I have took for granite . . . I knew right then I was in the sloop of despond. . . . Day one in the Congo, and here my brand-new tulip-tailored linen suit in Poison Green with square mother-of-pearl buttons was fixing to give up the goat."

Ruth May, the youngest, fearless and determined to "eat the world at one bite," gives voice to a five-year-old's version of the grown-up world:

> Back home in Georgia they have their own school so they won't be a-strutting into Rachel's and Leah and Adah's school. . . . The man in church said they're different from us and needs ought to keep to their own. Jimmy Crow says that, and he makes the laws. They don't come in the White Castle restaurant where Mama takes us to get Cokes either, or the Zoo. Their day for the Zoo is Thursday. That's in the Bible. . . .
>
> The grown-up Congo men are all named Tata Something. That one, name of Tata Undo, he is the chief. He wears a whole outfit, cat skins and everything, and a hat. Father had to go see Tata Undo to pay the devil his do. . . .
>
> Nelson says to think of a good place to go, so when it comes time to die I won't, I'll disappear and go to that place. He said think of that place every day and night so my spirit will know the way. . . . I know what it is: it's a green mamba snake away up in the tree. You don't have to be afraid of them anymore because you are one. They lie so still on the free branch; they are the same everything as the tree. . . . Your eyes will be little and round but you are so far up there you can look down and see the whole world. . . .

The Prices have been warned to leave the Congo, that the political situation is unstable, but Nathan is blind to anything but his own fierce need to convert the Congolese, to force his own truth on them. It is only when Ruth May's final vision comes horribly true that Orleanna and her daughters flee from Kilanga, while Nathan stays behind, growing progressively more determined and more insane, and the newly independent country unravels. Anatole explains to Leah the death of Patrice Lumumba and the American machinations in support of Joseph Mobutu this way:

Like a princess in a story, Congo was born too rich for her own good, and attracted attention far and wide from men who desire to rob her blind. The United States has now become the husband of Zaire's [Congo's] economy, and not a very nice one. Exploitive and condescending, in the name of steering her clear of the moral decline inevitable to her nature.

These are terms that Nathan Price's daughter can easily understand. The need to remake some exotic land or people over again in your own, the proper, image goes hand in hand with the need to acquire whatever wealth that land possesses. Nathan Price is Kingsolver's cautionary tale, a man who learned nothing, and from whom she would have us, if at all possible, learn something.

The Poisonwood Bible is probably the grimmest of Kingsolver's works, but she believes in hope, Emily Dickinson's thing with feathers, and its motif flits through even her darkest scenes. "To be hopeful, to embrace one possibility after another—that is surely the basic instinct," she says in "High Tide in Tucson." "Baser even than hate, the thing with teeth, which can be stilled with a tone of voice or stunned by beauty. If the whole world of the living has to turn on the single point of remaining alive, that pointed endurance is the poetry of hope. The thing with feathers." Adah sees it in the pet parrot Methuselah, and backwards in his death by carnivore. Appropriately, Adah, post-Africa, becomes a microbiologist, capable of seeing God as a virus and driver ants as God's housecleaning.

Rachel, by her own lights, fares the best of any of them, working her way through three questionable marriages to ownership of the Equatorial, a hotel in French Congo, a country still comfortably under European control. She has little but scorn for Leah, who "has had her brains washed by the Communists," and lives in a shack while Mobutu builds another palace with U.S. aid. But for Leah, ". . . it comes to me suddenly, from childhood, my first, stammering definition of communism to Anatole: They do not fear the Lord, and they think everybody should have the same kind of house. From where I'm standing, sister, it's hard to fathom the threat." Each finds her own version of the thing with feathers, the wings toward what she wants, or needs.

In her poem "Deadline (January 15, 1991)" Kingsolver reflects on the Gulf War: "In history you will be the vigilant dead/ who stood in front of every war with old hearts/ in your pockets, stood on the carcass of hope/ listening for the thunder of its feathers." In her essay "Jabberwocky" from *High Tide in Tucson*, she reflects on the question of "political" art. Kingsolver is an activist, and makes no apologies about it. Refused permission in a shopping mall to hand out leaflets protesting the Gulf War, she argued that the mall management allowed other groups to pass out yellow ribbons and "We Kick Butt" bumper stickers. "'Handing out yellow ribbons is public service,' they said, 'but what *you* want to do is *political*.'" This use of the word "political," she argues, means only that an idea is not endorsed by the majority. "If 60 percent of us support the war, then the expressions of the other 40 percent are political—and can be disallowed in some contexts for that reason alone." Artists in the U.S., Kingsolver says, censor themselves for fear of being labeled "political," as if being political meant that the art was no good. Point of view is bad. "When I'm interviewed about writing, I spend a good deal of time defending the possibility that such things as environmental ruin, child abuse, or the hypocrisy of U.S. immigration policy are appropriate subjects for a novel. I keep waiting for the interviewer to bring up art things, like voice and metaphor; usually I'm still waiting for that when the cows come home."

It is voice and metaphor that give Kingsolver's fiction its richness, its sense of being there, of being someone else, looking through someone else's eyes, or in their window, for a moment. If that experience induces us to be better behaved guests while we are using God's couch, to clean up the graves of our ancestors and the leavings of our own generation, or to see how one word may mean many things, it is because Kingsolver has brought us with her to Gracela Canyon or to Kilanga, and put into our nostrils the sharp smell of marigolds and the scent of frangipani, "flowers so sweet they conjure up sin or heaven, depending on which way you are headed."

In her fifth and latest novel, all these motifs return, twined into three stories that themselves braid together into a whole like a loaf of challah: the lost child, the found child, the full moon, the graveyard, the coyote, the pact with the gods of the earth. *Prodigal Summer* is about sex: people sex, bug sex, coyote sex; about pheromones and full moons, and the drive to pass on your genes. Lacewings, newly hatched, are "everywhere suddenly, dancing on sunbeams in the upper story, trembling with the brief, grave duty of their adulthood: to live for a day on sunlight and coitus." Hawks mate in midair, "coupling on the wing, grappling and clutching each other and tumbling curve-winged through the air in hundred-foot death dives."

Sex is urgent and dangerous, to the human heart as well as the lacewing. Deanna Wolfe is a late-forties, divorced biologist, come home to Virginia to work for the Forest Service, when she meets a man in the woods who has nothing to recommend him but the tide of her own hormones. Lusa Landowski is an entomologist with a bone-deep yen for the farms her Jewish grandfather and Palestinian mother lost in wars. She marries a farm boy with five maternal sisters and is left with the farm but not the boy when he is killed in a highway wreck. Garnett Walker is a elderly widower trying to bring back the American chestnut, guarding his seedlings against marauding insects with gallons of malathion. Nannie Rawley is his neighbor trying to raise organic apples, and lecture him into ecological harmony. All are linked in ways not apparent at first, by old connections of blood and marriage that in the end will not be ignored. They are like the giant saturniid moths that live in the hollows of the mountain. "Most people never knew what wings beat at their darkened windows while they slept," Lusa thinks, but they are there, old memories and yearnings as translucent as the pale wings of a luna moth. Luna moths and coyotes are both creatures of magic and some mystery, and in *Prodigal Summer* they are the embodiment of Kingsolver's vision of the world.

Deanna has found a den of coyotes, and she explains their necessity to Eddie Bondo, a coyote hunter and her summer lover, in the same terms that Nannie Rawley uses to Garnett Walker: Prey species, mammal or insect, reproduce faster and are more prolific than predator species. When you kill a predator you let loose on the world all the mice or rabbits or deer or caterpillars that that predator would have eaten. When you kill the prey, the plant-eaters, which is Garnett Walker's aim, you wipe out the predators with them. Then the plant-eaters rebound again with frightful speed, with no one left to eat them. Deanna's coyotes are here to take care of that, but they are still oddly endearing: they form lifelong pair bonds, and their courtship ritual involves much talking and licking and bringing each other presents of food. A den generally contains one breeding alpha female and her sisters, the aunties, who help raise the pups. They are intelligent and curious, and there are excellent reasons why the Native American trickster deity is Coyote.

All of this Deanna explains to Eddie Bondo, who remains unimpressed. But Deanna is a biologist, not a sentimentalist, and she has seen coyotes' dual role in the fact that hunted coyote populations rebound with the speed of prey. No one has ever been able to wipe out coyotes. To the contrary, they have lately moved into places they never inhabited before, scrounging garbage in New York, and settling happily in the suburbs on a diet of mice and unwary poodles. The key to coyotes, Deanna says, is that they are also prey, and their population explosion our cautionary tale against tinkering with the food chain. Wolves, hunted into near extinction, used to keep coyotes under control. Men are no match for them. "There's no such thing as killing one thing," Deanna tells Eddie. "Every dead animal was somebody's lunch or somebody's population control."

This notion is at the heart of *Prodigal Summer.* We are all linked, to other humans, to other mammals, to birds and blacksnakes and moths. Deanna carefully scoops a moth from the curtains of her cabin, and releases it, only to have a phoebe nesting in the eaves swoop down and snatch it from the air. "In a vivid brown dash she was gone again, off to feed her nestlings." This troubles Deanna only briefly. Predation is the way the world works, is supposed to work. But when the phoebe's nestlings are eaten by the blacksnake which Deanna has been happy to have in her attic eating mice:

> She breathed hard at the urge to scream at this monster or tear it down from the rafters and smash its head. Breathed three more times, blowing out hard through her lips each time, feeling a faint coil of nausea inside her anger. This was her familiar, the same blacksnake that had lived in her roof all summer, the snake she had defended as a predator doing its job. Living takes life. *But not the babies*, she cried in her mind. *Not these; they were mine. At the end of the summer the babies are all there will be.*

It is the babies that cry to her, the urge of everything to reproduce itself while there is still time. The thought of one coyote shot by Eddie Bondo is bearable as long as the pups are there, as long as there will be children. Children are always at the heart of Kingsolver's fiction: lost children, children regained, children found and adopted. In *Prodigal Summer*, Deanna mourns the loss of the phoebes and her own failing fertility:

> This was what she had. The beauty of this awful night. She listened for small yips in the distance, something to put in her heart beside the lost phoebes and the dread of another full moon rising with no more small celebrations from her body, ever again. She kept herself still and tried to think of coyote children emerging from the forest's womb with their eyes wide open, while the finite possibilities of her own children closed their eyes, finally, on this world.

It is only after she comes to terms with this that she discovers that her periods have stopped because she is pregnant by Eddie Bondo. Likewise, Lusa stops taking birth control pills after her husband is killed, and her periods return under a full moon in a cloud of phero-mones that drive all her brothers-in-law and a teenage nephew to indis-cretion. Nevertheless, it is not her own children that the night gives her, but the children of her divorced and dying sister-in-law and a way to keep the farm and the family both. Nannie Rawley's child, a fragile daughter with Down's syndrome whose father was Deanna's father too, was lost long ago. What the summer brings Nannie is Deanna's pregnancy, and the orphaned children adopted by Lusa, who are Garnett Walker's grandchildren. In the end, it doesn't matter how we reproduce ourselves, as long as we do. At the end of the book, we hear the coyotes begin to howl from the ridge top: "With voices that rose and broke and trembled with clean, astonished joy, they raised up a long blue harmony against the dark sky."

The last scene mirrors the first, with repeated phrases: someone, a female someone, is walking in the woods, silent and preoccupied. "But solitude is only a human presumption. Every quiet step is thunder to beetle life underfoot; every choice is a world made new for the cho-sen." In the first scene, the female someone is Deanna Wolfe; in the last, Aunt Coyote, hunting for her sister and the children. This then is what Kingsolver wants to tell us. We are all part of the same pattern. It interlaces, interlocks, and binds us to it. In return we get it all, luna moths, coyotes, children, blacksnakes.

The Missionary Position:
Barbara Kingsolver's *The Poisonwood Bible*_____

Elaine R. Ognibene

Elaine R. Ognibene places *The Poisonwood Bible* in the context of narratives that uncover the pious, missionary intentions of colonizers as being complicit with colonial imperialism. She investigates in detail the many parallels Kingsolver suggests between the larger movement of colonialism and the smaller circle of the Price family, in which Nathan is the colonizer and his wife and children are the colonized. The narratives told by the women of the Price family are, in part, chronicles of their incremental shedding of missionary and missionized identities, even as Nathan persists ever more intensely and obsessively in misunderstanding and misconstruing his cultural surroundings. For the rest of his daughters' lives, Nathan remains the antagonist against whom they measure themselves and their achievements. Ognibene links her observations to the larger cultural and moral role that she—and Kingsolver—envisage for the United States; a role that would finally "connect consequences with actions" and thus help to engage the Congo, and Africa as a whole, as a partner, not as a colonized entity.   — T.A.

In his history of the Congo during the reign of Belgium's King Leopold (1876-1909), Adam Hochschild tells a riveting and terrifying story of greed and terror, as well as what he terms the "politics of forgetting" the hard truths that have emerged over the last hundred years or so. He shows how a dominant European and American technique for diverting attention from the truth involved a language of righteous zeal and religious reckoning, a scriptural rhetoric used to hide the real story of imperial greed. Several scholars from contemporary critical schools—deconstructionists, Marxists, and postcolonialists address the issue in a similar fashion. In the words of Phillipa Kafka, they work at "(un)doing the missionary position" in literature, advancing new notions of "exclusionary identity, dominating heterogeneity and universality or in more blunt language, White supremacy" (1997, xv). Relying on Henry A. Giroux's words, Kafka defines the missionary position as "monolithic views of culture, nationalism and difference" (xvi).

In *The Poisonwood Bible*, Barbara Kingsolver illustrates the hypocrisy of religious rhetoric and practice that sacrifices the many for the good of the few in power, drawing a clear parallel between a missionary's attitude and colonial imperialism. To the author, Nathan Price does not represent the missionary profession: he "is a symbolic figure . . . suggesting many things about the way U.S. and Europe have approached Africa with a history of cultural arrogance and misunderstanding at every turn" (http://www.Kingsolver.com/dialogue/12questions.html). Nonetheless, Kingsolver does show how, contrary to popular opinion, religion and politics are not separate entities, but a powerful combined force used historically not only to "convert the savages" but to convert the masses to believe that what is done in the name of democratic, Christian principles is done for the greater good.

Even King Leopold understood the power of public relations: he knew "that what matters, often, is less the substance of a political event than how the public perceives it" (1998, 251), or, as Hochschild says, "If you control perceptions, you control the event" (251). Leopold used democratic, religious rhetoric to control his rape and pillage of the Congo; he "recognized that a colonial push . . . would require a strong humanitarian veneer," so he promised to abolish the slave trade and establish "peace among the chiefs . . ." (Hochschild 1998, 45). Building the infrastructure necessary to "exploit his colony," Leopold raised money through the Vatican "urging the Catholic Church to buy Congo bonds to encourage the spread of Christ's word" (92). Using Catholic and Protestant missionaries to set up children's colonies, theoretically to offer religious instruction and vocational information, Leopold's true goal was to build his own kingdom. "He deployed priests, almost as if they were soldiers . . . to areas where he wanted to strengthen his influence" (133-34). Describing 19th century colonizing behaviors,

Hochschild observes, "In the Congo the Ten Commandments were practiced even less than in most colonies" (138). Ironic how almost a century after Leopold, deceptive and destructive "missionary" rhetoric persists and prevents human rights.[1] In the United States, the rhetoric appears in a variety of groups from the Promise Keepers to the Kansas Board of Education, but the message is always one of righteous coercion. In postcolonial Africa, there is "still a form of neocolonialism" that denies human rights. As Raoul Peck, award winning filmmaker of *Lumumba*, states, "things haven't changed." Both at the time of Lumumba's decolonization movement and now, the Congo is "too rich in resources to be left to the Congolese" (Riding 2001, 13, 26).

Numerous contemporary novels, such as *Crossing the River* by Caryl Philips, *Mean Spirit* by Linda Hogan, or *Comfort Woman* by Nora Okja-Keller, provide examples of the missionary position gone awry. In these novels, authors often invert the journey motif. Men who see themselves as good Christians who lead good lives learn from their journeys that the concepts of Christianity upon which they have based their lives are inherently paradoxical. Some lose their way and sense of purpose, because neither scripture nor faith offers them an understanding of the disorder in their lives. Some ironically convert to "pagan" rituals and ways; others wander seeking answers to questions that have no answers and living isolated lives. Although locales shift and the specific religious affiliation, age and race of the missionary change, one recurring theme crosses culture and class lines: the men all see themselves as carriers of the "Word," superior to the populations they aim to convert. Over the course of the novels, most of the men alter their missionary position as their own words turn back upon them.[2]

One man who does not change is Nathan Price. In *The Poisonwood Bible*, Nathan's evangelical, self-righteous, judgmental attitudes threaten the lives of his family, as well as the people in the remote Congolese village of Kilanga. A zealot, Nathan risks lives in pursuit of his obsessive vision. An abusive father, Nathan goes mad for the second time in his life, as he tries to convert the natives over a year and a half period of hunger, disease, drought, witchcraft, political wars, pestilential rains, Lumumba, Mobutu, Ike, and the CIA. The effects of Nathan's missionary position on his wife, Orleanna, his four daughters, and the Congolese become clear as Kingsolver parallels Nathan's behaviors to imperialist actions in the Congo.

Kingsolver uses multiple narrators to construct her political allegory. Orleanna, Leah, Adah, Rachel, and Ruth May tell their stories in contrapuntal turns, offering personal versions of the consequences of the Reverend's taking them to the Congo. Despite dramatically different voices, all, even Rachel, Ms. Malaprop of the novel, tell stories of change as well as discovery. Most reveal specifics about intellectual and spiritual awakenings; the loss of one kind of belief and birth of another. All, even five year old Ruth, draw some parallel between the tyranny of politics in the Congo and the war in their private lives. And all expose the missionary tactics of the man Adah calls "Our Father" as monolithic, abusive, and destructive. As the characters tell their stories in interrupted sequences that move back and forth among speakers, the narrative point of view creates a field of reciprocal subjects, all crucial to the story but none exclusive or central. The heart of the novel emerges only by stacking multiple renditions and discerning the similarities and differences that together shape the broader view. As tension builds up to crisis, their stories accomplish one of Kingsolver's stated aims: they "connect consequences with actions" in the Price family and the broader world as well (Sarnatoro 1998, 1).

In the beginning, "God said unto them . . . have dominion . . . over every living thing that moveth upon the earth" (Genesis 1:28). The Prices' journey into the heart of the Congo begins with Nathan, like King Leopold, taking the words of "Genesis" literally. The daughters' stories come from decades of journal-keeping but are recounted as circumstances unfolded; Orleanna's story comes from a kind of guilty hindsight. The voice that opens each of the first five chapters ("Genesis," "The Revelation," "The Judges," "Bel and the Serpent," and "Exodus") where scriptural titles set the themes is that of Orleanna Price, the wife of a man "who could never love her," a woman who tells her story to the ghost of her dead child, and a person who sees herself as "captive witness" to events that occurred during her year and one-half (1959-61) in the Congo. To Orleanna, "hell hath no fury like a Baptist preacher" (Kingsolver 1999, 8). Her narrative focuses upon the family stepping down "on a place [they] believed unformed," on their desire to have dominion, on their limited knowledge of almost everything, and on the unnameable guilt that she still carries with her (9-10). Orleanna's story illustrates the complicity that comes with silence and the "common hunger" shared by Nathan and others out to conquer the Congo.

In "The Revelation," Orleanna explains her initial ignorance about bringing Betty Crocker cake mixes into the jungle and her slow learning about Congolese cultural practices. She wanted to be a part of Kilanga and be Nathan's wife, but she acknowledges her true position: "I was his instrument, his animal. Nothing more . . . just one of those women who clamp their mouths shut and wave the flag as their nation rolls off to conquer another in war" (Kingsolver 1999, 88). Orleanna muses retrospectively on her political mistakes as well as her cultural ones, recognizing parallel behaviors between Nathan and national leaders. Thinking about Eisenhower's need for control and retired diplomat George F. Kennan's belief that the U.S. should not have "'the faintest moral responsibility for Africa'" (96), she reconstructs Nathan's similar need for control, as well as his desire for distance from the consequences of his acts.

The longer she lives in Kilanga, the clearer Orleanna's vision becomes. Remembering a man who seduced her with promises of "green pastures," she now sees a "righteous" and unbending judge, an abusive husband and father for whom ownership is the norm. Trying to make sense of Nathan's transformation to a tyrant, Orleanna correctly identifies the turning point to be World War II and Nathan's escape from the Death March from Bataan that killed the rest of his company (Kingsolver 1999, 197). Returning home a man who blamed others for his own sense of "sin," Nathan refuses her touch. When she jokes, Nathan hits her. When she listens to stories about the war on the radio, he tells her not to "gloat before Christ" about her "undeserved blessing." When they have sex, he blames her for her "wantonness." When she stands still, he condemns her "idleness." When she or one of the girls suffers, he accuses them of "a failure of virtue." Occupied by Nathan's mission "as if by a foreign power," she falls prey, allowing him "full possession of the country once known as Orleanna Wharton. . . ." Drawing parallel behaviors between Nathan and the colonizers, Orleanna sees how her own "lot was cast with the Congo . . . barefoot bride of men who took her jewels and promised the Kingdom" (198-201).

Reconstructing the political espionage in the Congo, when America and Belgium "divided the map beneath [her] feet," the fifteen years after Independence, when Senator Church and his special committee looked into the secret operations in the Congo, Orleanna itemizes specifically the people and the politics involved. Appropriately she does so under the title heading of "Bel and the Serpent," a text from the Apocrypha; to most a book "of fear mongers who . . . want to scare people" (Kingsolver 1999, 328). Her history reveals the men who fit that description, including her husband. While the Congolese station chief, hired by CIA head Allen Dulles to arrange a coup, hired a scientist, Dr. Gottlieb, to make a poison that would kill or disfigure Patrice Lumumba, Orleanna was trying to protect her children and escape the "dreadful poison" raining down upon her from her husband's obsessive behavior. Sponging her five year old who was dying from malaria, Orleanna was oblivious to the "scent of unpleasant news" that she now knows: on that same August day, Mobutu Sese Seko was promoted to colonel in exchange for one million dollars in United States money to guarantee his loyalty; Lumumba is put under arrest in a house surrounded by "Mobutu's freshly purchased soldiers"; and, after Lumumba's execution in January, the Congo is "left in the hands of soulless, empty men" (320, 323). Tracking the history of that period, author Bill Berkeley confirms that the Congo was left in the hands of tyrants, white and black, who, throughout Mobutu's thirty-four years of "brutality unmatched" in the colonial era and after, "took the jewels" and killed the people (2001, 117).

Plagued by unanswerable "if" questions, Orleanna closes her narrative in the "Exodus" chapter on a note that is sad, insightful, and redemptive. Free of Nathan's control, she chooses to speak and in voice comes redemption. She begins by defining the need to understand the deceptive nature of words, a recurring theme in the novel: "*Independence* is a complex word in a foreign tongue. To resist occupation, whether you're a nation or merely a woman, you must understand the language of your enemy. *Conquest* and *liberation* and *democracy* and *divorce* are words that mean squat . . . when you have hungry children . . ." (Kingsolver 1999, 383). Orleanna's wisdom about the space between words moves her to change. She accepts responsibility for her complicity and acquires the words for her story. For Orleanna, telling her story is a syncretic process, as she aims to reconcile what has gone before.

Like Orleanna, the highly intelligent fourteen year old twins, Leah and Adah, stand still and silent under their father's autocratic rule for much of their time in the Congo. They stand, however, at different ends of the Nathan continuum. Leah, an avid conversationalist, likes spending time with her father more than she likes "doing anything else," pays him due homage, and vows "to work hard for His favor, surpassing all others." She is, as her twin sister notes with disdain, "Our Father's star pupil" (Kingsolver 1999, 36-38). Adah, the twin who suffers from hemiplegia, loves palindromes, and does not speak until she is an adult, ridicules her father throughout her narrative with a brilliant ironic wit. Both, however, capture Nathan's destructive behaviors in their narratives: Leah via unconscious irony that grows into conscious knowledge and Adah via conscious understanding of her father's pride and ignorance. Both undergird their "Father"story with a narrative of domination and greed in the Congo, demonstrating similarities. By the end of the novel, their diverse views connect, and each woman names herself a pagan of sort, an "un-missionary" (525). Like their mother they come to see that the Emperor, in this case "Our Father," is not wearing any clothes. Like their mother, they also believe that they are responsible in some way for the horrors that happen in Africa and they seek forgiveness.

Leah begins with stories about Nathan's arrogance and abuse. Watching Nathan correct Orleanna's mistaken notions about items to take to the Congo, she sees his disdain for the woman he associates with the "coin-jingling sinners" in the temple (Kingsolver 1999, 13). Leah next observes Rachel fall victim to a strap thrashing when she paints her fingernails bubble-gum pink, to Nathan a warning signal "of prostitution" (15). A third example appears as the family lands in Leopoldville, and Nathan arrogantly dismisses Reverend Underdown's kind efforts as an attack on his self-reliance. Leah's comments upon landing in Kilanga are ironic: "He led us out . . . into the light. . . . Our journey was to be a great enterprise of balance. My father, of course, was bringing the Word of God—which fortunately weighs nothing at all" (18, 19). Leah is both wrong and right about "light" and "balance" in ways that she cannot yet imagine.

In Kilanga, Leah's sisters prefer to be mother's helpers, but she prefers to help father "work on his garden." Her garden story becomes a parable of the minister's inability to harvest either seeds or souls. Nathan plans his Garden of Eden to be his "first African miracle" and instructs his daughter while they work with a moral paradigm about the balance of God's "world of work and rewards." He states, "Great sacrifice, great rewards!" (Kingsolver 1999, 37). When Mama Tataba cautions Nathan about both his method and the Poisonwood plant, he cites scripture and ignores her words. Next morning, with "a horrible rash" and swollen eye caused by the red dust from the tree, Nathan, one of "God's own," feels unjustly cursed. Denying responsibility for his own foolish acts, he screams out his rage at his family.

While Nathan heals, Mama Tataba reconstructs the garden, shifting the design from flat to hills and valleys so that the seeds will grow, and later Leah watches as an angry Nathan levels it again. When Nathan does follow Mama Tataba's design, plants do grow but bear no fruit, because they lack pollinators. To Leah, Nathan's failed efforts contradict his theory of balance and rewards, and his words about cause signify nothing: the Bible convention in Atlanta, Nathan tells Leah, "debated about the size of heaven . . ." and "there's room enough for everybody," especially the "righteous" (Kingsolver 1999, 78). Empty words, like empty vines, bear no fruit, Leah understands.

At fifteen, the more Leah learns about the ways of Kilanga, the more complicated her life becomes. As the sisters spy on Eeben Axelroot, securing information about the CIA, guns, tools, army clothes, and "distant voices in French and English" that she will later comprehend, Leah also learns the language of Kikango and begins to recognize the wide gap between cultures, between American games like "Hide and Seek" and the Congolese children's game of "Find Food" (Kingsolver 1999, 109, 114). Embarrassed by her father's ignorant and arrogant behavior, Leah shifts her ground. Catalysts are many, but the most important ones are her relationship with Anatole, an African teacher and co-worker whom she comes to love and marry; her increasing knowledge about war and politics, especially about Lumumba's revolutionary struggle; and her nursing Ruth May and Orleanna through a horrible bought of malaria. Each drives Leah to break the order of "Our Father" and join with "the inhabitants of this land" that she is coming to love (187).

The two episodes that solidify Leah's attitude about her father and her loss of his kind of faith are the election held by the villagers in Nathan's church and Ruth May's death. These two episodes also signify Kingsolver's testament to the power of language understood and her indictment of Nathan's rhetoric. During Sunday service, in the midst of Nathan's sermon about false idols from the "Apocrypha," the congregation is inattentive. Finally Tata Ndu, the tribal chief, stands and cuts Nathan off to hold "an election on whether or not to accept Jesus Christ as the personal Savior of Kilanga." Nathan shrieks that his behavior is "blasphemy," but Ndu hoists Nathan upon his own white imperialist petard. Ndu states that "white men have brought us many programs to improve our thinking . . . Jesus and elections" are two. "You say these things are good. You cannot say now they are not good." Leah feels a chill as her father begins speaking "slowly, as if to a half-wit" and then blows up, insulting the whole congregation. To Leah, Ndu "states truth" about Nathan's, and other white men's, ignorance: "You believe we are *mwana*, your children, who knew nothing until you came here" (Kingsolver 1999, 333). Explaining the foolishness of such thought, Ndu clarifies the history of his learning handed down across generations, the philosophy of cultural sharing, the politics of a tribal government that teaches the need to listen to each man's voice before making a choice and then to select only if the entire community agrees, and the dangers of a majority vote capable of excluding up to forty-nine percent of the people. The congregation votes and Jesus loses, eleven to fifty-six (334). Leah sees how Nathan has no sense at all of the culture he wants to civilize; his message is as irrelevant as his Kentucky seeds to the Congo environment.

Kingsolver cleverly weds the personal and political in both Leah's reflections and Tata Ndu's connection of Nathan's actions to other white colonizers whose "Christian" rhetoric resounds with bigotry. Interestingly, writing about ongoing evil in Africa today, Bill Berkeley like Ndu, rebuts the views of two authors who, like Nathan, continue to perpetuate stereotypes of African inferiority. He dismisses as "nonsense" their notions that current violence results from a lack of "'Western enlightenment,'" a "'new-age primitivism'"or the "'superstitions'" that "supposedly flourish in tropical rain forests" (2001, 9).

Leah loses any faith that she had left in both her father and his God when Ruth May dies from a venomous snake bite, and her father has no words to explain the child's death, except that his youngest daughter "wasn't baptized yet." Seeing an "ugly man" who desired the personal glory of baptizing his child with all of Kilanga's children, the daughter who had idolized her father, now could not stand to look at him. Amidst torrential rains, Nathan appears like Lear, a mad father abandoned by his daughters, wandering in the wilderness and speaking in words that few can understand. Leah notes the bizarre and almost humorous irony, when Bwanga, one of Ruth May's friends, asks, "Mahdah-mey-I?" The children remember Ruth May's game and echo her words, looking at her dead body and asking again and again in a rising plea: "Mother May I?" While the children chant to "Mother" seeking wisdom and permission, Father, Leah observes, continued his biblical oration without any clear idea of what was going on (Kingsolver 1999, 374-75). Nathan lacks the wisdom that Lear gained from his suffering; Nathan is deaf to the truth just as he is deaf to the language nuances of the Congolese culture.

When Leah sings her part of the "Song of the Three Children," the song that closes the novel becomes a history and a promise. She knows that there is no justice in the world, but she sustains her belief in a certain kind of grace. Like Brother Fowles, she listens to the people, trusts in a dynamic Creation which will not "suffer in translation," and remains with Anatole and their family in Africa, the land she chooses as her own.

Adah begins her journey in a much different way than Leah. Although they are identical twins, Adah sees herself as a "lame gallimaufry" who is definitely not her father's "star pupil." Associating herself with both "Jekyll and Hyde" because of her dark desires and crooked body, Adah chooses silence, recognizing its advantages in certain circumstances, especially in Kilanga. Yet she aligns herself most often with Emily Dickinson, using her poetry as a kind of personal philosophy that guides her narrative: both liked to "dwell in the darkness" (i.e., a world of secrets and revelation), and both "Tell All the Truth *but tell it slant*" (Kingsolver 1999, 34, 295, 407). Her slanted truth carries a skeptical tone, especially about "Our Father," who punishes his children for being female or for straying from his puritanical path with the "dreaded Verse." Adah's words about her father are brilliant and caustic; there is little that she does not notice.

"Our Father speaks for all of us, as far as I can see" (Kingsolver

1999, 32), Adah says as she begins her analysis of Nathan's behavior in Kilanga. Not only does Nathan silence his family, but he insults them and has since the time of the twins' birth. Adah sarcastically surmises her father's attitude about her own condition: "Our Father probably interpreted Broca's aphasia as God's Christmas bonus to one of his worthier employees" (34). She too comments upon her father's garden fiasco, his distance from and lack of concern about family members, and his passion for the Apocrypha. However, Adah's stories about "The Verse," her father's paradoxical sermons, and his persistent insult and abuse of family all connect, and each adds a specific dimension of Nathan's character that relates his behavior to broader public events.

"The dreaded Verse is our household punishment," states Adah, "we Price girls are castigated with the Holy Bible" (Kingsolver 1999, 59). Nathan writes some scriptural reference for the child-offender; the offense could be any act, from painting one's nails to saying damn, that "Our Father" considered a sin. Then the "poor sinner" must copy "Jeremiah 48:18 . . . and additionally, the ninety-nine verses that follow it" (59). Her satiric commentary on her father's preference for "his particularly beloved Apocrypha" slides into a *reductio ad absurdum* set of questions that parallel Nathan's "impressive" outcomes with her own "grocery sums in the Piggly Wiggly" to the case of the "cursing parrot" Methuselah who was "exempt from the Reverend's rules . . . in the same way Our Father was finding the Congolese people beyond his power. Methuselah was a sly little representative of Africa itself, living openly in our household." Adah concludes with delicious wit: "One might argue, even, that he was here first" (60).

From "Genesis" through "The Judges," Adah describes her father's ignorant errors as he attempts to convert the villagers to his point of view. Her palindrome for Nathan's sermonizing, his "high-horse show of force" is the "Amen enema" (Kingsolver 1999, 69). As the Reverend towers over the altar, Adah watches the congregation stiffen, and recalls the dead fish on the riverbank, one of her father's conversion mistakes. Nathan promised Kilanga's hungry people "the bounty of the

Lord, more fish than they had ever seen in their lives," but he executes "a backward notion of the loaves and fishes," sending men out to pitch dynamite in the river. The villagers did feast all day, but there was no ice to save the thousands of fish that went bad along the bank. Nathan's destructive act won him no converts. To Adah, he appeared incapable of understanding why, just as he could not understand how saying "words wrong" led only outcasts to his flock.

Nathan's method is his meaning and that is his mistake, according to Adah: "Our Father has a bone to pick with this world, and oh, he picks . . . it with the Word. His punishment is the Word, and his deficiencies are failures of words. . . . It is a special kind of person who will draw together a congregation, stand up before them with a proud, clear voice, and say words wrong, week after week" (Kingsolver 1999, 213-14). Adah observes the Reverend shouting: "TATA JESUS IS BANGALA!" every Sunday, while people sit scratching themselves in wonder. "*Bangala* means something precious and dear. But the way he pronounces it, it means the Poisonwood tree. Praise the Lord . . . for Jesus will make you itch" (276). The irony seems clear to all but Nathan. He fails to see how the language of the region, rich in tonal ambiguities, describes far better than his English the complex antitheses that face people in his congregation. He expects only that they, like his family, will do as he teaches.

After the Congo achieves independence, after the family loses its stipend and all contacts with the larger world, after Orleanna and Ruth May fall "sick nigh unto death," the girls had to endure Nathan's "escalating rage" and physical abuse. Adah remembers the "bruises" and connects her father's abusive behavior with the secrets she learns about Ike and the planned assassination of Lumumba (Kingsolver 1999, 219). Why the "King of America" wants a tall, thin man in the Congo to be dead is a shock to Adah. "How is it different," she wonders, "from Grandfather God sending the African children to hell for being born too far from a Baptist Church?" Adah wants to stand up in church and ask her father: "Might those pagan babies send us to hell for living too far from a jungle?" (298). Adah never asks her father those questions, but she carries them with her when she leaves the Congo and decides to speak.

Free from Nathan's righteous rage, Adah finds her voice in a language of self-definition and science at Emory University, where she finds a future as a neonatal physician and researcher on AIDS and Ebola. Profaning her father's religious obsession, she states, "I recite the Periodic Table of Elements like a prayer; I take my examinations as Holy Communion; and the pass of the first semester was a sacrament" (Kingsolver 1999, 410). When she commutes back to her mother's house, searching for Nathan's military discharge to provide her tuition benefits, she discovers that his medal was not for "heroic service" but for "having survived." Though the conditions were "technically honorable . . . unofficially they were: Cowardice, Guilt, and Disgrace" (414). Adah finally understands why the Reverend could not flee the same jungle twice. Sixteen years later, Adah, like Orleanna and Leah, asks, "How many of his sins belong also to me? How much of his punishment?" (491). She too tries to make sense of her complicity. Unwilling to engage in the "politics of forgetting," Adah tells the hard truth in her own poetic way.

The youngest and the oldest of the daughters, Ruth May and Rachel, lack the astute insight, sense of complicity for wrongs done in the past, and passionate commitment to make the world better for others that their twin sisters share. Both, however, each in her own humorous and sad way, show the evil results of their father's behavior, and both stories illustrate the consequences of white supremacy in ways the reader least expects.

Ruth May's time in the novel is short; she arrives in the Congo at age five and dies from the bite of a diabolical green mamba snake when she is six. Her words are few, but her naive voice reveals the prejudicial attitudes shaped by her father and a religious rhetoric of white superiority and biblical truth. Her statements about African people or blacks in general, her tales about parental conflict, and her "political" comments are never completely correct, but they illustrate well the outcomes of discrimination. Ruth May begins by repeating words of her father and expands into ordinary Georgia attitudes: "God says the Africans are the Tribes of Ham," the worst of Noah's three sons, and "Noah cursed all of Ham's children to be slaves forever. . . ." She thinks about "colored children" in Georgia, who are "not gifted" and, as Ruth May heard a man in church say, ". . . different from us and needs ought to keep to their own." Ruth May continues, telling readers about Jimmy Crow who "makes the laws" excluding blacks from stores, restaurants, and the zoo. She also tells about a classmate in Sunday school teaching her to talk like the "cannibal" natives: "Ugga bugga lugga" (Kingsolver 1999, 20-21). Ironically, these words parallel those of Khrushchev in a newspaper cartoon that appears in an article on Soviet plans for the Congo. Holding "hands and dancing with a skinny cannibal native with big lips and a bone in his hair," Khrushchev sings, "Bingo Bango Bongo, I don't want to leave the Congo!" words that sound amazingly like Ruth May's (161). A five year old's words, humorous as her mistakes may be, paralleled against the Khrushchev cartoon, illustrate the breadth of white supremacist attitudes and the depth of Kingsolver's anti-imperialist ideology that undergirds the narrative. Her story about parental conflict adds to this understanding.

Ruth May hears her parents taking different positions on a range of issues related to the natives. For example, she watches malnourished children with distended stomachs and comments, "I reckon that's what they get for being the Tribes of Ham." Father "says to forgive them for they know not what they do." Mama says, "You can't hardly even call it a sin when they need every little thing as bad as they do" (Kingsolver 1999, 50-51). When Ruth May notices the lost legs, arms, eyes, and other physical disabilities of the natives, Father says, "They are living in darkness. Broken in body and soul. . . ." Mama says, "Well, maybe they take a different view of their bodies." Ruth May observes that "Mama has this certain voice sometimes . . ." and when Father states that "the body is the temple," Mama says, "Well, here in Africa that temple has to do a hateful lot of work in a day. . . ." Ruth May sees Father "looking at Mama hard . . . with his one eye turned mean," for talking back to him (53-54). Even Ruth May recognizes the undertow of her parents' relationship, but Kingsolver uses Ruth May's voice for more. Ruth May's story shows how her father places the people of Kilanga alongside his family, always beneath his feet, as she consistently challenges Nathan's and other exploiters' sense of superiority.

Nathan's physical abuse of both her sisters and herself, his assignment of "The Verse," his trying "to teach everybody to love Jesus" but breeding fear instead, all these acts are visible to Ruth May. So too are the broader politics that bring destruction to Kilanga. Ruth May's story is "off the mark" in words but on target in meaning. She observes the Belgian Army arrive, recognizes that the "white one knows who is boss" and sees the shoeless "Jimmy Crow boys" who hide out and say "Patrice Lumumba!" (Kingsolver 1999, 123-24). She listens to the doctor who sets her arm argue with her father about those "boys" and "missionary work" in the same debate. When the doctor says that missionary work "is a great bargain for Belgium but . . . a hell of a way to deliver the social services," listing the abuses of slavery, such as cutting off hands in the rubber plantations, Father becomes angry and shouts, "Belgian and American business brought civilization to the Congo!" (121). Like other colonizers, Nathan associates "civilization" with his God, his language, and his culture.

These are the words Ruth May remembers; these are the words that make her "scared of Jesus" (Kingsolver 1999, 158). These are the words that tell her that her father isn't listening to anyone but himself. These are the words that when she has malaria make her believe she is sick "because of doing bad things" (273). These are the words that make Ruth May believe that "being dead is not worse than being alive" but different, because the "view is larger" (540).

Rachel, as clueless and morally neutral as she is, malaprops her way into the reader's critical vision, because she best represents America's material culture. Capable of entertaining her sisters with imitation radio commercials—"Medically tested Odo-ro-no stops underarm odor and moisture at the source!"—Rachel is "willing to be a philanderist for peace," but she can only go so "far where perspiration odor is concerned" (Kingsolver 1999, 148). For Rachel, fashion is more important than culture, politics, or moral issues that she neither sees nor understands. Ironically, however, Rachel sees truth about things that concern her. For example, from the moment the Prices arrive in Kilanga, she sees the truth about Nathan's position, as well as the family's place in the Congo. "We are supposed to be calling the shots here," Rachel begins, "but it doesn't look to me like we're in charge of a thing, not even our own selves" (22). Yet Rachel, like her father, takes for "granite" almost everything, although his assumptions are more serious than Rachel's expecting a "sweet-sixteen party" or a washing machine in their hut. Rachel's stories about the welcoming party planned by the natives and the Underdowns' visit, although only two of many often humorous tales, reinforce stories already told by her mother and the twins. But Rachel's narrative is different: her tone is one of contempt and her focus is on pragmatic issues, mainly her own gains and losses. Rachel finds herself a place among the exploiters. Even at the end of the novel, three marriages-of-sort later and not yet out of "the Dark Continent," Rachel still does not believe that "other people's worries" have "to drag you down" (516).

When the Prices arrive in Kilanga, Rachel feels shoved "into heathen pandemony" as men drum and women sing, welcoming the family. Seeing women dancing and cooking "all bare chested and unashamed," she observes Father "already on his feet" with "one arm [raised] above his head like one of those gods they had in Roman times, fixing to send down the thunderbolts and the lightning." When Nathan begins to speak, Rachel sees his speech "as a rising storm" (Kingsolver 1999, 25, 26). Initially the people cheer Nathan's passion, but Rachel's stomach knots because the Reverend "was getting that look he gets, oh boy, like Here comes Moses tromping down off of Mount Syanide with ten fresh ways to wreck your life" (27). Rachel, despite her mistake, describes well the poison her father uses to destroy the people's spirit. As Nathan preaches about nakedness and the "sinners of Sodom," the natives' expressions "fall from joy to confusion to dismay" (28). Nathan's words, unlike those of the Congolese, are not of welcome but of damnation, and throughout the novel, Nathan continues to use scripture as a weapon of attack.

When the Episcopalian Underdowns who oversee financial affairs for the Mission League bring news of uprisings and the need for the Prices to leave, Nathan's behavior shows how little he has changed. The Underdowns carry newspapers that cite Belgians as "unsung heroes" who come into a village and "usually interrupt the cannibal natives in the middle of human sacrifice" (Kingsolver 1999, 161). They also bring news about a Soviet plan for moving forward in the Congo, depriving "innocent savages of becoming a free society," and the election in May for June independence of the Congo. Rachel sees that for her father this news was a "fairy tale," and she states his response: "An *election* . . . [w]hy . . . [t]hese people can't even read a simple slogan. . . . Two *hundred* different languages . . . this is not a *nation*, it is the *Tower of Babel* and it *cannot* hold an election. . . . [T]hey don't have the . . . intellect for such things" (167-68). Rachel misses the similarities between her father's words and the articles about "savages"; instead, she becomes angry at having her own wishes for leaving the Congo dashed. Rachel does, however, capture cause: "Father would sooner watch us all perish one by one than listen to anybody but himself" (169). Refusing to heed any advice to leave, Nathan assumes his intractable position.

The remainder of Rachel's time in Kilanga is short. Under the pretense of engagement to Axelroot, the Afrikaner bush pilot, diamond smuggler, and CIA mercenary, Rachel learns about his espionage activities and eventually escapes with him to Johannesburg, South Africa, the beginning of her exodus experience. After three relationships, two real marriages, one divorce and one death, Rachel inherits her last husband's (Remy Fairley's) Equatorial Hotel for businessmen in Brazzaville and never leaves the continent she so much wanted to escape. She does, however, create her "own domain." Although she credits herself with never looking back, her final words show that the memory of her father-as-antagonist remains: "Oh, if Father could see me now, wouldn't he give me The Verse!" (Kingsolver 1999, 515). Congratulating herself for not being like her father, for sounding "un-Christian," Rachel ironically misses the point that she is in a way most like him in her singlemindedness (516). Although in her own malapropism, "It's a woman's provocative to change her mind," Rachel never does.

Kingsolver ends her complex novel, leaving the reader with an uneasy sense of balance between loss and salvation. Nathan dies guilty, wandering in the jungle, speaking his rote messages about his foreign God, and sustaining his myth of purpose. Ruth May dies, and her spirit hovers over her mother offering forgiveness. Rachel, who cares little about others, does understand that she can reap the financial rewards of her white South African hotel. Orleanna and the twins, however, experience a redemptive sense of worth. Each in her own way learns, in Robert Coles's words, how "to hold secure one's own moral and spiritual self" amidst the "crushing institutional forces of the state . . . the marketplace, and . . . the church. . . ." Each is "driven by particular interests" and "passions" (1999, 167). All three women become advocates for justice: civil rights, medical research on AIDS, and revolutionary educational practices for the poor people in the Congo. The novel ends, but Kingsolver's story is not over. The net in which the Prices and the Congo are caught still exists, because the exploitation embodied in the "missionary" position remains to haunt not only the Congolese but a broader world as well.

At the beginning of the twenty-first century, one hundred years after Stanley preached the "gospel of enterprise," seeking men to work in Africa who would be "missionaries of commerce" (Hochschild 1998, 68), conflict in Africa continues in daily acts of violence and failed efforts at peace. As Tamba Nlandu, professor of philosophy and native of the Congo, explained, the country is divided into antagonistic sections that include multiple warring factions and wars continue even after "peace" treaties are established. Citing tribal and cultural conflicts, as well as power and greed as dominant motives for both Africans and outsiders alike, he sees peace as only a remote possibility (see also Fisher 1999; Fisher and Onishi 2000; Hranjskj 1999, 2000; Shaw 1999; and Traub 2000).[3] Current information about wars appears in daily news stories about countless numbers of people succumbing to disease and hunger in burned, looted villages throughout the Congo. Citing the human toll of thirty-two months of war in "apocalyptic terms," Karl Vick estimates the dead at three million people, especially children (2001, A1, A5; see also Knickmeyer 2001, Nullis 2001). In late May 2001, Colin Powell, Secretary of State, traveled to Africa and promised to help combat disease and nurture democracy, a hopeful note. Yet Powell's promises are qualified by his own caution to avoid getting "too committed" and Defense Secretary Rumsfeld's desire for a sharp reduction in overseas commitments (Knickmeyer 2001, A1, A4). Richard Holbrooke, former ambassador to the United Nations, worked hard but with little success to reduce Congressional antipathy for international peace keeping (Crossette 2001, 2-3). Despite promises of money to fight AIDS, the triumph of human rights is precarious at best, because as journalist David Rieff notes, an "entrenched moral absolutism" limits actions "to identifying atrocities, not doing good deeds" (1999, 40).

The "monolithic cultural views" that Kingsolver questions reappear in a recent interview with George Kennan. Questioned by Richard Ullman about the U.S. role in Russia, Kennan urges detachment: "I would like to see our government gradually withdraw from its public advocacy of democracy and human rights," establishing a clear distinction between Europe which "naturally, is another matter" because "we are still a large part of the roots of a European civilization" and anywhere else where struggle and violence occur (Ullman 1999, 6). Half a century after Eisenhower, whether Russia or the Congo, Kennan feels "not the faintest moral responsibility."

The power of Kingsolver's novel lies in her ability to question that response. On the surface, *The Poisonwood Bible* seems different from earlier works, such as *The Bean Trees* or *Animal Dreams*, fiction set mainly in South or Southwest America and occurring in a short span of time. In all her fiction, Kingsolver grapples with clashing cultural values, social justice issues, ecological awareness, and the intersection of private and public concerns. *The Poisonwood Bible*, however, is more complex; its images resonate across levels of meaning, allusions are multiple, and the stories of its narrators carry deep spiritual meaning. As re-told narratives cross and refract, shedding different shades of light on the same truth, ethical questions multiply. Unlike authors such as Joseph Conrad,[4] who, as Chinua Achebe states, "eliminate the African as a human factor" and reduce "Africa to the role of props for the break-up of one petty . . . mind," Kingsolver reverses expectations and roles: it is not the Congolese who are ignorant or "savage" or say the wrong words but the colonizers (North 2001, 40). Words, Kingsolver warns, have multiple meanings, especially in the Congo. To decode those meanings, readers must "look at what happens from every side and consider all the other ways it could have gone" (1999, 8). Kingsolver dares us to do so and to discover the moments of truth in the telling. This essay offers one "particular" angled version of a multidimensional novel: it illustrates how in "(un)doing the missionary position," Kingsolver "connects consequences with actions" and challenges readers to do likewise.

From *College Literature* 30, no. 3 (2003): 19-36. Copyright © 2003 by *College Literature*. Reprinted by permission.

Notes

1. Examples of national political "missionary" positions vary but include the following: Promise Keepers, Southern Baptists, compassionate conservatism, the Kansas Board of Education, Citizens for God's Own Air, and World Church of the Creator (see Baker 1999, Benedetto 1999, Belluck 1999, Berkowitz 1999, Johnson 2000, Judis 1999, Lieblich 2000, Page 1999, Raspberry 1999, Teepen 1999, and Willis 1999).

2. See also Erdrich (1984), Silko (1999), Dorris (1987), Morrison (1970), and Walker (1982).

3. Information comes from a lecture that Tamba Nlandu delivered to my honors seminar on February 2, 2000. Emmanuel Dongala, novelist and professor of chemistry at Simon's Rock College, confirms that view in his story of escape from the Congo in 1997 (Blackburn 2000, 1, 3). Interestingly, in his new novel, *Little Boys Come from the Stars* (2001), he offers the ingenuous viewpoint of a child to satirize the world of adults and to show how one preserves one's values in a corrupt and violent society.

4. Hochschild comments that Conrad (born Konrad Korzeniowski) believed Leopold's mission was both "noble" and "civilizing" and states that because most critical schools are not comfortable acknowledging the "genocidal scale of killing in Africa," they free *Heart of Darkness* loose "from its historical moorings." Hochschild writes, "It was as if the act of putting Africa on paper were the ultimate proof of the superiority of European civilization" (1998, 132, 142, 148). Michela Wrong disagrees, maintaining that *Heart of Darkness* is "primarily a withering attack on the hypocrisy of contemporary colonial behaviors." She sees Conrad as a man "preoccupied with rotten Western values . . ." (2000, 10).

Works Cited

Baker, Ross K. 1999. "GOP Faithful Cling to Dated Religion." *Times Union*, 2 August, A7.

Belluck, Pam. 1999. "Board for Kansas Deletes Evolution from Curriculum." *New York Times*, 12 August, A1, 15.

Benedetto, Richard. 1999. "Spiritual Messages of Politics." *Times Union*, 17 August, A9.

Berkeley, Bill. 2001. *The Graves Are Not Yet Full: Race, Tribe and Power in the Heart of Africa*. New York: Basic Books.

Berkowitz, Peter. 1999. "A Measure of Compassion." *The New Republic*, 16 August, 26-27.

Blackburn, Doug. 2000. "Out of Africa." *Times Union*, 8 May, C1, 3.

Coles, Robert. 1999. *The Secular Mind*. Princeton: Princeton University Press.

Crossette, Barbara. 2000. "Holbrooke Agrees to Lead U.N. Delegation to Congo." *New York Times*, 15 April (http://www.nytimes.com/library/world/africa/041500congo-un.html).

Dorris, Michael. 1987. *A Yellow Raft in Blue Water*. New York: Henry Holt.

Erdrich, Louise. 1984. *Love Medicine*. New York: Holt, Rinehart and Winston.

Fisher, Ian. 1999a. "Brutal Bands of Rwandans Bar Way to Peace in the Congo." *New York Times*, 4 August, late ed., A1, 4.

_____. 1999b. "Congo Peace Accord Ailing as Rivals Jockey for Position." *New York Times*, 1 August, sec. International, 10.

_____. 1999c. "Rwanda and Uganda to Meet on Congo." *New York Times*, 17 August 1, sec. International, A9.

Fisher, Ian, and Norimitsu Onishi. 2000. "'Africa's First World War' Rages in, Around Congo." *Times Union*, 6 February, A4.

Hochschild, Adam. 1998. *King Leopold's Ghost: A Story of Greed, Terror, and Heroism in Colonial Africa*. Boston: Houghton Mifflin Company.

Hranjskj, Hrvoje. 1999. "Congolese Rebels Appeal to Their Allies." *The Daily Gazette*, 4 January, A8.

_____. 1999. "Forces in the Congo Battle for Control." *Times Union*, 16 August, A3.

_____. 2000a. "Devastated Congo City Welcomes a Cease-Fire." *The Daily Gazette*, 12 June, A1, 5.

_____. 2000b. "Fighters Withdraw in Congo." *The Daily Gazette*, 20 June, World, A6.

_____. 2000c. "Shelling in Congo Kills 150 Civilians." *The Daily Gazette*, 10 June, A8.

Johnson, George. 2000. "It's a Fact: Faith and Theory Collide Over Evolution." *New York Times*, 15 August, sec. 4, 1, 4.

Judis, John B. 1999. "Taking Care of Business." *The New Republic*, 16 August, 24-29.

Kafka, Phillipa. 1997. *(Un)doing The Missionary Position: Gender Asymmetry in Contemporary Asian American Women's Writing*. Westport, CT: Greenwood Press.

Kingsolver, Barbara. 1999. *The Poisonwood Bible*. New York: HarperFlamingo.

Knickmeyer, Ellen. 2001. "Congo Conflict Reveals Hidden Horror of War: 3 Million Dead." *The Daily Gazette*, 7 May, A1, A4.

Lieblich, Julia. 2000. "Southern Baptist Convention Says Women Shouldn't Serve as Pastors." *The Daily Gazette*, 15 June, A1, A9.

Morrison, Toni. 1970. *The Bluest Eye*. New York: Holt, Rinehart and Winston.

North, James. 2000. "African Heart, No Darkness." *The Nation*, 10 July, 39-41.

Nullis, Claire. 2001. "Red Cross Reacts to Death of Congo Aid Workers." *The Sunday Gazette*, 29 April, A11.

Page, Clarence. 1999. "Silent People Can Be the Most Deadly." *Times Union*, 10 July, Commentary.

Raspberry, William. 1999. "Working with the Constitution." *Times Union*, 27 July, A7.

Riding, Alan. 2001. "In a Mirror on Africa, a Hero Unfairly Tarnished." *The New York Times*, 24 June, Arts, 13, 26.

Rieff, David. 1999. "The Precarious Triumph of Human Rights." *The New York Times Magazine*, 8 August, 36-41.

Shaw, Angus. 1999. "Peace in Congo Remains Elusive." *The Sunday Gazette*, 11 July, A6.

Silko, Leslie Marmon. 1999. *Gardens in the Dunes*. New York: Simon and Schuster.

Teepen, Tom. 1999. "Killing Evolution Off By Fiat." *Times Union*, 18 August, A12.

_____. 1999. "Moralizing Doesn't Help Life." *Times Union*, 19 July, A7.

_____. 2000. "Matching Wits, Political Fund Agendas." *Times Union*, 19 June, Commentary, A7.

Traub, James. 2000. "Sierra Leone: The Worst Place on Earth." *The New York Review of Books* 47 (June 29): 61-66.

Ullman, Richard. 1999. "The US and the World: An Interview with George Kennan." *The New York Review of Books* 46, 13 (August 12): 4-6.

Vick, Karl. 2001. "Congo's Many Killers." *Times Union*, 3 May, A1, A5.

Walker, Alice. 1982. *The Color Purple.* New York: Harcourt Brace Jovanovich.

Wills, Gary. 1999. "GOP Should Dump the Religious Right." *Times Union*, 5 July, A7.

Wrong, Michela. 2000. *In the Footsteps of Mr. Kurtz: Living on the Brink of Disaster in Mobutu's Congo.* New York: HarperCollins.

The Neodomestic American Novel:
The Politics of Home in Barbara Kingsolver's
*The Poisonwood Bible*_____

Kristin J. Jacobson

Kristin J. Jacobson takes advantage of the surprisingly large number of topical similarities between Louisa May Alcott's *Little Women*
and Kingsolver's *The Poisonwood Bible* to explore the latter book as a
"neodomestic" novel—that is, a book specifically devoted to the examination of women's roles in the household—especially as it responds to nineteenth-century American versions of domesticity. Both
because of its encounter with the culture of the Congo and as a result
of its internal strife, the Price household does not produce stable domesticity. Orleanna reflects on the impossibility of shedding her
white skin and its attendant privilege in an African setting. Rachel's
hotel and Leah's home, established after the family's departure from
Africa, become test cases for a "recycled" domesticity necessarily
under the shadow of Ruth May's death. Against some critics' assertions that "domestic" fiction has run its course, Jacobson points to a
wide range of recent American texts aside from *The Poisonwood Bible* that successfully renegotiate or "recycle" concepts of domesticity.   — T.A.

Housekeeping ain't no joke.[1]

Compelling connections exist between Barbara Kingsolver's *The
Poisonwood Bible* (1998) and Louisa May Alcott's *Little Women*
(1868). Both stories are set in the "women's sphere" of the home and
narrate the Price and March women's domestic travails. The Price family in *The Poisonwood Bible* loosely but distinctly parallels the March
family in *Little Women*. Both stories have minister fathers and families
comprised of four girls. The Price girls' character flaws especially co-

incide with the March daughters' failings that set *Little Women*'s narrative in motion.[2] Rachel Price mirrors her precursor Meg March, who thinks too much of her looks and hates to work.[3] Both Leah Price and Jo March are tomboys who long to be somewhere else, and Adah Price and Amy March are similarly selfish, "defective" girls—Amy endures ridicule due to her nose, and Adah's noticeable birth defect sets her apart physically and emotionally.[4] Devoid of moral or physical defects, the family favorites Ruth May Price and Beth March die tragically young. The rich ways such parallels jumble together—Meg March, for example, ultimately represents a woman of domestic "faculty,"[5] whereas Rachel Price commercializes domestic faculty for profit— suggest exploring *The Poisonwood Bible* as a "neodomestic novel," or a revision of the nineteenth-century domestic novel, and merit attention for what this revision reveals about American domesticity, the domestic novel, and white women's privilege.

Little Women and *The Poisonwood Bible* agree with the March family housekeeper's tidy summation: "Housekeeping ain't no joke." How the serious business of keeping house plays out in the individual novels reflects not only the novels' distinct historical milieus but also significant generic and ideological changes within white American women's domestic fiction. This essay focuses on three generic features present in *Little Women*'s domestic narrative and then revised in *The Poisonwood Bible*'s neodomestic tale: (1) the home setting, (2) the search for, or pilgrimage toward, home that launches domestic fiction's plot, and (3) domestic ideology, especially as it relates to the "cult of true womanhood."[6] Together *The Poisonwood Bible*'s revised features demonstrate a shift from stability to instability as the foundation of quotidian American home life. This shift challenges domestic fiction's conventional cultural work. Nancy Armstrong explains domestic fiction's traditional politics in *Desire and Domestic Fiction*: "I believe it [eighteenth- and nineteenth-century domestic fiction] helped to formulate the ordered space we now recognize as the household, made that space totally functional, and used it as the context for representing normal behavior."[7] Where conventional domestic fiction orders, normalizes, and sustains the household, neodomestic fiction destabilizes the model home and the roles defined by it. Comparing *The Poisonwood Bible*'s neodomestic features with its historical and generic precedents in *Little Women* reveals the American home as a key site for white privilege's reproduction and as a place not necessarily doomed to reproduce forever its imperial history.[8]

Before comparing the novels, let me first briefly define domestic and neodomestic fiction. While the term "domestic fiction" is sometimes used interchangeably with "sentimental fiction" and "woman's fiction," for the purposes of this discussion the term refers specifically to novels written by women whose dramatic action focuses on homemaking.[9] As white, middle-class heterosexuality represents domesticity's image for the West generally, and America specifically, this model also dominates American domestic fiction. Conventional domestic fiction like *Little Women* celebrates the white, middle-class heterosexual family.[10] *The Poisonwood Bible* "recycles"—to borrow Rosemary Marangoly George's term–*Little Women*'s domestic tale, producing a neodomestic narrative with a revised admixture of domestic tropes.[11]

Building on George's concept of recycling domesticity, I have coined the term *neodomestic* to encompass the collection of generic and ideological renovations that both distinguish neodomestic fiction from and connect it to its nineteenth-century roots. George outlines her concept of "recycled domesticity" in the essay "Recycling: Long Routes to and from Domestic Fixes."[12] She explains,

> narratives and practices that responsibly recycle domesticity perform two tasks: first, they effect transformations that are attentive to the materials and the debris of past domestic edifices. Second, in being attentive to the material and historical factors that have enabled domesticity to flourish, such recycling narratives make the domestic a site from which counter-theorizations about seemingly "larger" and unrelated institutions and ideologies can be produced. (pp. 2-3)

Neodomestic fiction recycles the domestic novel in historically conscious ways that posit alternatives to the conventional white, middle-class home.

(Re)claiming domestic fiction for the twenty-first century becomes a vexed proposal when we consider previous criticism that argues against this generic moniker for nineteenth-century women's fiction. Both Nina Baym and Susan K. Harris, for instance, argue against the label "domestic fiction."[13] Baym explains, "the term 'domestic' is not a fixed or neutral word in critical analysis. For many critics, domesticity is equated with entrapment—in an earlier critical generation, of men by women and, more recently, of women by a pernicious ideal promulgated (so the worm turns!) by men" (p. 26). While the domestic may continue to have pejorative connotations, the term also succinctly describes a recognizable collection of novels focused on the home.[14] The label neodomestic helps distinguish significant changes in the genre's history while maintaining connections to its nineteenth-century roots. Understanding neodomestic fiction as a development from nineteenth-century domestic fiction helps map the genre's changing terrain, highlighting recycled features as writers continue to experiment with domestic fiction's form. *The Poisonwood Bible* provides an exceptional demonstration of this phenomenon because of the multiple ways it intersects with *Little Women*.

Recycling the Model American Home: Domestic Fiction's (Un)Stable Foundations

How do we aim to live with it?
Orleanna Price[15]

Set during the Civil War, *Little Women* follows the March girls' transition from practicing homemaking as daughters to producing domesticity as wives and mothers. Kingsolver's story recycles this familiar narrative in ways, according to George's argument, "attentive to the materials and debris of past domestic edifices" (p. 2). In brief, the Prices' story begins in 1959 in Bethlehem, Georgia, as this Baptist family prepares to leave for a mission in the Belgian Congo. The father's ego and subsequent difficulty converting the community, the family members' culture shock, communication problems, environmental disasters, along with political uprising and Ruth May's death conspire against the mission's success. What begins as a year-long pilgrimage to the Congo turns into three decades of stories mapping the aftermath of the family's experiences in Kilanga, the fictional Congolese community where the Price family moves. Unlike *Little Women*, *The Poisonwood Bible* does not have an omniscient narrator. All the Price women take turns narrating the events. The novel's structure promotes narrative and ideological instabilities because different voices with distinct perspectives narrate the same incidents.

The primary difference between the two novels—and domestic and neodomestic fiction generally—is that, unlike the March family, the Price women do not successfully reproduce a stable home. *Little Women* ends triumphantly with fall harvest, where Mrs. March symbolically reaps the fruits of her parenting. The final tableau of her three surviving daughters' happy marriages celebrates Mrs. March's successful reproduction of American domesticity. At the conclusion Mrs. March sees her married daughters and exclaims that she can wish for them no "greater happiness than this!" (p. 502). While the Price women share this goal for a secure home, they are ultimately less successful in fulfilling it. *The Poisonwood Bible* does not repeat *Little Women*'s happy family tableau. In fact, Orleanna asks at the novel's outset: "What do we know, even now? Ask the children. Look at what they grew up to be" (p. 10). Orleanna's children are scattered, and her knowledge is uncertain.

This reversal of fortunes may be seen in part as a product of the Prices' displacement, but it also suggests that the novels have fundamentally different views of the white, middle-class American home's redemptive possibilities and benign status as a model for all. The Prices' domestic breakdown highlights rather than attempts to mask American domesticity's connections to imperialism. Amy Kaplan in "Manifest Domesticity" clarifies these connections: "domesticity is more mobile and less stabilizing; it travels in contradictory circuits both to expand and contract the boundaries of home and nation and to produce shifting conceptions of the foreign."[16] The Price home emphasizes domesticity's "expansionist logic" by destabilizing conventional dichotomies between the domestic and the foreign.[17] Rather than functioning as oppositional constructions, these spaces encroach on each other's territory throughout the novel. *The Poisonwood Bible*'s setting in particular unmoors domestic fiction's celebration of stable domesticity, exposing its imperial drive and intimate connections with the foreign.

Where nineteenth-century domestic novels tend to mask what Toni Morrison terms the "Africanist presence" within American literature,[18] *The Poisonwood Bible* sets "Africa" at its most visible center, as its "foreign" destination. Placing its portrayal of American homemaking in the Belgian Congo and the Jim Crow South, *The Poisonwood Bible* locates the Africanist presence within its narrative in order to tease out American domesticity's connections to imperialism. Conversely, conventional domestic fiction in part reproduces American imperialism and white privilege by displacing the Africanist presence. In Kaplan's words, the Africanist presence "is intimately bound to the expansionist logic of domesticity itself."[19] *Little Women* does not foreground Africa, but its presence spurs the Marches' homemaking projects. For example, the Civil War necessitates the father's absence, and the slavery question remains an unspoken text. *Little Women* also does not explore the imperial implications of Hannah's largely invisible domestic labor or Mr. Laurence's desire for his grandson Laurie to become an "India merchant" (p. 148), but these details expand the Marches' ability to reproduce domesticity and to stabilize their domain. Rather than repeating this lacuna, the neodomestic novel accounts directly for domesticity's expansionist history and its ties to an Africanist presence. In addition to setting the novel in the Belgian Congo and the Jim Crow South, *The Poisonwood Bible* highlights domestic ideology's hidden connections to an Africanist, or foreign, presence by deconstructing homemaking's promotion of good works.[20]

The "cult of true womanhood," which the domestic novel advances, requires helping others successfully produce white, middle-class domesticity. The March women's charity work represents this aim, joining true womanhood's virtues of domesticity and piety. The March women embody "The Women of America, in whose hands rest the real destinies of the republic," to which Catharine E. Beecher and Harriet Beecher Stowe dedicate their domestic handbook, the *American Woman's Home* (1869).[21] Beecher and Stowe explain a (white) woman's domestic teaching and example should demonstrate "the peculiar privilege of woman in the sacred retreat of a 'Christian home,'" which is "to lift up the fallen, to sustain the weak, to protect the tempted, to bind up the broken-hearted, and especially to rescue the sinful" (p. 433). To these ends, the March family assists local foreign and destitute families, thereby furthering their Christian and patriotic missions. For example, early in the novel they take a poor German family under their wing and informally adopt the motherless Laurie (pp. 17-19). Such acts of Christian charity promote the cult of true womanhood, making the March women good Christians and citizens.

The March women embrace their "peculiar privilege" by (re)producing a stable Christian home and community. The Price women produce, at best, a poor imitation. For example, the Price family also adopts a local boy, Nelson, into their household. However, they ultimately depend more on the aid provided by Nelson and Mama Tataba, a local woman who assists Orleanna with the cooking and housekeeping, than the Congolese depend on and benefit from their relationship with the Price family (pp. 90-98).[22] Analyzing the mother's narrative role to promote the cult of true womanhood within domestic fiction provides further insight into the novels' reproduced and recycled domestic ideologies as they affect white privilege. As mothers, Orleanna and Mrs. March share the "peculiar" responsibility to model domesticity for their daughters. Mrs. March self-assuredly takes up this role, explaining that following one's duty produces happiness: "I gave my best [referring to her husband] to the country I love. . . . Why should I complain, when we both have merely done our duty and will surely be the happier for it in the end" (p. 84). *The Poisonwood Bible* also presents the mother as an exceptional character. Like her nineteenth-century counterpart, Orleanna serves as a fundamental source of knowledge. Orleanna enjoys a complete historical consciousness—she always narrates from the present—whereas her daughters narrate their stories chronologically. Orleanna's retrospectives faintly echo the confident, fully formed wisdom Mrs. March shares with her girls. However, Orleanna lacks Mrs. March's righteousness, or Christian confidence. Where Mrs. March turns to God as the legitimizing source of her actions (pp. 84-85), Orleanna does not share faith as her duty's justification. As a result, Orleanna exhibits less confidence about her homemaking and parenting. Where Mrs. March understands her "peculiar privilege" as Christian duty, Orleanna wrestles with how to live with white privilege—with the legacies and realities of what Kaplan terms "manifest domesticity."[23]

Orleanna, however, is not Mrs. March's complete opposite or a failed mother. She models a compelling recycled ideology that negotiates American domesticity's imperial past, present, and possible future incarnations. Orleanna does not cleanly reproduce the rhetoric of manifest destiny or domesticity, and yet she recognizes its power and deep connections to the Africanist presence. Reflecting on her family tragedies and her personal losses, for instance, Orleanna understands that despite her troubles she still has the "peculiar privilege[s]" afforded her by her birthplace and her race. She explains to her reader:

You'll say I walked across Africa with my wrists unshackled, and now I am one more soul walking free in a white skin, wearing some thread of the stolen goods: cotton or diamonds, freedom at the very least, prosperity. Some of us know how we came by our fortune, and some of us don't, but we wear it all the same. There's only one question worth asking now: How do we aim to live with it? (p. 9)

Orleanna questions her family's and her role in the Belgian Congo, complicating duty's connection to privilege and to the domestic. The passage demonstrates Orleanna's awareness of her geopolitical privilege and a concomitant uncertainty about her role. Orleanna's questioning epitomizes neodomestic ideology's emphasis on historical consciousness, as opposed to Christian duty, and instability, as opposed to stability, as central features of the domestic. Orleanna's recognition of her privileged position, a position dependent on "stolen goods," also discloses the Africanist presence domestic novels historically tend to conceal. Her plea suggests that white American women can no more eliminate their privilege than they can shed their white skin.[24] To the extent that privilege is a function of race—as well as gender and class—truly moving out of the site one is often born into is an extremely difficult, if not impossible, task. The passage concludes with a key question about how to construct homes that are critical and mindful of the varying forces that (re)produce privilege.

Orleanna's question pinpoints the problem with which neodomestic fictions by white women struggle: *how can one move beyond imperial history without forgetting or ignoring it?* How will and how should (white) Americans negotiate their privilege on the domestic and global scale? Seyla Benhabib in her essay "Sexual Difference and Collective Identities: The New Global Constellation" poses a similar question about the construction of home. She asks, "Can we establish justice and solidarity at home without turning in on ourselves, without closing our borders to the needs and cries of others? What will democratic collective identities look like in the century of globalization?"[25] Orleanna suggests that the goal to eliminate white privilege altogether fails to take adequate account of the present and historical factors that form (white) privilege. Unable to reproduce or eliminate white privilege, she must recycle.

I have begun to show how *The Poisonwood Bible*'s recycled domestic setting and ideology distinguish it, in Biddy Martin and Chandra Mohanty's words, as "a text that speaks from within 'Western feminist discourse' and attempts to expose the bases and supports of privilege even as it renegotiates political and personal alliances."[26] By acknowledging the white middle-class home's reliance on an Africanist presence and its role in the reproduction of white privilege, neodomestic novels destabilize the model American home. *The Poisonwood Bible*'s self-reflective pilgrimage plot further sets it apart from conventional domestic fiction's celebratory narrative about first-world domesticity's expansion and its "civilizing" effects on subaltern groups.

(Un)Packing Empire's Burdens: (Neo)Domestic Fiction's Pilgrimage Home

We struck out for Africa carrying all our excess baggage on our bodies, under our clothes.

Leah Price (1959; p. 15)

We only took what we could carry on our backs.

Leah Price (1961; p. 389)

Both the Price and March families embark on pilgrimages at the beginning of their tales. Dispossession in some form, as Baym points out, frequently begins the domestic novel's plot (p. 35).[27] The female protagonist must overcome her homeless state in order to complete her quest successfully and stabilize her environment and identity. The

March girls' burdens—their character flaws—represent their impediments to completing their pilgrimages to individual homes. Jo, for instance, loves her independence too much to get married: "I don't believe I shall ever marry. I'm happy as I am, and love my liberty too well to be in any hurry to give it up for any mortal man" (p. 374). However, even Jo eventually marries. Modeling their journey on *Pilgrim's Progress*, the March girls learn to carry their burdens and achieve stable, happy homes reproduced according to their mother's model. Whereas the March girls take up their burdens and learn to carry them in order to establish a "Celestial City," the Price family's burdens bury them in cultural baggage. As missionaries in the Belgian Congo during the latter half of the twentieth century, the Price family ostensibly continues a tradition of cultural imperialism, furthering the civilizing reach of the White House. However, *The Poisonwood Bible*'s historically conscious recycling tweaks the "pilgrims' progress." The Prices' actual luggage symbolizes the (un)packing of their imperial burdens, or the dual predicament and promise embedded in their revised domestic pilgrimages.

The Prices' journey begins with the problem of transporting their imperial burdens to the Belgian Congo. In "The Things We Carried" Leah narrates their troubles coping with airline weight restrictions. Because they are sixty-one pounds over the limit, they carry the extra weight on their bodies (p. 15). Their material possessions, which include wearing several layers of clothes and packing "other goods, tools, cake-mix boxes and so forth" in pockets and under waistbands, encase the family "in a clanking armor" (p. 15). These comic rather than stoic Christian soldiers literally pack domesticity's burdens on their backs, looking as out of place and ill-equipped as "Eskimos plopped down in a jungle" (p. 18). Leah claims that what they carried with them from Georgia to Kilanga comprises "the full measure of civilization's evils" (p. 14). More than relating the Price family's naivete about the Congo, Leah's critique—like her remarks (quoted at the beginning of this section), which frame the family's entrance to and exit from Kilanga—pays homage to American imperialism's intimate connections to homemaking. Arriving with surplus luggage is coded as material excess that must be trimmed back.

Rather than promoting a flourishing empire, the Prices' conscientiously packed supplies "seem to represent a bygone world" (p. 14). In fact, commercial American culture ultimately fails in the Congo: the Betty Crocker cake mixes turn as hard as lead, and Nathan's carefully transported garden seeds produce infertile plants (p. 65, 80). Orleanna laments, "We brought all the wrong things" (p. 65). The less tangible imperial burdens the family brings, such as racism, also contribute to their failure to reproduce American domesticity. Ruth May's death, which coincides with Patrice Lumumba's murder, ultimately changes the Price women's domestic practices.[28] After Ruth May's death, which occurs in the middle of *The Poisonwood Bible* as opposed to Beth's death near the end of *Little Women*, the women cease trying to reproduce domesticity and begin recycling it. Ruth May's death becomes a catalyst for dramatic changes. Beth March's death, in contrast, reinscribes the domestic novel's familiar endings: marriage or death. While both Ruth May and Beth may be seen to epitomize "female virtue, a being literally too good for this world," Beth's death reinforces true womanhood.[29] Soon after Beth dies, Jo marries and her destabilizing role as a tomboy becomes less prominent.

When things fall apart in Kilanga, the Price family cannot be put together again just as they were. The Price women recycle to survive. For instance, Orleanna gives away much of what the family owns (pp. 371-72) and finally gathers the courage to leave her husband and Kilanga. In this symbolic and material act, Orleanna relinquishes the material trappings of her house of privilege: "My household would pass through the great digestive tract of Kilanga and turn into sights unseen" (p. 382). The Price women unpack white privilege, a key step in the shift from reproducing to recycling home. While they cannot eliminate white privilege, they can change how they carry it. Balancing their respective ideological and material burdens informs the Price women's exit from Kilanga and comprises part of the process of deconstructing white privilege and the model American home.

Unpacking white privilege requires that the Price women find ways to live responsibly with their privileges and histories. While Orleanna successfully distributes a portion of her material privileges, her redemptive act cannot so simply produce a more egalitarian society. Leah understands her mother's actions as a "farewell gift to Kilanga. . . . My pagan mother alone among us understood redemption" (p. 456). However, the limited extent of this "redemption" reveals itself through the burdens the Price women carry out of Kilanga. When the women leave, they are traveling much lighter than they were when they arrived. Nevertheless, the section "What We Carried Out" emphasizes that traveling with less material luggage and incorporating new domestic and traveling strategies does not eliminate the Price women's imperial loads. In Leah's case, adopting new traveling modes initially produces clear benefits. As she leaves Kilanga, Leah implements the Congolese women's carrying method, placing her burden on her head. She had never tried this before: "What a revelation, that I could carry my own parcel like any woman here! After the first several miles I ceased to feel the weight on my head at all" (p. 390). Her sense of weightlessness contrasts sharply with the burdens that weigh down the family upon their arrival. The weightlessness is not permanent. Leah's sister Adah reveals, "What I carried out of [the] Congo on my crooked little back is a ferocious uncertainty about the worth of a life" (p. 443). Adah struggles to reframe her existence. How will the Price women live now that "Africa has slipped the floor out from under [their] righteous house" (p. 443)?

Recycling the Retreat:
The Prices of Stable Homes

But in my dreams I still have hope, and in life, no safe retreat. If I have to
hop all the way on one foot, damn it, I'll find a place I can claim as home.

Leah Price (p. 506)

Constructed after they leave Kilanga, Rachel's "bad" commercial
hotel and Leah's "good" charitable home appear to provide two contrasting models that realign *The Poisonwood Bible* with conventional
domestic ideology. The previous section begins to illustrate a sacred,
stabilizing dichotomy within conventional domesticity that sets commercial concerns against domestic ones. As Baym writes, the cult of
true womanhood and, by extension, domestic fiction place the home
against commercial culture: "Domesticity is set forth as a value
scheme for ordering all of life, in competition with the ethos of money
and exploitation that is perceived to prevail in American society" (p.
27). The Marches' stable, happy home and genteel poverty construct
themselves against commercial culture. *The Poisonwood Bible* seems
to reproduce this tradition because commercial American culture's
burdens contribute to the Prices' failed Kilanga home. Rachel and
Leah's distinctive homemaking also appear to promote this tenet of
conventional domesticity.

Rather than reestablishing the commerce/domesticity dichotomy,
Rachel and Leah's homes ultimately undercut it. As will be seen, the
home's material security cannot be decoupled from its emotional security and vice versa. While neodomesticity favors Leah's noncommer-
cial homemaking, it also demonstrates that as long as Rachel and Leah
share the same goal—domestic security—neither material nor emotional security presents a genuine choice. Their distinctive homes emphasize domestic security's two sides: one economic and the other
emotional. In this sense, their recycled search for a safe retreat demonstrates what Judith Williamson calls "the supreme trick of bourgeois

ideology," which "is to be able to produce its opposite out of its own hat."[30] Their homemaking practices connect domestic stability to imperialism and white privilege, teasing out economic and emotional security's costs and consequences.

Were she a character in a conventional domestic novel, Rachel would be tragically flawed for refusing to cure her materialism. Unlike Jo, Rachel never realizes the error of the personal pursuit of money and power (*Little Women*, p. 354). Rachel, sinning against a fundamental tenet of the cult of true womanhood, profits for individual gain. Within the neodomestic novel's context, Rachel's character flaws turn conventional domesticity against itself, connecting imperialism, commercial culture, and American domesticity. In fact, in true colonial form, Rachel describes her home and business as a "little *country*":[31]

> Then why not go back [to America]? Well, now it's too late, of course. I have responsibilities. First there was one husband and then another to tie me down, and then the Equatorial, which isn't just a hotel, it's like running a whole little *country*, where everybody wants to run off with a piece for themselves the minute you turn your back. (p. 512, emphasis in original)

Rachel's remarks suggest she understands how imperialism works. She recognizes, in typical colonial fashion, that the land and its resources are up for grabs. She takes advantage of her situation and builds a home for personal financial gain. Aptly named The Equatorial, her hotel-home reflects Rachel's central position as an American, an authority she gains at the expense of the Congolese. Ironically, her failure as a true woman underscores the deep connections between commercialism, imperialism, and domesticity that domestic fiction attempts to mask.

Rachel's domestic practices and ideology represent the worst in American domestic and foreign policy: she couches her individual economic gain as a cultural improvement. Jo builds a school with her inheritance, and Rachel correspondingly incorporates commercialized culture in her hotel-home. However, where Jo instructs for community good, Rachel clearly works for personal profit. She explains, for example:

> The restaurant is for paying guests only, which is, needless to say, whites, since the Africans around here wouldn't earn enough in a month to buy one of my *prix-fixe* dinners. But I certainly am not one to leave anyone sitting out in the rain! So I built them that shelter, so they wouldn't be tempted to come in and hang about idly in the main bar. (pp. 461-62)

In effect, Rachel will serve the Black Congolese if they stay out of the main bar. As a result, Rachel replicates segregated Georgia in her miniature empire through her "separate but equal" and "you get what you pay for" exploitative services. Rachel's racist practices may also be a reproduced version of apartheid; after leaving Kilanga she moves to Johannesburg, South Africa, where she lives for at least four years (c. 1960-64). Rachel thus reproduces white privilege in her colonial retreat's construction. In fact, she conflates the aims of capitalist enterprise and aid organizations when she complains, "Mother's group has never raised one red cent for me, to help put in upstairs plumbing at the Equatorial, for example" (p. 476). Rachel's imperial hotel serves herself. Her narcissism, in turn, characterizes American domesticity: beautiful and worth protecting at all costs. However, money does not protect her absolutely.

The Poisonwood Bible presents a witty critique that recognizes Rachel's position under a patriarchal eye while it simultaneously criticizes her attempts to stabilize her precarious position with increasing degrees of separation from Black Congolese culture. The cult of true womanhood punishes women's entrance into commercial spheres by questioning their morality. Jo, for example, learns this lesson when she writes "sensation stories" (pp. 354-69). Before too long, Jo reflects, "They *are* trash. . . . I've gone blindly on, hurting myself and other people, for the sake of money" (p. 365). The cult of true womanhood

---

haunts Rachel too. Unlike Jo, who takes personal responsibility, Rachel places the blame on the viewer:

> Every so often a group of fellows will stop by in the afternoon on a sightseeing tour, and receive a mistaken impression of my establishment. . . . And guess what: they'll take me for the madam of a whorehouse! Believe you me, I give them a piece of my mind. If this looks like a house of prostitution to you, I tell them, that just shows the quality of your own moral fiber. (pp. 514-15)

Rachel abnegates personal responsibility for her business's outward appearance and the history that informs why men may misinterpret her trade. The viewer's moral fiber is questioned, not Rachel's. While Rachel may not escape a patriarchal, imperial gaze, which often views independent women as sexual objects, she still benefits from her place within the system: "I'm making a killing" (p. 512). Unlike her girlfriends in Georgia, Rachel has "opportunities as a woman of the world" (p. 514). Her economic and racial privileges promote her "success" (p. 514).

Ultimately, Rachel's knack for brushing off worries helps her construct a retreat from the outside world. Combined with her economic capital, her "amnesia" allows her to retreat from "bad luck." For example, when Rachel learns about diamond mines, she thinks, "Gee, does Marilyn Monroe even know where they come from? Just picturing her in her satin gown and a Congolese diamond digger in the same universe gave me the weebie jeebies. So I didn't think about it anymore" (p. 127). The last sentence underscores Rachel's domestic logic; she refuses to think about troubling issues: "If there's ugly things going on out there, well, you put a good stout lock on your door and check it twice before you go to sleep. You focus on getting your own one little place set up perfect, as I have done, and you'll see. Other people's worries do not necessarily have to drag you down" (p. 516). Rachel thus represents white privilege's ultimate "luck" (p. 367) with her conscious ability to forget and her economic means to lock herself away. Luck, in this case, functions as a synonym for colonialist opportunity. Her neocolonial retreat resembles a gated compound, requiring constant surveillance to ensure that no one can "run off with a piece for themselves the minute you turn your back" (p. 512).

This indictment of Rachel, however, fails to take into account the ways in which she also resists or, at least, complicates a neocolonial model of American domesticity. The above condemnation, after all, does not address how Rachel's nostalgic longing for America changes after Ruth May's death: "Until that moment I'd always believed I could still go home and pretend the Congo never happened. . . . The tragedies that happened to Africans were not mine. We were different, not just because we were white and had our vaccinations, but because we were simply a much, much luckier kind of person" (p. 367). Prior to Ruth May's death, "luck" in Rachel's lexicon—like "duty" in Mrs. March's worldview—ultimately justified her racial, class, and national privileges. After Ruth May's death, however, Rachel realizes luck may not always be on her side. Her lot in life leads Rachel to understand "sometimes life doesn't give you all that many chances at being good" (p. 515). While she still does not concern herself with the material factors that might influence luck or her "peculiar privilege," she knows from personal experience sometimes all possible choices are bad.

Rachel's shifts between facile and astute understanding resist straw woman constructions. Rachel is not simply evil. Her likeable qualities and keen insights hinder the reader's too easy dismissal of her as "unlike" me. Her Americanisms make her especially difficult to ignore. To paraphrase Rachel, you don't have to like her, but you sure have to admit she's out there.[32] Rachel's homemaking highlights the historical amnesia required to carry out American domesticity's inequitable economic and imperial agendas.

Conversely, Leah's character explores a recycled version of true womanhood's self-sacrifice for a greater good. Echoing Mrs. March's remarks about duty (p. 84), Leah values her marriage not only for its individual and family comforts but for its "world[ly]" effects as well. For example, Leah hopes that her marriage, despite its difficulties, means something in the world: "But hasn't our life together *meant more to the world* than either of us could have meant alone?" (p. 473, my emphasis). Leah's homemaking recycles Mrs. March's philosophy, but her unorthodox family ultimately undercuts conventional domesticity. Thus, Leah resembles fellow tomboy Jo, who balks at traditional gender roles throughout *Little Women* and makes an unconventional marriage.

Jo and Leah both marry men who are ethnically different—resisting the cultural taboos against mixed marriages. This textual wrinkle underscores *Little Women*'s gender and ethnic complexities. Although Jo eventually marries and is thereby recontained by conventional narrative expectations, her marriage—like Leah's—is unconventional. Even as the story marks Friedrich Bhaer, the German professor Jo marries, as ethnically different in his speech and demeanor, it also demonstrates how this unique match benefits both Jo and Professor Bhaer. This elder man, who is forty while Jo is still in her twenties when they marry, takes Jo's "improprieties" in stride. Furthermore, their school, like Leah and Anatole's relief work, provides stimulating work for them both (pp. 494-97). *Little Women* thus presents a conventional domestic narrative, but it should not be dismissed as a simple reproduction of patriarchal and racist ideologies. Likewise, Leah does not blindly reproduce the conventional home. She resists its imperial and commercial roots, recycling an alternative model home.

Even before Ruth May's death, Leah questions her privileged position and begins to break away from traditional gender roles that would confine her to the home.[33] Later, her biracial family hints at a significant mutiny against white privilege and other legacies of imperial history. Observing her children, for example, Leah remarks, "I look at my four boys, who are the colors of silt, loam, dust, and clay, an infinite palette for children of their own, and I understand that time erases whiteness altogether" (p. 526). Her children document possible redemption, proof that whiteness and, by extension, imperialism will not endure. The fact that her children appear fairly well adjusted to their lives in the United States and Africa attests to her hope's veracity.[34] Leah flips white privilege's familiar script: "[I] work my skin to darkness under the equatorial sun" (p. 526). Rachel, in fact, accuses Leah of being brainwashed by communists (p. 503).

A less generous reading might suggest Leah engages in what Minnie Bruce Pratt calls "cultural impersonation"; she borrows, in other words, "the identity of the Other in order to avoid not only guilt but pain and self-hatred."[35] Leah's self-conscious awareness of her position as a white American, however, disproves or at least softens this argument. For example, Leah and Anatole's sons are all named for men lost to war (p. 497). History lives within their household. Unlike Rachel, Leah does not attempt to mask her white privilege or use her home for personal profit. She does not construct security behind a door with stout locks. Rachel, like conventional domestic ideology, masks fissures to achieve stability. Leah, epitomizing neodomestic ideology, recognizes how the historic and present forces of cultural and economic capital converge to form privilege. For example, describing her 1974 Kinshasa home, Leah explains, "Our house is sturdy, with a concrete floor and a tin roof. We live in what would be called, in America, a slum, though here it's an island of relative luxury in the outskirts of *la cité*, where the majority have a good deal less in the way of roofing, to say the least" (p. 446). Contrasting American slums with the Kinshasa housing illustrates Leah's ability to distinguish the cultural and economic differences between the two urban environments and notions of a "good home."

The home depends on both discursive and material elements, and Leah's experiences emphasize Linda McDowell's point that "in all societies . . . the home is much more than a physical structure."[36] Rachel struggles to fabricate security through conscious forgetting and material hotel improvements. Leah struggles to construct a family and home able to withstand a nomadic life. Leah, Anatole, and eventually their children live a nomadic life through a series of homes in Africa and the United States. While Leah like Jo finds a good mate, she is not as successful in finding her place in the world. As the quotation that begins this section demonstrates, Leah attempts extreme acts to achieve a safe retreat. Despite their distinct homemaking, Rachel and Leah ultimately share a core definition of home: both seek security.[37]

Where Rachel pursues financial control and security in running her business, Leah seeks emotional security for herself and family. The time Leah's family spends in the United States demonstrates the complex ways in which economic and cultural, specifically racial, politics influence one's sense and experience of home. Where Rachel replicates segregation, her sister and her biracial family suffer from its legacies. In America, their home's material comforts are beyond what Leah's family has ever experienced. Nevertheless, living in the married student housing, "a plywood apartment complex set among pine trees" (p. 468), Leah and Anatole have trouble adjusting to the American home sensibility:

> the singular topic of conversation among our young neighbors was the inadequacy of these rattletrap tenements. To Anatole and me they seemed absurdly luxurious. Glass windows, with locks on every one and two on the door, when we didn't have a single possession worth stealing. Running water, hot, right out of the tap in the kitchen, and another one only ten steps away in the bathroom! (p. 468)

Modern conveniences like hot water from the tap seem luxurious considering the home Leah and Anatole recently left behind in Africa. Their experience demonstrates that material comforts and physical security—in the form of window and door locks—do not successfully produce a safe home or retreat. While their relative economic status improves in America, racial prejudice prevents Leah's family from feeling comfortable. Leah explains, "The citizens of my homeland regarded my husband and children as primitives, or freaks. On the streets, from a distance, they'd scowl at us, thinking we were merely the scourge they already knew and loathed—the mixed-race couple, with mongrel children as advertisement of our sins" (pp. 468-69). Racism against biracial families prevents her family from feeling at home.

Leah does not seem to belong anywhere, and this holds true when the family decides to return to Africa (pp. 468-74). Anatole's arrest upon reentry forces Leah to make a home without him: "Cloaked in my *pagne* and Anatole, I seemed to belong. Now, husbandless in this new neighborhood, my skin glows like a bare bulb" (p. 472). Alone, Leah does not feel at home in Kinshasa either. Nevertheless, she understands her Kinshasa neighbors' reserved manner: "They know just one thing about foreigners, and that is everything we've ever done to them" (p. 472). Leah recognizes the historical justification behind her Kinshasa neighbors' behavior and dreams "to leave my house one day unmarked by whiteness" (p. 504).

Leah and Rachel's mutual search for a safe retreat may be traced back to their lost American home; once again we see "the materials and debris of past domestic edifices" recycled in their homes (George, "Recycling," p. 2). Feminist geographer Doreen Massey best contextualizes their search for security: "Those who today worry about a sense of disorientation and a loss of control must once have felt they knew exactly where they were, and that they *had* control."[38] Massey goes on to clarify, "There is, then, an issue of whose identity we are referring to when we talk of a place called home and of the supports it may provide of stability, oneness and security" (p. 167). Leah's final chapter in book six suggests she eventually strikes a balance between a safe retreat and the access to privileges she desires for others: "There's the possibility of balance" (p. 522). Significantly, *Little Women* points to balance as a mark of domestic success (p. 121). However, neodomestic balance is not predicated on stasis but rather on movement. Leah finally understands her mother's wisdom: "As Mother used to say, not a thing stands still but sticks in the mud" (p. 526).

Conclusion: "Bangala" Homes

Home is where all justice begins.[39]

According to Orleanna, if we can embrace change and let go of our need to conquer space and people, then we will experience "the only celebration we mortals really know" (p. 385). Unlike Mrs. March, Orleanna does not rejoice in domestic stability. In fact, she suggests the desire for stability will cause colonialists to fail and ultimately curse us all (p. 384). Insisting upon domestic stability risks sorrow. Orleanna explains, "In perfect stillness, frankly, I've only found sorrow" (p. 385). Thus, the novel's neodomestic politics argue for change and instability. The neodomestic novel gives up the happy family tableau that concludes *Little Women*, gaining a foundational instability that potentially balances the desire for security and the need for fair access to domestic privileges.

The Poisonwood Bible recycles domesticity in novel ways. From this story, counter-versions of Anglo-American homemaking arise, ones not always dependent on patriarchal or (neo)colonial standards. Domestic fiction is a *bangala* term. Like the meanings of *bangala* that depend on the word's pronunciation—one referring to "something precious and dear" and another the name of the dangerous Poisonwood tree—the American home depends upon at least two seemingly contradictory drives: crystallizing emotional and economic security and providing access to these privileges (p. 276). The novel suggests American homes—in their ideological and material manifestations—can change for the better as well as continue on well-worn destructive paths. Domestic stability serves as a linchpin.

Not surprisingly, when the model American home undergoes scrutiny, Americans bristle. Critiquing the American home brings the American Dream, in essence the very ideology that is America, under question. Placing stout locks on this ideal, however, risks much more. Gwendolyn Wright in "Prescribing the Model Home" explains the problems that result when the model American home remains a singular proposition: "Confronting the problems of those for whom 'home' is lost or denied can intensify the potency of this ideal, making one's own 'perfect home' seem all the more essential and precarious. This fear prompts large numbers of Americans to turn away from the injustice they see around them."[40] She cautions that the American model home can become a "form of bondage" when it fails to fit a variety of family types (p. 223). Rachel, for example, never returns to the United States because she cannot meet traditional American domestic expectations. Simultaneously, Leah's search for a safe retreat threatens to doom her ability to experience "the only celebration we mortals really know" (p. 385). Recycling American domesticity holds the potential to produce "poisonous" as well as "precious" homes; the American home for the foreseeable future will contain some mix of both.

In addition to challenging domestic fiction's stabilizing cultural politics, neodomestic novels like *The Poisonwood Bible* can have an impact on the history and study of American fiction. Scholars such as Baym suggest domestic fiction "had run its course" by 1865 (p. 13).[41] The emergence of the "New Woman" challenged conventional domestic ideology, and domestic fiction gave way to novels like Edith Wharton's *The House of Mirth* (1905) that portray the home as a trap. While the politics have shifted, this essay suggests that useful comparisons emerge when we trace domestic fiction throughout the twentieth century. *The Poisonwood Bible* represents one of a critical mass of late twentieth-century and early twenty-first-century novels that (re)consider the geopolitical space of the American home. Toni Morrison's novels, for example, also recycle conventional domesticity in neodomestic fashion. In Morrison's neodomestic *Paradise* (1997) the various residents of an abandoned embezzler's mansion successively refurbish the property. Nuns first attempt to erase the embezzler's lascivious decor, setting up a boarding school to civilize Arapaho girls. When the school closes, the mansion, located at the outskirts of the fictional all-black town of Ruby, Oklahoma, becomes a temporary safe house for wayward women from the local community and abroad. Each resident attempts to create a safe haven and eventually fails. As in *The Poisonwood Bible*, the significance and folly of the occupants' actions lie in unexamined notions about the conventional American home.

Thus, this comparison between *Little Women* and *The Poisonwood Bible* is not meant to suggest that white women categorically define the genre of domestic fiction and the model American home. Other neodomestic novels that posit and explore instability as a key component of American domesticity include: the exiled homes in Lan Cao's *Monkey Bridge* (1997), the migrant home in Helena María Viramontes's *Under the Feet of Jesus* (1995), the postmodern expanding and contracting home in Mark Z. Danielewski's *House of Leaves* (2000), the queer homes in Michael Cunningham's *A Home at the End of the World* (1990), and a divorced father's suburban home in Richard Ford's *Independence Day* (1995). Thus, writers of various ethnic and cultural backgrounds, including male writers, experiment with domestic fiction's form in the late twentieth century. While the heterosexual home continues to dominate the genre, broadening domestic fiction's geography to include urban and rental domestic settings frequently recovers "queer" space as part of domestic fiction's architecture. Urban homes, moreover, comprise the prominent settings in much male gay fiction (for example, Jaime Manrique's *Latin Moon in Manhattan*, 1992), and rental properties (for example, Dorothy Allison's *Bastard Out of Carolina*, 1992) often provide the settings for nontraditional families. Analysis of *The Poisonwood Bible* only begins to scour the wide-ranging recycled or neodomestic narratives in contemporary American literature.

While continuing our homework in the field of domestic fiction, we would do well to remember what Kingsolver writes in her essay "Household Words": "Home is where all justice begins."[42] Both *Little Women* and *The Poisonwood Bible* confirm this statement with a shared understanding of the home's significance and power for American culture and politics. As an American emblem of success and the prime location for identity formation, the home offers a critical site for feminist redefinitions and activism. Neodomestic fiction promotes the radical ideology that we can gain security when we cease to depend on policed boundaries and locked doors. My analysis of the fictional American home's histories and present incarnations, especially regarding security and access, supports the neodomestic argument for a flexible, more mobile definition of home—one that does not craft domestic security at the individual or national scale through an ever-increasing level of exclusion and segregation. Whether or not this twenty-first-century fiction will reflect a future reality remains to be seen.

From *Tulsa Studies in Women's Literature* 24, no. 1 (2005): 105-127. Copyright © 2005 by the University of Tulsa. Reprinted by permission.

Notes

Thank you to Deborah Clarke at the Pennsylvania State University for initially pointing out to me the rich connections between *Little Women* and *The Poisonwood Bible*— and for granting me permission to consider this relationship in my work.

1. Louisa May Alcott, *Little Women* (1868; rpt. Boston: Little, Brown and Company, 1994), p. 114. Subsequent references will be cited parenthetically in the text.

2. *Little Women* begins by revealing each of the March girls' flaws, which they in turn plan—as in John Bunyan's *The Pilgrim's Progress* (1678)—to resolve. *Little Women*, in this sense, narrates the March girls' journeys to recognize and accept their burdens, or flaws, and correct them. See chapters one and two in *Little Women*, "Playing Pilgrims" and "A Merry Christmas."

3. Rachel Price and Amy March also resemble each other because both are guilty of misusing language; Rachel's frequent malapropisms and Amy's mispronunciations connect their characters.

4. Regarding Amy's disability, Alcott writes, "If anybody had asked Amy what the greatest trial of her life was, she would have answered at once, 'My nose.' When she was a baby, Jo had accidentally dropped her into the coal-hod, and Amy insisted that the fall had ruined her nose forever" (p. 42).

5. Ann Romines explains that domestic "faculty" is a nineteenth-century term that refers to the collection of skills that make "a housekeeper of exemplary competence," in *The Home Plot: Women, Writing and Domestic Ritual* (Amherst: University of Massachusetts Press, 1992), pp. 4-5.

6. In *Dimity Convictions: The American Woman in the Nineteenth Century* (Athens: Ohio University Press, 1976), Barbara Welter explains that the "four cardinal virtues—

piety, purity, submissiveness and domesticity" define True Womanhood in the nineteenth century (p. 21). Her essay "The Cult of True Womanhood: 1820-1860" originally appeared in *American Quarterly*, 18, No. 2 (1966), 151-74. Clearly, religion—specifically Protestant morality—is a fourth point that demands attention. An essay could be written that analyzes the ways *The Poisonwood Bible* revises the Protestant morality promoted in *Little Women*. Unfortunately, this task is beyond the scope of this essay; in the forthcoming sections, my essay only hints at the various ways *The Poisonwood Bible* recycles Protestantism. My larger project examining twenty-first-century neodomestic fiction, of which this argument represents a part, takes up this issue in greater detail.

7. Nancy Armstrong, *Desire and Domestic Fiction: A Political History of the Novel* (New York: Oxford University Press, 1987), pp. 23-24.

8. I am not the first to trace the intimate connections between imperialism and domesticity. Numerous literary scholars, cultural critics, and feminist geographers connect home with nation and empire, and this essay is indebted to their work. Amy Kaplan's work in particular emphasizes American imperialism's reliance on domestic cultures. See Kaplan's "Left Alone with America: The Absence of Empire in the Study of American Culture," in *Cultures of United States Imperialism*, ed. Kaplan and Donald E. Pease (Durham: Duke University Press, 1993), pp. 3-21; "Manifest Domesticity," *American Literature*, 70, No. 3 (1998), 581-606; and "Nation, Region, and Empire," in *The Columbia History of the American Novel*, ed. Emory Elliott et al. (New York: Columbia University Press, 1991), pp. 240-66. Other scholars who connect the home with empire and particularly influence my work include: Mona Domosh and Joni Seager, "Nations and Empires," *Putting Women in Place: Feminist Geographers Make Sense of the World* (New York: Guilford Press, 2001), pp. 140-73; the essays collected in *Writing Women and Space: Colonial and Postcolonial Geographies*, ed. Alison Blunt and Gillian Rose (New York: Guilford Press, 1994); and Rosemary Marangoly George's edited collection *Burning Down the House: Recycling Domesticity* (Boulder, CO: Westview Press, 1998) and her critical study *The Politics of Home: Postcolonial Relocations and Twentieth-Century Fiction* (Berkeley: University of California Press, 1996).

9. See Nina Baym, *Woman's Fiction: A Guide to Novels by and about Women in America, 1820-1870* (1978; rpt. Ithaca: Cornell University Press, 1980), pp. 23-24. Subsequent references will be cited parenthetically in the text.

10. Protestant morality comprises another key component. See n. 6.

11. Barbara Kingsolver purposefully drew from *Little Women* while writing *The Poisonwood Bible*. On her website at HarperCollins she responds to the question, "Were you consciously trying to create a parallel to *Little Women*, in this story of a mother and four daughters?": "Certainly I considered that other famous family of 'little women,' as I was writing this. It was one of the most beloved books of my childhood. But the parallels don't go too far. Louisa May Alcott didn't put any snakes in her book." See "Frequently Asked Questions," HarperCollins Publishers, http://www.Kingsolver.com/faq/answers.asp (accessed 13 June 2003).

12. George, "Recycling: Long Routes to and from Domestic Fixes," in *Burning Down the House: Recycling Domesticity*, pp. 1-20. Subsequent references will be cited parenthetically in the text.

13. See Susan K. Harris, *Nineteenth-Century American Women's Novels: Interpretive Strategies* (1990; rpt. New York: Cambridge University Press, 1992), p. 20.

14. My larger project examining twenty-first-century neodomestic fiction takes up these issues in greater detail.

15. Barbara Kingsolver, *The Poisonwood Bible* (New York: HarperPerennial, 1999), p. 9. Subsequent references will be cited parenthetically in the text.

16. Kaplan, "Manifest Domesticity," p. 583.

17. Kaplan suggests in "Manifest Domesticity," "the expansionist logic of domesticity . . . turns an imperial nation into a home by producing and colonizing specters of the foreign that lurk inside and outside its ever shifting borders" (p. 602).

18. Toni Morrison, *Playing in the Dark: Whiteness and the Literary Imagination* (Cambridge: Harvard University Press, 1992), p. 6. I am indebted to Kaplan's essay "Manifest Domesticity" for first connecting nineteenth-century American domesticity to Morrison's notion of the "Africanist presence" (p. 602).

19. Kaplan, "Manifest Domesticity," p. 602. Much early Anglo-American prose and poetry explicitly celebrate a narrow conception of domesticity while implicitly and sometimes explicitly articulating fears about non-American family and home structures. *A Narrative of the Captivity and Restoration of Mrs. Mary Rowlandson* (1682), for example, recounts early Anglo fears about Native Americans dispossessing "good" (white) Christians of their homes. In the nineteenth century, Catharine E. Beecher and Harriet Beecher Stowe's domestic advice and resource book, *American Woman's Home* (1869; rpt. New Brunswick: Rutgers University Press, 1998), assumes that a white, middle-class readership is the "Women of America" to whom the book is inscribed and "in whose hands rest the real destinies of the republic" (n.p.). Subsequent references will be cited parenthetically in the text. Native American women, such as Sarah Winnemucca Hopkins (*Life Among the Piutes: Their Wrongs and Claims*, 1883) and Zitkala-Sa (*American Indian Stories*, 1921), narrate the exacting costs of becoming acculturated to white American domestic norms, and African American women, such as Harriet Jacobs (*Incidents in the Life of a Slave Girl*, 1861), narrate the barriers erected against their access to American domestic ideals. Furthermore, Sarah A. Leavitt notes in "Americanization, Model Homes, and Lace Curtains" that at the turn of the century immigrant women were the primary target for much domestic advice. See her *From Catharine Beecher to Martha Stewart: A Cultural History of Domestic Advice* (Chapel Hill: University of North Carolina Press, 2002), p. 75. She also notes, "most domestic-advice texts left out black women. For most domestic advisors, black women existed only as servants" (p. 75).

20. My emphasis here on the "Africanist presence" should not discount Kingsolver's political agenda to make her readers aware of American involvement in the Congo, especially in terms of America's role in Patrice Lumumba's assassination.

21. Once again, literary, cultural, and feminist scholars provide an array of scholarship on domestic advice and fiction and the white, middle-class, heterosexual domestic ideal. For example, in addition to Leavitt's study *From Catharine Beecher to Martha Stewart* and George's *Politics of Home*, see Jeannette Batz Cooperman, *The Broom Closet: Secret Meanings of Domesticity in Postfeminist Novels by Louise Erdrich, Mary Gordon, Toni Morrison, Marge Piercy, Jane Smiley, and Amy Tan* (New York:

Peter Lang, 1999); Marjorie Garber, *Sex and Real Estate: Why We Love Houses* (New York: Pantheon Books, 2000); George's *Burning Down the House: Recycling Domesticity;* Dolores Hayden, *The Grand Domestic Revolution: A History of Feminist Designs for American Homes, Neighborhoods, and Cities* (Cambridge, MA: The MIT Press, 1981) and *Redesigning the American Dream: Gender, Housing, and Family Life* (1984; rev. New York: W. W. Norton and Company, 2002); Roberta Rubenstein, *Home Matters: Longing and Belonging, Nostalgia and Mourning in Women's Fiction* (New York: Palgrave, 2001); and Catherine Wiley and Fiona R. Barnes, eds., *Homemaking: Women Writers and the Politics and Poetics of Home* (New York: Garland Publishing, Inc., 1996).

22. Although beyond the scope of this essay, *The Poisonwood Bible* also works a subtle critique of the African domestic sphere into the narrative. Ruth May, for example, describes a conversation she overhears about a "Circus mission," and Leah notes how the women in Kilanga marry young (p. 271, 107). Rachel and Orleanna record the toll the body, especially the female body, endures as a result of those early marriages (pp. 53-54, 126). The novel also balances this subtle critique with Mama Tataba, an icon of domestic prowess who "cursed our mortal souls as evenhandedly as she nourished our bodies" (p. 94).

23. "Manifest domesticity" plays on the term "manifest destiny" and refers to the "pervasive imperial metaphor" in the nineteenth century, linking domesticity to "the contemporaneous geopolitical movement of imperial expansion" (Kaplan, "Manifest Domesticity," p. 583).

24. Biddy Martin and Chandra Talpade Mohanty make a similar point about Minnie Bruce Pratt's narrative in their "Feminist Politics: What's Home Got to Do With It?," in *Feminisms: An Anthology of Literary Theory and Criticism*, ed. Robyn R. Warhol and Diane Price Herndl (New Brunswick: Rutgers University Press, 1997), pp. 293-310. They discuss a passage where Pratt realizes she cannot abnegate responsibility for her father's history (pp. 301-02).

25. Seyla Benhabib, "Sexual Difference and Collective Identities: The New Global Constellation," *Signs*, 24, No. 2 (1999), 355. Martin and Mohanty similarly outline "the consolidation of the white home in response to a threatening outside" as the rhetoric of home's dark underbelly (p. 303). The series of foreign and domestic policy initiatives undertaken after September 11th add even greater magnitude to Orleanna, Benhabib, and Martin and Mohanty's remarks. America frequently uses violence to respond to the backlash against its privileged position within the global community.

26. Martin and Mohanty, p. 296.

27. Interestingly, French postmodern theorists, such as Gilles Deleuze and Félix Guattari, and Anglo feminist theorists, such as Rosi Braidotti and Caren Kaplan, have returned to the notion of leaving home or "deterritorialization." In turn, feminist theorists, such as George, critique such uses for the ways they reproduce the privileges deterritorialization claims to leave behind. *The Poisonwood Bible* suggests historically conscious deterritorialization will not uncritically reproduce white privilege. See Deleuze and Guattari, "What Is a Minor Literature?," *Kafka: Toward a Minor Literature*, trans. Dana Polan (Minneapolis: University of Minnesota Press, 1986), pp. 16-27; Rosi Braidotti, *Nomadic Subjects: Embodiment and Sexual Difference in Contem-*

porary Feminist Theory (New York: Columbia University Press, 1994); Caren Kaplan, "Deterritorializations: The Rewriting of Home and Exile in Western Feminist Discourse," *Cultural Critique*, 6 (Spring 1987), 187-98; and George's chapter "Home-Countries: Narratives Across Disciplines," in *The Politics of Home*.

28. Explicit parallels between home and nation (such as Ruth May and Lumumba's deaths) occur throughout *The Poisonwood Bible*. Orleanna especially emphasizes the connections between domestic and national politics in her chapter that opens book four, "Bel and the Serpent" (pp. 317-24).

29. Welter, *Dimity Convictions*, p. 11.

30. Judith Williamson, "Woman Is an Island: Femininity and Colonization," *Studies in Entertainment*, ed. Tania Modleski (Bloomington: Indiana University Press, 1986), pp. 100-01.

31. See George, "The Authoritative Englishwoman" in *The Politics of Home*, pp. 50-56, for a detailed discussion of the home abroad's replication of the empire.

32. Rachel says, "The way I see Africa, you don't have to like it but you sure have to admit it's out there" (p. 516). This passage suggests she too recognizes the Africanist presence within her own narrative.

33. For example, Leah's participation in the Congolese hunt, a practice reserved for boys and men, challenges traditional gender roles (pp. 335-42, 348-49).

34. While beyond the scope of this essay, a fuller reading of this passage would interrogate how African children of white and black parents fit into African and American societies.

35. Martin and Mohanty, p. 306. Martin and Mohanty quote Pratt's term.

36. Linda McDowell, *Gender, Identity, and Place: Understanding Feminist Geographies* (Minneapolis: University of Minnesota Press, 1999), p. 92.

37. To clarify, Baym does not include women's fiction before the Civil War as advancing the home as a separate sphere or retreat from the world (p. 48). After the Civil War, Baym explains, "the Gilded Age affirmed profit as the motive around which all of American life was to be organized. Home now became a retreat, a restraint and a constraint, as it had not appeared to be earlier" (p. 50). My use of the term "retreat" more broadly encompasses the security both pre-Civil War and antebellum women's fiction sought.

38. Doreen Massey, *Space, Place, and Gender* (Minneapolis: University of Minnesota Press, 1994), p. 165. Subsequent references will be cited parenthetically in the text.

39. Kingsolver, "Household Words," *Small Wonder: Essays* (New York: HarperCollins Publishers, 2002), p. 201.

40. Gwendolyn Wright, "Prescribing the Model Home," *Social Research*, 58, No. 1 (1991), 223. Subsequent references will be cited parenthetically in the text.

41. Blythe Forcey's entry "Domestic Fiction" in *The Oxford Companion to Women's Writing in the United States*, ed. Cathy N. Davidson and Linda Wagner-Martin (New York: Oxford University Press, 1995), p. 253, clarifies, "While the genre has never died out, it became an object of near-constant disdain in the first half of the twentieth century as it was made the icon of everything that modern literature strove *not* to be."

42. Kingsolver, "Household Words," p. 201.

The Revelatory Narrative Circle in Barbara Kingsolver's *The Poisonwood Bible*_____

Anne Marie Austenfeld

Anne Marie Austenfeld focuses her attention on the narrative techniques Kingsolver employs in *The Poisonwood Bible*. Austenfeld argues not only that the multiple narrators, or focalizers, all female, provide differing perspectives on a topic—a postcolonial, feminist, religiously influenced, backward-looking family history—that requires such multiplicity but also that the narrators together form a circle of storytellers. The narrators' emphasis on their personal stories also marks this narrative as different from traditional forms of history writing and writing about Africa directed toward Western audiences. Austenfeld shows how the circle of narrators enacts a particular rhetorical appeal to the reader, one that replaces traditional persuasive rhetoric, based on the exchanging of controversial viewpoints, with invitational rhetoric, a dialogic structure open to multiple perspectives.   — T.A.

Imagine a novel related not by one, not by two, but by five narrators, all female, one dead. In novels written near the turn from the 20th to the 21st century readers and scholars encounter a richness of new fictional tools, among them narratives like the one described above—Barbara Kingsolver's *The Poisonwood Bible* (1998)—that depart both from traditional social views and from familiar literary forms. Ansgar Nünning describes what he calls "revisionist historical novels," which have significantly extended the boundaries of the historical novel to include, among other elements, "the history of mentalities, women's history, oral history, history from below, and the history of everyday life" (362), often using narrative tools such as "several character-focalizers whose limited perspectives project highly subjective views of history" (363) to challenge conventions of the realist novel. Kristin Jacobson's definition of "neodomestic fiction" describes a genre that "recycles the domestic novel in historically conscious ways that posit alternatives to the conventional white, middle-class home" (106). Narrative theory provides a valuable resource in achieving a useful critical reading of revisionist and neodomestic fiction. Bakhtin suggests the value of a "diversity of individual voices" in telling a story (262), and Foss and Griffin's concept of "invitational rhetoric" describes the effectiveness of a model in which each successive speaker offers a viewpoint, but also listens openly to those of all other speakers (5). Whereas a single, externally observing, extradiegetic narrator, sometimes in conjunction with a single homodiegetic, or character-narrator formerly sufficed to offer what was considered a balanced perspective, contemporary authors have found a complex story may require multiple homodiegetic narrators, practicing invitational rhetoric, in order to achieve the desired effect of balanced narration.

The subject of this essay, Barbara Kingsolver's *The Poisonwood Bible*, is a prime example of an established author employing new tools in the treatment of a complex sociohistorical moment: the transformation of an American missionary family's modes of existence and self-perception, foregrounded against the corresponding political transition of the Congo from colony to self-governing entity. The narrative tool used is what I will call a *revelatory narrative circle* of five character-narrators, who speak by turns in an orderly way, each filtering events, themes, and dialogue throughout the novel. The five female, American narrative voices offer a feminist alternative, first, to historical writing, which tends to be male-centered, focusing on political and military events and key public figures, second, to male-written and narrated European fiction about Africa, typified by Conrad's *Heart of Darkness*, and third, to the technically conventional use of a third person narrator found even in thematically African works such as Chinua Achebe's *Things Fall Apart*.[1] By examining Kingsolver's work in light of narrative theory, we find that it is precisely the personal, revelatory tone of the five narrative voices that marks *The Poisonwood Bible* as an important milestone in contemporary narrative practice.

Mary Jean DeMarr suggests that Kingsolver's experiences as a young child living in the Congo with her parents spurred her to write this novel and informed both its thematic concerns and its shape (117-118). The result is a family-centered structure which marks *The Poison-wood Bible* as an innovative treatment of the topic of post-colonialism. Kingsolver adds a personal depth that is lacking in the accounts of the birth of the Republic of Congo usually taught in history class, and she delivers what history books rarely do: examples of how a variety of in-dividual human beings act and are acted upon every day in the context of rapid and difficult social, political, and economic changes. Because Kingsolver has participated in her own family's sharing of stories about how Congolese people and American aid workers lived and in-teracted during the 1960s, she is able to use narrative to compose a pic-ture of everyday life in the fictional village of Kilanga, a picture of which the political situation is only one part. Her narrators' detailed renderings of village life make a valuable contribution to our under-standing of the plight of the individual underneath, or within, the politi-cal system. In this novel, the ordinary person is the most important per-son, and each narrator serves not only as a focal vehicle for telling the story but also as a determining agent whose choices of whom and what to include in her portion of the story shape the overall message and the-matic slant of the entire work.

By developing a circle of five character-narrator personalities and assigning different responsibilities to each one, Kingsolver builds pat-terns of focalization within each voice. "Focalization," as defined by Mieke Bal, shows "the relations between the elements presented and the vision through which they are represented" (142), that is, between events and analysis and the entity who perceives them. Peter Messent suggests the term "focalization" to describe how an author controls and orients narrative through the narrator (21ff). According to these defini-tions, what readers "see" and "hear" in a narrative is focalized, or cho-sen, colored, and interpreted by the narrator as constructed by the au-thor.

Kingsolver uses five character-narrators to focalize in five distinct ways, thus avoiding what Bal has noted as a chief drawback of the character-narrator, "If the focalizor coincides with the character, that character will have an advantage over the other characters" (146). In structuring her novel, Kingsolver not only uses the names of Biblical books for some section headings, but also "redacts" material from several sources, much as the compilers of Scripture have done, enriching the story in the process. Orleanna sees through the eyes of wife and mother, focuses on the reasons for deeds and events; examining, for instance, American and Congolese conventions guiding the behavior of wives and mothers. Rachel sees the world through the eyes of a literal-minded, materialistic teenager, but she renders human relationships, material details, conversations, and emotions with great accuracy. Her descriptions of scenes such as a theological debate between Nathan and Anatole (128-133) and the Hollywood-style cigarette lighting and kiss scene with Eeben Axelroot (290-93) employ a degree of minute physical and verbal detail that reveals the value she places on recognizable behavioral formulas. By contrast, Leah, who sees with the eyes of an intelligent, flexible learner, presents historical and cultural details, describes relationships and emotional connections, and generally seeks to integrate all types of knowledge into her narratives. Particularly memorable are Leah's account of the Independence Day ceremonies near the end of "Revelation" (181ff), and her later analysis of Independence Day events in "Exodus" (415ff). Sardonic, palindrome-spouting Adah complements Leah's narrative by showing the world through the eyes of a physically handicapped, but intellectually gifted young person. Her social marginalization by both society and family, noted by Stephen D. Fox (3), leaves her free to ponder the wonder of the natural world, the absurdity of the human-made world, and the currents of language, biology, and political intrigue flowing around her. Adah is the last living voice to speak in the novel, as she critiques the elusive qualities of truth, both personal and absolute, and the intimate relationship of truth to falsity in human thought and behavior, concluding, "We are the balance of our damage and our transgressions" (533). Baby sister Ruth May, who sees with the all-observing eyes and limited comprehension of a five-year-old, offers us a broad sample of all she sees, hears, smells, dreams, and feels. Her voice is perhaps the most straightforward and positive one, and it is this voice that closes the story. In the last paragraphs of the novel, Ruth May's spirit-voice admonishes her mother, "Move on. Walk forward into the light" (543). Each of these five voices has its own distinct pattern of language and angle of viewing people and events, providing a variety of focalizations or filters and reminding the reader that no one person can know all.

By the late 1980s, Gérard Genette suggested the possibility, but found no example, of a narrative told by a "secondary" character (102). What we find in *The Poisonwood Bible* is an advance past the perceived need for a secondary character-narrator to a hero-less circle of what Genette calls "autodiegetic" characters, each by turns primary and secondary. In the novel we see intentional shifts of narrators back and forth: between the world of the past and the narrative present, between narrator in one section and observed character in another narrator's section. The "metalepsis," or blurring of distinctions between narrative levels (Genette, 88) thus achieved might lead Genette to place *The Poisonwood Bible* in the realm of the fantastic. The repeated reframing of the narrative of the ants, in particular, moves away from the standard construction of a "récit premier," or "level A" telling containing other levels, towards a non-hierarchical shared telling, in which none of the individual narrators dominates at the top level, but rather each narrator takes up the thread of the narrative in the same place the previous narrator began, producing a more subtle layering of narratives, all at the level of direct relation to the audience. This structure typifies the "invitational rhetoric" defined by Foss and Griffin as an alternative to persuasive rhetoric that strives to set up a dialogic structure of open sharing of multiple ideas or perspectives in place of the usual structure of argument from one viewpoint or another (5). According to Foss and Griffin, invitational rhetoric arises from the work of bell hooks and JT Woods and is motivated primarily by "a commitment to the creation of relationships of equality and to the elimination of the dominance and elitism that characterize most human relationships" (4). Jeanette Riley et al. point out how a character in an earlier Kingsolver novel "participates in creating a network of justice" by taking responsibility for the people in her life (100), and Kingsolver herself has stated, "I believe the creation of empathy is a political act" (*Address*, par. 12), indicating that the turn-taking, hero-lacking narrative structure of *The Poisonwood Bible* is founded in her desire to achieve a politically and socially effective rhetoric. Kingsolver's assertion clearly marks this novel as a conscious act of innovation; she has used a recognizably feminist mode of discourse both to model the use of invitational rhetoric in the novel and to create reader empathy.

An as yet under-explored source of the multi-voiced narrative, or "polyphony" (Kundera 73), in *The Poisonwood Bible* is Kingsolver's non-fiction work. In a 1997 KET interview ("Messing") the author recounts her experiences working with the Sanctuary Movement for political refugees during the 1980s. She explains how she would first listen to the stories of her friends and neighbors, refugees who had fled brutal regimes in Chile, El Salvador, and Guatemala; then she would write articles and broadsides to disseminate those stories in the community (312). She describes the important process of learning the language of a place—Arizona in this case—while researching *Holding the Line*, her 1997 book about the Arizona mine workers' strike thus, "It was in those hundreds of hours I spent sitting on people's front porches, . . . listening to them tell their stories about their ancestors. . . . These women suffered unbelievable injustices. And I had to record that" (317). Biographer Linda Wagner-Martin assesses the effect the extensive interview process has on the tone of *Holding the Line*, saying, "For Kingsolver . . . the individual stories of the hundreds of people caught in the dilemma . . . were the core of the event" (55). Kingsolver's form of social activism, listening to individual stories and writing them into coherent prose, deeply informs her fiction writing as well. Just as she performed what she calls "front porch research" in preparation for writing *Pigs in Heaven* (320), she has converted a lifetime of conversations heard in Africa and about Africa into the personal-toned narrative layers of *The Poisonwood Bible*. The front porch, the place where people tell their versions of the story, is the center of Kingsolver's life and of her fiction. What women reveal to one another on the front porch are their own foundational truths, the subversive currents of personal truth that run underneath the official version, and this truth is the very substance of this novel.

The fact that *The Poisonwood Bible* consists entirely of *what women say*, moreover, puts into perspective the social and political conditions under which the characters in the novel live, and does so in ways unprecedented in novels about Africa written by male authors. In the course of her narratives, Orleanna compares herself to the Congo: colonized, stripped of valuables (198-201), and to the earth itself: "changing hands, bearing scars" (89). According to Elaine Ognibene, "The longer she lives in Kilanga, the clearer Orleanna's vision becomes" about her husband, politics, and her situation as it parallels that of the Congo (22). This clear-sightedness allows Orleanna to explore the position of the individual within, or under, the political system. Orleanna expands upon this theme in the opening pages of "Exodus," saying of women like herself and her Congolese counterparts,

> Don't dare presume there's shame in the lot of a woman who carries on. On the day a committee of men decided to murder the fledgling Congo, what do you suppose Mama Mwanza was doing? Was it different, the day after? Of course not. Was she a fool, then, or the backbone of a history? When a government comes crashing down, it crushes those who were living under its roof. People like Mama Mwanza never knew the house was there at all. (383)

She goes on to critique the usefulness of abstract concepts to village women like Mama Mwanza, and to ordinary woman in general, saying, "*Conquest* and *liberation* and *democracy* and *divorce* are words that mean squat, basically, when you have hungry children and clothes to get out on the line and it looks like rain" (383). Orleanna expresses these thoughts as she explains why she left the Congo with her children, leaving Nathan there on his own. The value of these observations is twofold. First, they link the lot of all women, American and African, who, like Orleanna consider themselves ordinary, and second, they underscore one of the driving truths of the novel: that ordinary people often fail to see a meaningful connection between themselves and the larger political movements and systems at work in the world in which they live. Jacobson points to key questions brought up by Orleanna in her portions of the narrative: not only how to live with having survived and gone back to the privileged life of a white Southern lady, but also how to move beyond imperial history without forgetting it, and how white Americans should negotiate privilege on domestic and global scales (110-11). Kingsolver uses the voice of Orleanna to deliver observations that consider philosophical positions not normally covered in the news or historical accounts, so Orleanna's voice reminds us not to rely on our assumptions or on what we have learned before, but to consider those who live with—or despite—the revolution.

Of the narratives of Orleanna's daughters, Pamela Demory observes that unlike Conrad's Marlow, these women have no audience or opportunity to tell their own stories within the world of the novel. "In giving them a voice, Kingsolver comments on the political, social, and family constraints that keep them from speaking, and at the same time comments on *Heart of Darkness*, pointing out by implication the absence of women's points of view in Conrad's story" (186). Demory argues persuasively that Kingsolver's novel is a critical retelling of *Heart of Darkness*, but even more interesting to this study is Kingsolver's critical tool: the way in which the narratives are framed.

Diane Kunz points out that in the narrative structure, Orleanna's

voice is "retrospective," while those of the girls are "contemporaneous" (246). In pondering why, we should note that Orleanna's voice
functions in our present, but invites us to visit the past, leading us into
the time and place of the story. Rather than encountering diaries or
overhearing front porch conversations, we, the readers, find ourselves
functioning as the friends on the front porch, receiving the narratives
directly, within the heart of the story. The narrative circle reflects in the
fictional context what scholarship has noted in communication practices, namely that the most effective method of conveying a story is determined by the nature of those telling it. Renee Curry cites behavior
studies showing that girls who are silent in public are more articulate
"in private, with each other, or with their own writings" (97), a truth reflected in the limitation of this narrative to familial voices. Marianne
Cave's discussion of chronotopes suggests that women's narratives
about the world are necessarily related to self-construction of identity
and are therefore personal (121), a feature borne out by the varied ways
the narrators bring the events, thoughts, and feelings of the past into the
narrative present. Additionally, Walter Fisher asserts that narrative can
effectively replace argumentation in the position of persuasive device
(2), opening up the area of "recounting" or story-telling as a valid way
of telling truths about the human condition. Taken together, the insights of the theorists indicate that to attend to the tales recounted by
the circle of revelatory female narrators in *The Poisonwood Bible* is to
open oneself to a large dose of philosophical truth. While the novel is
what Monika Fludernik calls a "pseudo-oral" form rather than an
"oral" form, the art of the author is the use of a structure that imitates an
intimate circle of storytelling, in a domestic setting, to a listener
(reader) who voluntarily joins that circle and agrees to give credence to
the truths expressed there.

Not only does the narrative circle reflect observed characteristics of
female story-telling, it also reflects acculturation. A contemporary
American or Western reader is able to recognize the series of personal
narratives from outside the genre of the novel, from the intimate setting

of the front porch or kitchen, from the interview-based women's television program, and from the similarly interview-based investigative journalism practiced by Kingsolver herself in work such as *Holding the Line*. In this light we may identify the collective, turn-taking, layered narrative structure of Kingsolver's novel as an organic female form: a group of female voices sharing a story that is of vital importance to them. The reader is drawn into a private circle, implicitly a place where the truth can be told without silencing influences from the world at large. The construct of the speaker/reader private circle is only that—a construct—but it is a powerful tool signifying the integration of the sympathetic reader, male or female, into the story-telling process.

We may look to Kingsolver's stated intentions for insight into why she uses the private circle construct. Curry has complained about the historical position of female narrators in general, saying, "As readers, we often succumb to the idea that girls with knowledge must either be silenced or disbelieved. We label them 'untrustworthy narrators,' and we doubt the stories they tell" (103). With reference to *The Poisonwood Bible*, Wagner-Martin points to "the striking convention of choosing as narrators of the events characters who are, initially, powerless" (108). In fact, Kingsolver seems to count on turning on its head any notion that girls are untrustworthy or powerless as narrators. Her explicitly stated aims to create "chick books" (DeMarr 21) and to write books that speak from female experience (Epstein 34) suggest that her use of female narrators in *The Poisonwood Bible* arises from a lack of confidence in the adequacy of *male* voices that have told us about the Congo so far, especially Conrad's Marlow. Moreover, Kingsolver's girl narrators, abruptly removed from the innocence-protecting atmosphere of highly religious 1959 Georgia, USA, and deposited in a Congo ravaged by political and cultural flux, find themselves forced to refashion their identities to some degree in order to make sense of what is happening around them and to them. Yet, the value they continue to place on truthfulness and seeking to do what is right should be seen as enhancing their value as narrators. A narrative theory approach indicates that while none of them is capable of revealing the whole truth, as a group these narrators can be relied upon to achieve as true a story as possible about life in the post-colonial Congo and to offer a valuable counterbalance to other versions we have heard.

Much like the real-life voices we hear throughout *Holding the Line*, the voices of Kingsolver's fictional narrators gain power and credibility partly through their numbers. On her website, the author explains her use of multiple narrators by describing the requirements of philosophical discourse. "The four sisters and Orleanna, "she says, "represent five separate philosophical positions, not just in their family but also in my political examination of the world. This novel is asking, basically, 'What did we do to Africa, and how do we feel about it?' . . . There are a hundred different answers along a continuum, with absolute paralyzing guilt on the one end and 'What, me worry? I didn't do it!' on the other end" (FAQ). Kingsolver goes on to explain where each character falls on the continuum, with Orleanna at the paralyzed end and Rachel at the blithely unconcerned end. Like the true story of the Arizona mine strikes, the fictionalized story of an American family in the Congo involves many perspectives. The reader of *Holding the Line* could not begin to understand the scope and complexity of what went on in Arizona in 1983 without hearing the many eyewitness accounts from different towns and different mines, nor without learning about events that took place simultaneously in different locations. In the same way, the reader of *The Poisonwood Bible* could not possibly begin to understand the complexity of the motives underlying the actions and words of different individuals, private and public, which affected the lives of every person living in the Congo in 1959 and 1960 without hearing from all five of the Price family females. From her circle of non-fiction sources for *Holding the Line*, women such as Berta Chavez, Diane McCormick, and Mrs. Delgado and her daughters, Kingsolver has learned that the truth doesn't speak with one voice, but with many. The force of this knowledge shapes the narrative structure of *The Poi-*

sonwood Bible and enriches the author's ability to tell in a work of fiction truths as deep and complex as she has told in her non-fiction work.

Had Kingsolver been able to enter the former Belgian Congo in the early 1990s to perform interviews, she would have done so (FAQ). Since the volatile political situation made researching a non-fiction piece impossible, she used her talents as a fiction writer to tell the story of America's involvement in the post-colonial Congo in an innovative way. Weaving together memory, history, linguistics, and interview material obtained in surrounding countries she has formed the fictional Congolese village of Kilanga, center of the novel's narrative circle. The five female voices of this circle, gentle and ungentle by turns, express a range of truths, privileging the philosophical positions of those who live their lives by loving and respecting other people, even those who are so "other" that it may at first seem impossible to find any ground for mutual understanding. The varied angles of view, the varied intellects and spirits, the varied ages and personalities of the narrative voices give *The Poisonwood Bible* its vital depth, enhance its historical quality, and provide a high level of tellability, that quality that makes a tale well worth sharing.

Note

1. For those interested in comparing Kingsolver's work to that of Chinua Achebe, Jonathan Cott's 1981 interview in *Parabola*, reprinted in Bernth Lindfors' *Conversations with Chinua Achebe* (UP of Mississippi, 1997), provides biographical and personal information. Achebe's information sources are interestingly similar to Kingsolver's, in that Achebe describes how he has based much of his writing on stories told to him by the women of his family as well as on folk tales, legends, jokes, riddles and proverbs (76).

Works Cited

Bakhtin, M. M. *The Dialogic Imagination: Four Essays*. Ed. Michael Holquist, Transl. Caryl Emerson and Michael Holquist. Austin: U of Texas P, 2002.

Bal, Mieke. *Narratology: Introduction to the Theory of Narrative*, 2nd Edition. Toronto: U of Toronto P, 1997.

Cave, Marianne. "Bakhtin and Feminism: The Chronotopic Female Imagination." *Women's Studies* 18 (1990), 117-127.

Curry, Renee. "'I Ain't No Friggin' Little Wimp'—the Girl 'I' Narrator in Contemporary Fiction." In *The Girl: Constructions of the Girl in Contemporary Fiction by Women*. Ed. Ruth O. Saxton. New York: St. Martin's Press, 1998. 95-105.

DeMarr, Mary Jean. *Barbara Kingsolver: A Critical Companion*. Westport, CT: Greenwood Press, 1999.

Demory, Pamela H. "Into the Heart of Light: Barbara Kingsolver rereads *Heart of Darkness*." *Conradiana Lubbock* 34.3 (2002): 181-193.

Epstein, Robin. "Barbara Kingsolver." *The Progressive* 60.2 (1996), 33-37.

Fisher, Walter R. "Narration as a Human Communication Paradigm: The Case of Public Moral Argument." *Communication Monographs* 51 (March 1984).

Fludernik, Monika. *Towards a 'Natural' Narratology*. New York: Routledge, 1996.

Foss, Sonja K., & Griffin, Cindy L. "Beyond Persuasion: A Proposal for an Invitational Rhetoric." *Communication Monographs* 62 (March 1995).

Fox, Stephen D. "Barbara Kingsolver and Keri Hulme: Disability, Family, and Culture." *Critique* 45.4 (2004), 1 Feb 2005. http://proquest.umi.com/pdqweb?did_682680121&Fmt=3&clientId=30327&RQT=30d&Vname=PQD.

Genette, Gérard. *Narrative Discourse Revisited*. Transl. Jane E. Lewin. Ithaca, NY: Cornell UP, 1988.

Hardy, Barbara. *Tellers and Listeners: The Narrative Imagination*. London: Athlone Press, 1975.

Jacobson, Kristin J. "The Neodomestic American Novel: The Politics of Home in Barbara Kingsolver's *The Poisonwood Bible*." *Tulsa Studies in Women's Literature* 24.1 (Spring 2005): 105-127.

Kingsolver, Barbara. "FAQ Answers." *Kingsolver Webpage*. HarperCollins 2003. 22 February 2005. http://www.Kingsolver.com/faq/answers.asp#question11.

_____. *Holding the Line: Women in the Great Arizona Mine Strike of 1983*. Ithaca, NY: Cornell ILR Press, 1989.

_____. *Address to the 1993 American Booksellers Convention*. Accessed 5 June 2006 via: http://www.readinggroupguides.com/guides/animal_dreams-author.asp.

_____. *The Poisonwood Bible*. New York: HarperCollins, 1998.

Koza, Kimberly, A. "The Africa of Two Western Women Writers: Barbara Kingsolver and Margaret Laurence." *Critique* 44.3 (2003), 19 Feb 2005. http://search.epnet.com/direct.asp?an=99108066&db=aph.

Kundera, Milan. *The Art of the Novel*. New York: HarperCollins, 2000.

Kunz, Diane. "White Men in Africa: On Barbara Kingsolver's *The Poisonwood Bi-*

ble." In *Novel History.* Ed. Mark C. Carnes. New York: Simon and Schuster, 2001. 285-297.

Messent, Peter. *New Readings of the American Novel: Narrative Theory and Its Application.* Tuscaloosa: U of Alabama P, 1998.

"Messing with the Sacred: An Interview with Barbara Kingsolver." Dir. Guy Mendes, KET, the Kentucky Network, 1997. Transcript: *Appalachian Journal* Spring 2001: 304-324.

Nünning, Ansgar. "Where Historiographic Metafiction and Narratology Meet: Towards an Applied Cultural Narratology." *Style* 38.3 (Fall 2004): 352-403.

Ognibene, Elaine R. "The Missionary Position: Barbara Kingsolver's *The Poisonwood Bible.*" *College Literature* 30.3 (2003): 19-36.

Riley, Jeannette E.; Torrens, Kathleen M.; & Krumholz, Susan T. "Contemporary Feminist Writers: Envisioning a Just World." *Contemporary Justice Review* 8.1 (March 2005): 91-106.

Wagner-Martin, Linda. *Great Writers: Barbara Kingsolver.* Philadelphia: Chelsea House Publishers, 2004.

Barbara Kingsolver and Keri Hulme:
Disability, Family, and Culture_____

Stephen D. Fox

Beginning with a description of the emerging field of literary disability studies, Stephen D. Fox looks at *The Poisonwood Bible* alongside New Zealand author Keri Hulme's widely read novel *The Bone
People*. Using a comparatist approach and invoking earlier texts that
thematize disability, Fox uncovers how Hulme and Kingsolver transform the patterns of writing about disability from a merely exploitative practice toward a practice that grants disabled characters complex subjectivity and agency. Fox sees Kingsolver's portrayal of Adah
and her transformative changes in Africa as part of the author's larger
social and political agenda, yet he also offers a substantiated critique
of Kingsolver's probably romanticized portrayal of African culture in
its relation to disability. By examining disability in a postcolonial context, both Kingsolver and Hulme suggest the extent to which the reception of disability is socially constructed.   — T.A.

Two recent popular novels, Barbara Kingsolver's *The Poisonwood
Bible* and Keri Hulme's *The Bone People*, explore postcolonial situations—in Africa and in New Zealand—and present pivotal characters
with disabilities who eventually define the relationships of disability to
each of the two cultures. Although the two novels have different perspectives, each appears to depart from traditional literary representations of disability that have been exploitative and highly limiting. But
do they really break new ground?

Disability studies is an emerging field, still defining its theories and
parameters and borrowing much of its methodology from gender, racial, postcolonial, and queer studies, which often derive from theorists such as Foucault and Derrida, but with an important difference.
Whereas the other studies may overlap—lesbian writing in India could
conceivably be studied by all four of the above methodologies—only

disability studies is universal in its application. Disability is one of the most pervasive markers ("Bodily Criticism," Thomson 284-86). Anyone in any group could be, could have been, or could become a person with a disability, and everyone will experience some form of disability if he or she lives long enough. Yet critics in this new field find that authors have traditionally used, and abused, the concept of disability merely as a literary convenience, a handy metaphor for Otherness or for alternative social disturbance. David T. Mitchell and Sharon L. Snyder argue that alternatives in gender, race, and sexual orientation have often been demonized by marking those groups with physical or intellectual abnormalities. Martha Stoddard Holmes sees nondisabled individuals historically defining themselves as normal by using disability as a universal metaphor for abnormality. That is, if people with disabilities did not exist, nondisabled people would have to invent them. However, the situation for characters with disability differs from other frequently marginalized groups in that they have "a plethora of representations in visual and discursive works. Consequently, disabled people's marginalization has occurred in the midst of a perpetual circulation of their images" (Mitchell and Snyder 6). Although other groups may suffer a lack of literary exposure, people with disabilities get plenty of fictional press, usually of a negative kind.

Not surprisingly, characters in fiction with disabilities almost always are flat and static. Because they most often function as symbols, their perspectives are not developed and are unimportant to the development of the plot. Physical aberration in a literary character is indicative of mental, emotional, social, or spiritual aberration or any combination of those states. Physical difference marks the outsider or the monster, who rages or is isolated and dying inside unseen, for example, Ahab in *Moby-Dick* or the deaf narrator in *The Heart Is a Lonely Hunter.* Dracula and his heirs, including the latest Anne Rice creation, are pigment deficient, dentally freakish, and daylight-challenged—in the best nineteenth-century tradition of the "freak" sideshow.[1] These figures, in literature as in real life, allow nondisabled people to shiver with horror as they congratulate themselves on their own normality. Because of his or her convenient symbolism, a disabled character who is given a full voice and complex personality and subjective perspective is difficult to find.[2]

* * *

Barbara Kingsolver and Keri Hulme, appearing to split from this exploitative tradition, offer realistic, complex disabled characters, not simply metaphors. Kingsolver has a highly politicized agenda in *The Poisonwood Bible*: She critiques European and American imperialist policies toward Africa, oppressive patriarchal attitudes toward women, racial oppression in the American South, and alienating cultural assumptions about disabled people. Nonetheless, she gives us full characterizations and complete subjective experiences. Her characters, including Adah, who is disabled, are not symbolic pawns. They live on their own.

In *The Poisonwood Bible*, Nathan Price, a Southern preacher, drags his wife and four daughters to the Congo to fulfill his messianic visions. He is the only one in the novel not granted a subjective voice. The result is that he appears to be a stock character, a wild-eyed religious fanatic. Eventually his motivation is revealed to be a hellish World War II experience that left him with an overwhelming sense of evil and guilt that now compel him to confront the world and remold it, a prime situation for displaying a series of major and minor oppressions and alienations, through complex flesh-and-blood people.

The overriding theme of alienated "Otherness" and the cultural rejection of it manifests in the issue of disability. Kingsolver is aware of recent scholarship in disability studies,[3] and in *The Poisonwood Bible*, she dramatically uses disability to depict cultural fear of the Other and the necessity of having the Other to define normality. The twin sisters Leah and Adah Price are the novel's examples of physical otherness. Leah's fetus is supposed to have consumed half of the brain of Adah's fetus while the two were still in the womb, thus marking both as abnormal almost from conception. The two children are assumed to be retarded and are treated as such until a sympathetic educator discovers that, on the contrary, both are geniuses. Adah with her half-brain has an extraordinary talent for languages, one quirk of which is a preference for creating, thinking, and writing in palindromes. Suspension of disbelief is strained here because medical opinion finds the coupling of hemiplegia with high-end intelligence to be extremely unlikely.[4] Kingsolver may be stretching probability, but she has a point to make. The pendulum in the story swings the other way, and the two are still seen as freaks, now for being too smart. The irony of their situation foregrounds the fact that retardation and genius are not simply facts of nature or of medical opinion, but are culturally defined. Society uses the extremes, the nonaverages, to define what is to be called normal. Suspicion of the disabled and the superabled provides an opposing cohesion that unifies the majority as standard. Unity comes from exclusion so society must mark some individuals for exclusion. Alienation by definition is a requirement for maintaining the social fabric.

Adah is also electively mute. She chooses not to speak because she accepts her role as outsider. That is, she will not communicate with a society that does not see her as a person. Later, when she chooses her own path in life (college and medical school), instead of acquiescing to social definition, she achieves selfhood and begins to talk. She discovers that her extreme lameness had been only a cultural marking, an unconscious manifestation of her acceptance of her social monstrosity. She begins to walk almost normally.

Her family also marks her. Like all the female Prices, her wishes count as nothing against the monomania of her father, who is so obsessive and unrelenting that, against the advice of the villagers, he refuses to stop pulling up Poisonwood shrubs even when their sap causes his skin to erupt painfully. He must impose his will on nature and on humankind, no matter what the consequences. In fact, his insistent imposition of his will puts both the villagers and the women in his family in the position of the colonially oppressed. In the terms of postcolonial scholarship, Nathan Price is the "dominant discourse":

> The dominant discourse constructs Otherness in such a way that it always contains a trace of ambivalence or anxiety about its own authority. In order to maintain authority over the Other in a colonial situation, imperial discourse strives to delineate the other as radically different from the self [. . .]. The other can, of course, only be constructed out of the archive of "the self," yet the self must also articulate the other as inescapably different. [. . .] Of course, what such authority least likes, and what presents it with its greatest threat, is any reminder of such ambivalence. (Ashcroft, Griffiths, and Tiffin, *Empire* 103)

Even Adah's mother Orleanna, faced with having to decide which child to save during a devastating invasion of army ants, hesitates, then chooses the nondisabled child, Ruth May, leaving slow-moving Adah to probable death. Adah's family marginalizes her; she is doubly oppressed, as a woman and as a disabled person.

Some feminist critics recommend considering Adah's situation from the perspectives of class and race.[5] Nathan Price comes originally from the lowest level of Southern white society but gains some limited status through becoming a religious figure. He transports his Southern racism to the Congo and, at least in his own mind, translates the African villagers into another social stratum below himself. His attempts to impose his will on the villagers can be seen as efforts to manufacture and sustain his own classist and racial superiority, and from the angles of postcolonial studies and disability studies, he puts his daughters on the same inferior level as the Africans. In Price's hierarchy, African males, American females, and the disabled all occupy a lower social rung. His refusal to have any dealings with village women puts them on an even lower rung. The villagers, however, politely but firmly reject Nathan Price's constant assertions, seeing them as weirdly inappropriate. By their rejections they script their own selfhood and their equality to him. In the face of their assertions, he must continue to demand acquiescence or lose all pretense of superiority. Cora Kaplan notes the coordination in fiction and politics of feminine degradation with the oppression also of working classes and colonized cultures:

> The unfavourable symbiosis of reason and passion ascribed to women is also used to characterize both men and women in the labouring classes and in other races and cultures. [. . .] Through that chain of colonial associations, whole cultures became "feminized," "blackened" and "impoverished"— each denigrating construction implying and invoking the others. (602)

Price's extreme obsession, which leads eventually to his abandoning his family, to insanity or at least insane behavior, and death, is the outcome of his desperate need to maintain his social, gendered, and nationalistic supremacy.

Fortunately, Adah slowly becomes aware that the African society would, on the contrary, not close the option of family to her: "I did know that many women in Kilanga were more seriously disfigured and had husbands notwithstanding" (*Poisonwood* 72). African culture, specifically the Congo's, liberates Adah and most of the Price women. The name "Price" is itself tempting: is it the price they pay as women, or the price—the death of youngest daughter Ruth May by snake bite, the self-destruction of their father—that Africa demands for freeing the others from their cultural chains? Rural Georgians see Adah, whether retarded or genius, as an atypical horror and reject her, and her physical difference identifies her alien nature. But in the Congo Adah finds that disability, in a sense, does not exist; it is so prevalent that it is seen as a normal, integrated part of life. Because disability is inevitable, people accept it and get on with their lives, like Mama Mwanza in the hut next door, who continues as an enthusiastic wife and mother despite a lack of legs. It is assumed that given the harshness of this life, everyone will be disabled in some way, sooner or later. Thus, disability is accepted here as alternate ability. Adah is not marked as different, and her inclusion allows her to pursue selfhood when she returns home. This is a refreshing break with the long literary tradition in which the disabled individual remains pitiable because he or she functions as a symbol, not a person and either self-destructs as the abnormal should, or is destroyed by representatives of an enraged normality. True, Kingsolver plays with another stereotypical trap, the rescue by a nondisabled mentor. An older doctor persuades Adah that her lame leg is a psychosomatic reaction to social expectation. This mentor even becomes her lover, summoning up ghosts of other rescuers from *Johnny Belinda* to *Dark Victory* to *The Miracle Worker*. In all of those the caretaker receives most of the credit. However, Kingsolver is aware and astute. She has Adah recognize that no matter how many good intentions both parties have a relationship can never escape the trap of a patronizing pity. Adah drops her doctor-mentor and goes off to live life on her own terms.

We can, of course, regard this plot solution in two ways. The first, implied above, is to see Kingsolver's critique of attitudes toward disability. It is clear that Adah's dysfunctions are completely socially marked. When she redefines herself as unique and worthy, the stigma of her disability vanishes. Just as European and American business and religious interests "colonized" (in the pejorative sense used in postcolonial critical methodology) the Congo—exploiting the country with the justification that its people were Other and inferior—so the cultural perceptions of the nondisabled people of Georgia colonized Adah. They expected a monster; so they created one. Their labels became part of her manifest flesh. In an ironic reversal, it is possible to say that the Congolese culture, by allowing Adah to reinvent herself, recolonizes her by its more appropriate physical expectations. The colonized become the colonizers, to the benefit of all.

It is wise to remember that "for Kingsolver, writing is a form of political activism."[6] As Kingsolver's themes reject traditional cultural attitudes toward the disabled, so her literary structures deconstruct traditional exploitations of disabled characters.

Or do they? It would be possible to argue alternatively that this plot twist is a sellout that allows a relatively happy ending. Worse, we find that the disability never really existed except as a figment. Leslie Fiedler warned that certain kinds of fiction indicate a desire to erase disabled people—either "by kill or by cure"; that stories evoking pity for the handicapped also express "a wish that there were *no* handicapped, that they would all finally go away" (46, emphasis in original). Perhaps Kingsolver has had it both ways. Initially Adah is the weapon for ironizing American cultural attitudes—a useful metaphor once again. Then, after suffering Adah's disability with her for more than four hundred pages, we find our empathy and our growing critique of culture both unceremoniously dumped. We might say that this twist of events is only fair, for now we, as readers, can feel exploited by our own assumptions, just as Adah has always been. I doubt Kingsolver intends anything that devious. What saves the story from betrayal (of its themes or its characters or its readers) is the fully subjective perspective given to Adah throughout. She is a total personality and she evolves. As a person, she evades the role of metaphor because she does not simply erase her disability. Rather, she continues to acknowledge that, although she is no longer silent and limping, her past is still her: "Tall and straight I may appear, but I will always be Ada [the palindromic name that she used to identify her disabled self] inside. A crooked little person trying to tell the truth. The power is in the balance: we are our injuries, as much as we are our successes" (*Poisonwood* 496). Here she offers a poignant recognition that we are all the totality of ourselves, present and past, and in so doing she transcends any suspicious machinations of plot.

That full characterization may help compensate for another regrettable aspect of the story as well. In her portrayal of happy, integrated, fully functioning disabled people in the Congolese village, Kingsolver is debunking one metaphor (the Otherness of disabled people) while promoting another one (the colonial romanticizing of Africa). As James Charlton's study of disability in developing countries indicates, whatever problems that Americans with disabilities may have, the situation is worse elsewhere. A real Mama Mwanza would be treated simultaneously as both pitiful and a pariah, forbidden to marry or work because she would bring bad luck and is an offense to gods and ancestors, economically oppressed and shunned, probably bereft of support services (Charlton 25, 59-60). One African word for "cripple" has even worse connotations than its English equivalent: *chirema* means someone not only with mobility issues but also utterly useless, a complete failure in life (66). The rural nature of the village would make the circumstances not more bucolic as in the novel, but worse in all regards. The sense of oddity as ritual pollution and affront to the gods of natural forces would be even stronger, the shunning by family and tribe more certain and rigid, and practical assistance almost unknown (108).

We must ask if Charlton's sources can reliably speak for all African people with disabilities, and, because, as postcolonial studies point out, the African continent is by no means homogeneous,[7] we must also ask if Charlton's sources can be applied specifically to Kingsolver's Congolese culture. Charlton notes that data about the numbers and situations of individuals with disabilities in the various sectors of the planet Earth are not a problem; reliable sources such as the United Nations and independent agencies have had accurate numbers "for twenty years." On the other hand, he acknowledges that his study is limited in that it does not describe living conditions of all sectors or all disabilities. Specifically, he chooses to set AIDS aside: politics and difficulties with access have hampered his work. In fact, his African information depends on thorough interviews with numbers of people with disabilities who are also disability rights advocates, specifically in South Africa and Zimbabwe (xv). Clearly such people will emphasize problems, but Charlton's study has credibility nonetheless by constant reference to specific circumstances and facts, not just personal narratives.

The second question is trickier: can information from sources in formerly British South Africa and Zimbabwe be stretched to apply to the formerly Belgian Congo? Actually one of the consulted organizations, the Southern Africa Federation of the Disabled (SAFOD), is transnational and works in many other areas of Africa, including Botswana, Malawi, Mozambique, Namibia, Swaziland, Zambia, and others, albeit apparently not in the Congo. At a conference organized by SAFOD in 1991 in Harare, Zimbabwe, "forty delegates came *from all over Africa* to discuss disability issues" (Charlton 146-47, emphasis added). That fact suggests that individuals with disabilities share a similar fate in the various African cultures. Current African thinking in most regions supports a general emphasis on political and social commitment and a common aesthetic despite local "ideological differences" (Ashcroft, Griffiths, and Tiffin, *Empire* 132).

Given the Africa-wide applicability of Charlton's information, it probably is fair to say that Kingsolver's liberal intentions have created an African utopia for disability similar to how Europeans in earlier centuries fancied a New World El Dorado inhabited by Noble Savages. As a writer in the New World giving readers a romantic Africa where people are naturally compassionate and tolerant, Kingsolver has now partially reversed the earlier process. Kingsolver claims not to draw her characters from real life[8] and has said that she does not remember her experience of Africa as a child of seven, in 1963.[9] The villagers she describes in her novel seem quite generalized, almost completely lacking in noteworthy or unique customs. For example, the issue of which African language they use never arises. Her credits at the end of the novel (perhaps intended to add political ballast to the story) include Nigerian fiction about the Ibo and Igbo people (Chinua Achebe's *Things Fall Apart*), Conrad's nineteenth-century *Heart of Darkness* (ostensibly about the Congo), other books on the Congo, as well as works on snakes in Southern Africa, ritual and magic from all over Africa, birds in east Africa, and folk tales from the entire continent. She also professes to have relied on friends' reports and on her own travel in other parts of Africa, but not in the Congo/Zaire (author's note ix-x). Clearly, although the history and politics in the story are Congolese, the indigenous people are (intentionally or by lack of information) generically sub-Saharan pan-African. Only the specifics about some rather vicious flora and fauna (crocodiles, Poisonwood, army ants, asps) makes them African at all. Because of this fogging of ethnicity, applying Charlton's information about individuals with disabilities seems as reasonable for Kingsolver's villagers as for any real-life African group.

In addition, unfortunately for Kingsolver, the task of portraying the feelings of real African village women may be, according to feminist critics such as Cora Kaplan, impossible from the beginning:

> The subjectivity of women of other classes and races and with different sexual orientations can never be "objectively" or "authentically" represented in literary texts by the white, heterosexual, middle-class woman writer, however sympathetically she invents or describes such women in her narrative. (602)

This criticism seems all too applicable to *The Poisonwood Bible*, as Kingsolver has projected a fantasy of her own libertarian ideals onto Mama Mwanza. Indeed, it might be fair to say that Mama Mwanza (and the fingerless Tata Zinsana, the goitered Mama Nguza, and others) reveal more about Kingsolver's own liberal, middle-class desire for political intervention than about the true situation of rural, disabled Congolese.

The result in the novel is a mixed success. Kingsolver is able to humanize metaphors that elsewhere exploit people with disabilities, but she trades them for romantic (and romantic Marxian) metaphors about Africans. In the process she does a grave disservice to individuals with disability in developing countries by minimizing their actual plights.[10] Is Kingsolver, in effect, establishing a Western humanistic ideal as a universal norm and then, after deriding its absence in the West, projecting it imperialistically onto African peoples? The entire process of colonial imposition required just such a sleight of hand as the one made by Kingsolver, involving a "naturalizing of constructed values" on "the unconscious level" that, instead of promoting the values of the colonized, actually makes them "peripheral" or "marginal" (Ashcroft, Griffiths, and Tiffin, *Empire* 3). Ironically, by idealizing the Congolese in her pursuit of particular humanistic goals, Kingsolver erases those people's true natures and actual needs.

* * *

The Bone People also has family and cultural concerns, but Keri Hulme goes far beyond those concerns to an infusion of culturally appropriate mythic spirituality. For Maoris, family is culture is cosmic spirituality, in a series of widening vibrations (Te Awekotuku 49). The three areas are not distinguishable or separable, and the link is intergenerational as well. A Maori cut off from his or her family, as are all three main characters in the story, becomes ontologically isolated and a self divided. So the three characters, before they find salvation by fusing into a spiritual and psychological triad, are initially self-destructive. Kerewin extrudes horrific art that ingests the light like her Suneater or pours forth as nightmare images on paper. Joe reels under the impact of incessant drinking, his sense of his lost wife, and a constant teetering on the edge of violence. Simon, orphaned by storm and shipwreck and adopted by Joe, insists on his elective muteness and rebelliousness. In addition to their individual angst, the three form a dysfunctional family that is physically abusive, a parody of father-mother-child relationship. Joe regularly beats Simon and tries to beat Kerewin, who, to her horror, is eventually provoked into beating Simon. On one occasion, she thoroughly beats Joe as well, and Simon deliberately provokes the beatings. As a negative triad, they are a study in self-hate and mutual flagellation.

As the two try unsuccessfully to merge, they also manifest the divided culture, the disturbed coexistence of colonial European (*Pakeha*) societies with Maori ones. Kerewin is genetically and culturally half and half, Joe is almost completely Maori, and Simon is European, perhaps even Scottish nobility. The violence and alcoholism are seen as outgrowths of their mutual loss of roots, of having lost a source that they have not replaced. All the major characters in the novel, not just Simon, find verbal communication unacceptable or insufficient, preferring instead visual art, drunkenness, silence, and extreme physical action. Reaching across the boundaries between people requires an effort too strenuous to be borne by mere words. Hulme's rhetoric is a fractured pastiche of half-thoughts and flash descriptions, which befits the splintered relationships.[11] The characters' individual, familial, and cultural lives are negative because each of them lacks the spiritual infusion necessary for unity and growth, a unity that they eventually achieve after much suffering and mythic revelation. Hulme indicates that the violence, especially Joe's, represents misdirected energy and aggressiveness now split apart from the "strongly hierarchical, strongly spiritual system" of the traditional Maori family:

> Once a rural and tribal people, Maoris have now become urban and divided into very small family groups. [. . .] In the cities, you are cut off from the life of the land, the sea, your family marae, from your ancestral roots. (Hulme, "Maori" 293)

Reestablished convergence with "'the spiritual world,' or numinous world, which all of us are part of whether we will or not" is what Hulme hopes will reconcile Maori and Pakeha societies and render the violence obsolete (Hulme and Turcotte 140, 153).

The three characters eventually solve their problem, and Simon, the child with a disability, is the pivot. Disability here is a spiritual as well as a cultural wound. Simon has a special secret ability to see human auras, those natural spiritual energies that emanate from each individual but which partake of the whole of nature. At one point he tries to explain this talent to Kerewin:

ON PEOPLE? scratching his head with the pencil, frown still in place, writing again finally, ON PEOPLE.

"I don't see anything on people. Do you?"

He nods wearily. Then he keeps his head bent, apparently unwilling to look at her.

Kerewin's turn to frown.

What the hell would you see on people in the dark. Shadows in the daytime, yeah, but at night?

It's the word shadows that gives her the answer.

"Wait a minute . . . Sim, do you see lights on people?"

Head up fast, and his bright smile flowering. O Yes.

[. . .]

In the library, the books spread round them,

"Well, that's what they are. Soul-shadows. Coronas. Auras. Very few people can see them without using screens or Kirlian photography." [. . .]

He touches by her eyes.

"No, I can't see them. I'll bet Joe can't either."

Right, says the boy, grinning wolfishly. He writes quickly, SCARED SAID NOT TO SAY. (*Bone People* 93)

Thus Simon is marked not as a disabled mutant (although the local town folk see him as that) but as a young shaman, of European origin but in touch with the islands' energy and spirit. He does not communicate through speech because the situation is skewed and people are incapable of understanding each other. In such negative circumstances, violence is the only viable communication, people can only contact each other physically; and Simon is the self-appointed lightning rod for that violence. Forbidden to tell of his ability to see the souls of others, violence is his way of "speaking" and of allowing others also to "speak" through their violence toward him. His "disability" becomes a bridge between the two adults and between the two cultures. Simon is completely conscious of using violence for mediation. He chooses this role and becomes the agent that creates a new, united community to replace the fragmented old one:

> All morning the feeling had grown, start a fight and stop the illwill between his father and Kerewin. Get rid of the anger round the woman, stop the rift with blows, with pain, then pity, then repair, then good humour again. It works that way . . . it always did. There isn't much time left for anything to grow anymore. It must be in this place or the break will come, and nothing will grow anymore.
>
> So start a fight. (192)

Simon is sensitive to the precise status of the relationship, to its fractures and fault lines, and he knows just when to apply the ameliorating explosion.

Kerewin and Joe are first aware of each other in a bar. Joe is drunk and loud; Kerewin feels contempt for him, and they do not make contact. The two are brought together only when Simon invades Kerewin's isolated tower home, forcing Joe to come for him. Simon continues to be the agent that propels them out of their shells and into each other's lives. Like Kingsolver's Adah, Simon is supernormal and would generate fear in both cultural communities if knowledge of his talent were to be widespread. He must reach people, not through his divine gifts, which they would reject, but through physical action, the only means they are able to understand and to accept.

All the major characters in the novel are disabled in the sense that they are emotionally and psychologically crippled. Literally, the eponymous "bone people" are the displaced bones of the Maori ancestors, but more generally they signify all the displaced people "orphaned" by family schism (Tawake 330). Additionally the "bone people" can denote the totemic *wairua* in the story: the mystical disfigured person Kerewin encounters; the old man, Tiaki Mira, who helps Joe; and Simon himself (Hulme and Turcotte 142). Because everyone has a *wairua*—"an unseen double, a soul-shadow, your own spirit"—these figures can be seen as extensions or doubles of Kerewin and Joe (Hulme, "Myth" 33). And everyone's invisible soul doubles, the auras, are seen as well, by Simon.

Thus Hulme seems to agree with the perspective of the African villagers in *The Poisonwood Bible* that sees disability not as sinister Other but as something positive. Both books direct attention to postcolonial situations and attitudes, and both seem to posit non-Western spiritualities, a cultural oneness with the land, as a rebuttal to Western fragmentation and compartmentalization. The village of Kilanga has a solid culture that both accepts and respects the laws of the surrounding jungle. The spiritual beliefs of the villagers accord with the natural forces around them. Nathan Price with his strict Christian fundamentalism is utterly at odds with those forces. His insistence, against local advice, on growing Western vegetables by Western farming methods leads only to humiliating failure. Perhaps the best example of his being at odds with African natural forces is his demand that all children be baptized in the local river, ignoring the very real problem of crocodiles. That idea is politely but firmly rebuffed, and the credibility of his Western god declines still further.

Adah's empathy for the truths of the village enables her to free herself of injurious Western definitions: "In the way of the body and other people's judgment I enjoy a benign approval in Kilanga that I have never, ever known in Bethlehem, Georgia" (*Poisonwood* 72). Later she adds, "In that other long-ago place, America, I was a failed combination of too-weak body and overstrong will. But in Congo I am those things perfectly united: *Adah*." Disability is natural—literally part of the spirit of nature. Adah is normal because her essence transcends her body:

> The Bantu speak of "self" as a vision residing inside, peering out through the eyeholes of the body, waiting for whatever happens next. Using the body as a mask, *muntu* [self] watches and waits without fear, because *muntu* itself cannot die. The transition from spirit to body and back to spirit again is merely a venture. (343)

These comments late in the book corroborate what her mother Orleanna had said to Nathan early after their arrival in Kilanga about the prevalence of disability among the villagers:

> Father said, "They are living in darkness. Broken in body and soul, and don't even see how they could be healed."
> Mama said, "Well, maybe they take a different view of their bodies."
> Father says the body is the temple. [. . .]
> She took the pins out and said to him, "Well, here in Africa that temple has to do a hateful lot of work in a day." She said, "Why, Nathan, here they have to use their bodies like we use *things* at home—like your clothes or your garden tools or something. Where you'd be wearing out the knees of your trousers, sir, they just have to go ahead and wear out their *knees*!" (53, emphasis in original)

Georgia Christians wrote shame onto Adah's existence: "Recently it has been decided, grudgingly, that dark skin or lameness may not be entirely one's *fault*, but one still ought to show the good manners to act ashamed" (493, emphasis in original). The alternative African mystic vision of the eternal self beyond temporary physical aberration "abled" Adah.

Similarly in *The Bone People*, Kerewin and Joe move out of isolation—and the self-destructive behavior that goes with it—only after near-death visions that are accepted by the text as mystic. Kerewin's cancer goes away when she sequesters herself in a natural retreat appropriately owned by her estranged family, and Joe's vision of the underground water prepares them to join the Triad with Simon. They become the triple-headed figurine, created in a fire by Kerewin, with their three faces and hair entwined. The three people are shriven in preparation for rebirth: Kerewin's cancer is a diseased, false pregnancy that will be replaced by a true son, Simon, who is also the "sun child" who replaces the destructive Suneater, her artistic monstrosity. Joe must survive a belly wound, making him a kind of Fisher King whose renewal will be tied to that of the land itself. And Simon must transcend a near-fatal beating.

The Maori see themselves as one with the land, and, until the British arrived, they had no concept of land as commodity, as something to be owned:

> Papatuanuku is the Earth Mother, combining all elements of the planet; her immediate form is *whenua*, the land. Continuing the organic metaphor, *whenua* is also the Maori word for the placenta, which is promptly buried with simple ritual after birth. The practice is still observed today, even in cities; thus the word itself reflects the relationship between people and the land [. . .]. (Te Awekotuku 33)

Each character must reunite with the land before he or she can merge again with family and society, for "the Maori relationship to the land is intense" and "everything growing or moving on the land [. . .] has a relationship with humanity" (Hulme, "Maori" 302-04).

It is appropriate that when she goes into retreat and cures herself Kerewin leaves the Triad sculpture buried in embers and takes a small bag of earth from near her tower. Her connection with the Earth Mother and with the concept of home will go with her, as the Triad is baked in what is both a funeral pyre and a phoenix's rebirth. Hulme's emphasis on place also suggests the general privileging of space over time noted by postcolonial scholars:

> Post-colonial literary theory, then, has begun to deal with the problems of transmuting time into space, with the present struggling out of the past, as it attempts to construct a future. [. . .] Place is extremely important in all models, and epistemologies have developed which privilege space over time as the most important ordering concept of reality. (Ashcroft, Griffiths, and Tiffin, *Empire* 36-37)

In the novel, Hulme's awareness of the Maori past evolves into the vision of a syncretic future that encompasses both Maori and European derivations. Because Kerewin considers entering the fire herself, it is both an image of death—the dissolution of self—and of necessary purgation (*Bone People* 330-31). In fact, transformations occur for a number of properties connected with the three characters. All three have haircuts, and because hair is one of the oldest symbols of the life force, the loss of their hair suggests the shriving of their old lives. Meanwhile, the painful fishhook in Simon's thumb is supplanted by the jade hook Joe gives Kerewin, said by Kerewin to be set into her heart. A braid from Simon's hair is attached to the jade ("greenstone"), which is the color of his eyes and a substance the Maoris consider mystical (Hulme, "Maori" 307). Clearly Simon is marked as transcendent.

After Kerewin returns, she destroys the tower in which she had lived in isolation and constructs instead a spiral house along the lines of the chambered nautilus. Here the shellfish theme that recurs in the novel is a superb symbol of inclusion. The concept of family in the larger Maori sense is thereby fulfilled: Kerewin is reconciled to her own family on all levels, from a nuclear family of parents and child to her whole tribe and to humanity and the entire Earth. Individual selves are preserved within the separate chambers, all within the unity of the society in accord with the natural, spiritual realm, the nautilus.[12] Simon is the agent of this fruitful evolution, which unfortunately puts him squarely in the tradition that views people with disabilities in the other extreme, as links with the divine. Again, the norm is defined by contrast with the abnormal, only in *The Bone People*, it is the supernormal. Therefore, Hulme's treatment of disability is problematic, as is Kingsolver's. Treating difference as heroic or mystical is in keeping with Maori beliefs as well as with those of many other peoples (for example, the Yoruba of Nigeria). But that treatment has the unfortunate side effect of placing people with disabilities above others and hence regarded as separate and abnormal. Hulme, like Kingsolver, allows her character with disability to emerge as a fully complex individual with a personal perspective on events and an evolution of self. These characters are saved from the traditional literary exploitation, but only by the implementation of yet another traditional metaphor, the disability as divinely linked. This problem with disability may be countered, however, by postcolonial benefits; Hulme is privileging precolonial beliefs and so subverting the European domination of her people.

In the process of this unification, Hulme also creates bridges across lines of class, race, and gender. The three main characters represent the three social strata: European aristocracy (Simon, probably of Scottish nobility), New Zealand middle class (Kerewin, who is educated, has traveled and has studied martial arts), and New Zealand working class (Joe). At the same time those three represent the two races, Pakeha and Maori (Simon and Joe) and the hybridization of the two (Kerewin, who at the close of the novel is also the fulcrum for the hybridization of all cultures and personalities in the new nautilus structure). Finally Kerewin completely subverts Joe's attempts at male domination, both physically and emotionally, attaining gender equality. The resulting synthesis is sweeping, encompassing all perspectives.

Hulme is in an excellent position to rescript the cultural concept of disability and other Western perspectives. As residents of a "settler colony," the Maori are "doubly marginalized,"

> pushed to the psychic and political edge of societies [. . . they] have experienced the dilemma of colonial alienation. For this reason they demonstrate a capacity, far greater than that of white settler societies, to subvert received assumptions about literature [. . .]. (Ashcroft, Griffiths, and Tiffin, *Empire* 144)

We might add, "assumptions" about culture in general. Thus Hulme's hybridized, syncretic cultural solution is typical of the literature from her kind of postcolonial situation: "This is a strategy of subversion and appropriation" (Ashcroft, Griffiths, and Tiffin, *Empire* 154). In this case, disability provides the means.

Thus, Barbara Kingsolver and Keri Hulme are proceeding toward inclusiveness. Their novels reject past Western concepts of disability as their writings move beyond the traditional literary use of disabled figures as metaphors by which to define normal society. Adah and Simon are representational—symbolic, if you like—but no more so than other major characters. Their human complexity is as deeply portrayed as that of the nondisabled characters; they are allowed their own subjective viewpoints and development. Regrettably, Kingsolver romanticizes African disability; and, much more understandably given Maori tradition, Hulme associates disability with mysticism. Both attitudes are distortions. In sum, the portrayal of disability in the two novels may not be entirely naturalistic, but it displays a fullness and respect for the characters with disability not traditionally found in literature.

Notes

This study began as a project under Dr. Paul Longmore at the National Endowment of the Humanities Summer Institute on Disability Studies, San Francisco State University, July-August 2000.

1. On the significance of freak shows, see Thomson, *Extraordinary Bodies* 284-86.

2. Mitchell and Snyder, *Narrative*; Lennard Davis, *Enforcing Normalcy* (London and NY: Verso, 1995); Thomas G. Couser, *Recovering Bodies: Illness, Disability, and Life Writing* (Madison: U of Wisconsin P, 1997).

3. Barbara Kingsolver, letter to the author, 27 Sept. 2000.

4. Sander Gilman, e-mail to the author, 9 Jan. 2001. See Kaplan 593-94. See a summary of other such feminist critics in Ashcroft, Griffiths, and Tiffin, *Empire* 175-76.

5. See Kaplan 593-94. See a summary of other such feminist critics in Ashcroft, Griffiths, and Tiffin, *Empire* 175-76.

6. Barbara Kingsolver. *About Barbara*. HarperCollins Publisher. 28 Aug. 2001, http://www.Kingsolver.com.

7. For example, Ashcroft, Griffiths, and Tiffin, "Introduction: Issues and Debates" and "Introduction: Language" and Aijaz Ahmad, "Jameson's Rhetoric of Otherness and the 'National Allegory,'" in Ashcroft, Griffiths, and Tiffin, *Post-Colonial* 2, 283, 77-82. See also Ashcroft, Griffiths, and Tiffin, *Empire* 3: "While the idea of an 'African' literature, for instance, has a powerful appeal to writers and critics in the various

African countries, it has only limited application as a descriptive label. African and European critics have produced several regional and nation studies which reflect the widespread political, economic, and cultural differences between modern African countries."

8. Barbara Kingsolver. *About Barbara*. HarperCollins Publisher. 28 Aug. 2001, http://www.Kingsolver.com. Also Kingsolver, author's note, *Poisonwood* ix.

9. "Barbara Kingsolver," interview and biography, producer Guy Mendes, Signature Series on Contemporary Southern Writers, Annenberg/CPB Project 203, 15 May 1997.

10. Kingsolver performs a similar enhancement on the American Indian families in *Pigs in Heaven* (New York: HarperCollins, 1993), in which the family structure is depicted as outrageously flawless in terms of unity, love, caring, tradition, and spirituality. Doubtless there is a certain core of truth in these portraits, but Kingsolver loses credibility by her extreme idealization of these groups and ultimately does them no favor.

11. The psychological and emotional suggestiveness of this style also subverts the imperial English by the consistent intrusion of glossed or untranslated Maori terms, thus creating an "English" that recognizes the usefulness of the colonial tongue yet amalgamates a localized hybrid uniquely suitable to New Zealand. The reader, thereby, is confronted with a gap between the old colonial center and the present postcolonial nation and at the same time provided with a bridge over that gap. For a discussion of this kind of subversion and appropriation of English into "English," see Ashcroft, Griffiths, and Tiffin, *Empire* 62-65.

12. This healing process seems to be a vision not only in Hulme's work but also in some modern Maori literature (see Murray S. Martin, "Forging an Identity: The New Zealand Literary Experience," *ACLA Bulletin* 24.2 [1993]: 79). The healing can begin in Maori novels only when the characters reestablish their links with Earth and family, as for example in Witi Ihimaera's *Tangi*, in which a young Maori man goes home for a funeral and ends by permanently forsaking his Westernized urban success in favor of reunion with the Maori community.

Works Cited

Ashcroft, Bill, Gareth Griffiths, and Helen Tiffin. *The Empire Writes Back*. London: Routledge, 1989.

_____, eds. *The Post-Colonial Studies Reader*. London: Routledge, 1995.

Charlton, James I. *Nothing About Us Without Us: Disability, Oppression, and Empowerment*. Berkeley: U of California P, 1998.

Fiedler, Leslie. "Pity and Fear: Images of the Disabled in Literature and the Popular Arts." *Tyranny of the Normal: Essays on Bioethics*. Boston: Godine, 1996. 33-47.

Holmes, Martha Stoddard. "Wasted Tears and Wasted Objects: Disability and Affect." *How We Feel About Our Bodies*. Roundtable Discussion, MLA Convention, Marriott Hotel, Washington, DC, 29 Dec. 2000.

Hulme, Keri. *The Bone People*. Baton Rouge: Louisiana State UP, 1985.

_____. "Maori: An Introduction to Bicultural Poetry in New Zealand." *Only Connect*. Ed. Guy Amirthanayagam and S. C. Harrex. Adelaide and Honolulu: Centre for Research in the New Literatures in English and East-West Centre, 1981. 290-310.

_____. "Myth, Omen, Ghost, and Dream." *Poetry of the Pacific Region: Proceedings of the CRNLE/SPACLALS Conference*. Ed. Paul Sharrad. Adelaide: Centre for Research, 1984. 31-38.

Hulme, Keri, and Gerry Turcotte. "Reconsidering *The Bone People*." *Australian and New Zealand Studies in Canada* 12, Writer's Choice Series. Sydney, Australia: U of Sydney P, 1 Aug. 1989. 135-54.

Kaplan, Cora. "Pandora's Box: Subjectivity, Class, and Sexuality in Socialist Feminist Criticism." *Contemporary Literary Criticism: Literary and Cultural Studies*. Ed. Ronald Schleifer. New York: Longman, 1998. 593-610.

Kingsolver, Barbara. *The Poisonwood Bible*. New York: HarperPerennial, 1999.

Mitchell, David T., and Sharon L. Snyder. "Introduction: Disability Studies and the Double Bind of Representation." *The Body and Physical Difference: Discourses of Disability*. Ed. David T. Mitchell and Sharon L. Snyder. Ann Arbor: U of Michigan P, 1997. 1-31.

_____. *Narrative Prosthesis: Disability and the Dependencies of Discourse*. Ann Arbor: U of Michigan P, 2000.

Tawake, Sandra Kiser. "Reading *The Bone People*—Cross-Culturally." *World Englishes* 12 (1993): 325-33.

Te Awekotuku, Ngahuia. "Maori: People and Culture." *Maori Art and Culture*. Ed. D. C. Starzecka. Chicago: Arts Media Resources, 1996.

Thomson, Rosemarie Garland. "Body Criticism as a Context for Disability Studies." *Disability Studies Quarterly* 17.4 (1997): 284-86.

_____. *Extraordinary Bodies: Figuring Physical Disability in American Culture and Literature*. New York: Columbia UP, 1997.

The Southern Family Farm as Endangered Species:
Possibilities for Survival in Barbara Kingsolver's *Prodigal Summer*_____

Suzanne W. Jones

Suzanne W. Jones examines how two key elements of Kingsolver's biography—her original academic training as a biologist and her family heritage as a child of Appalachia—come together in *Prodigal Summer*. The novel fictionalizes an urgent concern shared by southern environmentalist writers: namely, the need to inculcate the spirit of sustainability into the entire bioregion and its human inhabitants. Jones makes a regional argument by inviting us to see Kingsolver's novel in the company of Kentucky's Wendell Berry and Georgia's Janisse Ray. Yet *Prodigal Summer*'s special force, according to Jones, resides in Kingsolver's having achieved a new literary quality previously unreached in her work and traceable in particular through the novel's controlling metaphors. In this text, published at the turn of the millennium, literary, environmental, and feminist qualities unite as Kingsolver's character Lusa begins to think and farm like a bioregionalist, herself advocating what Jones, following Aldo Leopold, calls an "environmental ethic of care."   — T.A.

In your father's day all the farmers around here were doing fine. Now they have to work night shifts at the Kmart to keep up their mortgages. Why is that? They work just as hard as their parents did, and they're on the same land, so what's wrong?

—Barbara Kingsolver, *Prodigal Summer*

At the same time some southern studies scholars are positioning the U.S. South in a larger cultural, historic, and economic region that encompasses the Caribbean and Latin America, some southern environmentalist writers, such as long-time essayist and novelist Wendell Berry and activist-turned-memoirist Janisse Ray, are finding a pressing need to focus on smaller bioregions and the locatedness of the human subject.[1] These writers believe that agribusiness and consumer ignorance are driving small farmers out of business and that clear-cutting timber and farming practices dependent on chemicals are threatening local ecosystems.[2] Best-selling novelist Barbara Kingsolver has joined their ranks. With her most recent novel *Prodigal Summer* (2000), Kingsolver returns to her home region and her academic roots to explore both the crucial ecological issues that most interest the South's environmentalist writers and some of the transnational questions that currently preoccupy literary critics. Setting her novel in southern Appalachia,[3] where she grew up and where she now owns a cabin, she fictionalizes problems that she has since published impassioned essays[4] about: failing family farms, fragmented communities, ecosystems out of balance, and rural-urban, insider-outsider tensions.

In *Prodigal Summer* Kingsolver's academic training in evolutionary biology and ecology, her abiding concern for community and family, and her intimate knowledge of a particular place combine to produce no less than a blueprint for saving the small family farm and for restoring ecological balance in a southern Appalachian bioregion that is struggling to survive. Kingsolver, who is at the height of her verbal powers in this novel, employs elaborate Darwinian conceits to link human and natural worlds, both to show how they are connected and how they are similar in needing variety to sustain the health of a complex interdependent ecosystem. Near the end of the novel, Kingsolver places an important Darwinian principle in the mouth of the organic apple grower, Nannie Rawley: "There is nothing so important as having variety. That's how life can still go on when the world changes" (390). And the world of southern Appalachia has changed dramatically. The majestic chestnut trees that once provided a livelihood for some and shelter for many have succumbed to an Asian fungal blight, farming can no longer be relied on to support a family, rural people commute long hours to work in factories or to supplement meager farm income, and their children know little about the ecosystem they inhabit.

Kingsolver thinks of place in much the same way as Arif Dirlik, who has argued that to focus on the groundedness of places through ecology and topography is "not to return to some kind of geographic determinism or bounded notion of place" or to posit an "immutable fixity." For Dirlik, place is the "location," "where the social and the natural meet, where the production of nature by the social is not clearly distinguishable from the production of the social by the natural" (18). He argues that "[a] place suggests groundedness from below, and a flexible and porous boundary around it, without closing out the extralocal, all the way to the global" (22). As Darwin pointed out, difference becomes an important resource for survival. In *Prodigal Summer* Kingsolver employs non-native human and animal species to suggest solutions to local economic and ecological problems in southern Appalachia.

At the same time Kingsolver reveals how introducing exotic species into the southern landscape can harm the nonhuman ecosystem, she demonstrates that not all exotics are necessarily invasive—thereby providing biological background for the human social parallel that she sets up. Certainly kudzu, which has no natural enemy in the South, and the Asian fungus that has killed off the American chestnut are damaging, invasive species. But some exotic species, such as Asian daylilies, which escaped from flower gardens, now beautify the roadside without taking over the fields and pastures. Other non-native species such as the Chinese chestnut have been imported on purpose by retired agriculture teacher Garnett Walker because their resistance to fungus may prove beneficial in breeding a blight-resistant American chestnut hybrid. To give one more prominent example, forest ranger and wildlife ecologist Deanna Wolfe does not judge coyotes, which are migrating to southern Appalachia, "invasive" as most readers might expect, because her research shows that coyotes will help restore the imbalance in the ecosystem caused by the loss of larger predators (wolves and mountain lions) in this habitat.[5] With such examples from the natural world, Kingsolver breaks down simplistic oppositions between natives and non-natives, preparing readers to see the beneficial nature of the human exotic that she introduces in the character of Lusa Maluf Landowski, an urban intellectual with ancestral roots in Poland and Palestine and a family religious heritage of Judaism and Islam.

Rural Appalachia is wary of variety but not totally averse to change. Kingsolver ironically points out that southern Appalachia suffers as much because of the agricultural changes farmers have embraced as because of their resistance to change. Insecticides that the local U.S. Agricultural Extension Service has promoted to protect cash crops such as tobacco are harming other crops, killing the beneficial pollinators so necessary to organic orchard growers like Nannie Rawley. The high cost of chemical herbicides and insecticides has driven many farmers out of business, and more than a few inhabitants of the fictional town Egg Fork have succumbed to cancer. Kingsolver suggests that imbalances in the natural environment caused by human ignorance are creating complex environmental problems that few understand. She uses her main female characters—Nannie, Lusa, and Deanna—to teach these lessons, both to her readers and to the locals, emphasizing the need for an environmental ethic of care to bring balance to the ecosystem and prosperity to local farmers.[6]

The Widener family farm is bordering on extinction. The farm can no longer support the extended family because the drop in governmental price supports has diminished tobacco's profitability. But Cole Widener, the only family member willing to experiment with new crops, has not found a legal crop more profitable than tobacco. His experiment with growing such vegetables as cucumbers and bell peppers for an urban population fails because nearby markets are not large enough to make perishable vegetables maturing at the same time an economically viable alternative. When Cole learns of a potato-chip factory in Knoxville, he hopes that potatoes, which store and ship almost as well as tobacco, might become his cash crop, but the variety that grows best in his soil has too much sugar to make good potato chips. So Cole falls back on tobacco, but he must supplement his farm income by hauling grain for the agricultural conglomerate, Southern

States. Wendell Berry would say that Cole's agricultural practices have failed because he has not come up with "good local solutions to local problems" (*Citizenship Papers*, 159). And yet Cole is far from the stereotypical provincial farmer. Hoping to find ways to improve his agricultural practices and thus keep the family farm solvent, he enrolls in a workshop in integrated pest management at the University of Kentucky, which is where he meets Lusa.

Kingsolver shows the importance, indeed the necessity, of human variety in an ecosystem when Lusa takes over the farm after Cole's death in a hauling accident. Because Lusa is a "religious mongrel" (438) with a knowledge of Judaism and Islam that the locals do not possess, she knows that the holy days of these religions will converge during her first year of farming and create a demand for goats, necessary for the religious celebrations. Conscious too of the health risks associated with tobacco, she decides not to plant tobacco but to raise goats and sell them to a cousin in New York. To her surprise and that of the Widener family, she succeeds. And at the same time she provides a good solution to another local problem, for the county is overrun with unwanted goats that the children have raised for a 4-H project.

But this happy ending is neither a final solution to the vicissitudes of small family farms nor a conclusion facilely produced. Following Wendell Berry's rule of thumb, Kingsolver has Lusa recognize that "good" farming practices will always require flexibility, or the "ability to adapt to local conditions and needs."[7] Lusa is not so naïve as to think that goats can become her sole cash crop; she knows that next year "she might raise no goats at all, depending on the calendar" (438). Instead she contemplates growing grass seed to take advantage of the fact that the U.S. government, in trying to rectify an ecological mistake, has begun to pay people to plant native bluestem grasses in place of the previously championed non-native fescue, which has destroyed the habitat of native birds such as the bobwhite. Kingsolver has Lusa think like a bioregionalist, rather than an agri-industrialist, and in so doing highlights current problems in agribusiness practices, which ignore bioregional differences in favor of supposed universal solutions. The novel illustrates how some of the worst so-called "solutions" to agricultural problems, such as the use of broad-spectrum insecticides, have been dispensed by the county Agricultural Extension Service agents with the imprimatur of the U.S. government.

As Martyn Bone has pointed out, Kingsolver's agrarianism is not the subsistence farming praised by the *I'll Take My Stand* Agrarians, nor is Egg Fork's failing agricultural community emblematic of "the pastoral idea of farmers at one with Nature" (246). Bone argues that the farming advocated in this novel "is not just post-Agrarian or even postsouthern: it is transnational" (248). Certainly Bone is right that this novel takes an important transnational turn with Lusa's immigrant background and Nannie Rawley's Mexican migrant apple pickers. Kingsolver's agrarianism does not come with a capital "A." At the same time, however, although Kingsolver's view of present and past farming practices is more complex and nuanced than that of the Agrarians, it shares some characteristics. As she says in her foreword to Norman Wirzba's *The Essential Agrarian Reader*, "the decision to attend to the health of one's habitat and food chain is a spiritual choice. It's also a political choice, a scientific one, a personal and convivial one. It's not a choice between living in the country or the town; it is about understanding that every one of us, at the level of our cells and respiration, lives in the country and is thus obliged to be mindful of the distance between ourselves and our sustenance" (xvii). In *Prodigal Summer* Kingsolver certainly advocates growing subsistence crops along side cash crops. Lusa cans and freezes organic fruits and vegetables from her large garden in order to avoid shopping at Kroger, and she patiently explains to her niece Crys why purchasing less flavorful and healthful foods from a supermarket chain is problematic—they come from who-knows-where and are grown under who-knows-what conditions. The community of Egg Fork has not yet become a transnational space, with big box stores that have made the town's architecture placeless and have driven all the local merchants out of business. Indeed the Amish farmers' market is thriving because of their much sought-after homemade baked goods as well as their pesticide-free produce and that of invited organic growers like Nannie Rawley.

But Kingsolver suggests that the Wideners' dependence on Kroger has diminished the quality of their food and changed the nature of their relationship with the land. Crys and her brother are more closely connected to the worlds they see on television than to their own habitat, a point Kingsolver makes when Crys cannot identify the butterflies that captivate her. This single example cannot support the spiritual and ideological weight that Lusa attributes to it. But Kingsolver clearly shows throughout the novel that not understanding the interconnections between the natural and the human world damages the ecosystem, as Nannie's argument with Garnett about broad-spectrum insecticides and Deanna's argument with western bounty hunter Eddie Bondo about coyotes demonstrate. In other words, although these farmers are not living a pastoral ideal, Kingsolver thinks they could and should be trying, for the good of themselves and their ecosystem.

Thus Barbara Kingsolver's larger point is as much ecological as it is agricultural. She uses principles of ecology to question and to illuminate human behavior, and not just the Widener family's actions but Lusa's own. To survive and prosper, this rural farming community, which has become an endangered species, needs more information about the interconnectedness of their world. At the same time Lusa, whom the locals view as the "outsider," needs to understand the properties of non-native species, like herself, in order to live in happy relation to the natives. If the insiders, like Garnett Walker and the extended Widener family, have identified Lusa as the Other because of her non-Christian background, her bookish ways (she openly reads Darwin for pleasure), her urban roots, and her feminist practices (she does not change her name when she marries), she too has stereotyped and distanced herself from them because of their accent, their rural folkways, and their lack of formal education. This stereotypical response on both sides causes problems in Lusa and Cole's marriage.

Philosopher Norman Wirzba suggests that a world view which has perceived soils, waterways, and forests as "simply resources to feed cultural ambition" has led to "an animosity between the country and the city, each side claiming for itself moral purity or human excellence": "Farming folk have routinely described their way of life as conducive to peace, balance, and simple virtue, and the ways of the city as promoting strife, ambition, and greed. City folk, on the other hand, have considered cities as the entry into sophistication, creativity, and enlightenment, and farms as places of ignorance, provincialism, and limitation" (6). *Prodigal Summer* attempts to deconstruct these simplistic oppositions. Lusa is not simply a "city person" as her husband and his family pigeonhole her, but someone who spent her childhood "trapped on lawn but longing for pasture" and "sprouting seeds in pots on a patio" but "dreaming" of the expansive garden she realizes on the Widener farm (35, 375). Deanna Wolfe was raised on a farm in Egg Fork, but as the local forest ranger she practices what she has learned from her degree in wildlife ecology at the University of Tennessee. When Deanna first gets to know Eddie Bondo, Kingsolver writes, "She was well accustomed to watching Yankee brains grind their gears, attempting to reconcile a hillbilly accent with signs of serious education" (11). Like Eddie, Lusa brings the same prejudices to Zebulon County.

In order to raise goats successfully, Lusa must critically examine her own practices[8] as an aloof and rather condescending urban outsider, who because she has an advanced degree in biology assumes she knows much more than the locals. Kingsolver gives Lusa what Wendell Berry has called the "provincial . . . half-scared, half-witted urban contempt for 'provinciality,'" a contempt for farmers that Kingsolver herself encountered when she left Kentucky.[9] At the beginning of the novel, which opens at the beginning of summer, Lusa fights with Cole about his desire to pull down the fragrant honeysuckle vine crawling up the side of their garage; by the end of the novel and the end of that summer Lusa discovers that he was right to be concerned because the vine has completely devoured the garage. Lusa realizes that honeysuckle, which to her urban sensibility looks lovely and smells heavenly, is in her new rural habitat merely "an invasive exotic, nothing sacred" (440).

Throughout *Prodigal Summer* Kingsolver is at pains to point out that some things in life can be known from experience, without the abstract knowledge of scientific theories. Deanna is proud of the fact that her farmer father, who never went to college, knew as much about the natural world as many of her professors. Cole's knowledge of how invasive honeysuckle is in his environment is another example. Lusa acknowledges the error in her own thinking after his death: "*You have to persuade it two steps back everyday*, he'd said, *or it will move in and take you over*. His instincts about this plant had been right, his eye had known things he'd never been trained to speak of. And yet she'd replied carelessly, *Take over what? The world will not end if you let the honeysuckle have the side of your barn*. She crossed her arms against a shiver of anguish and asked him now to forgive a city person's audacity" (360). In the course of the novel, Lusa must face up to the fact that she has romanticized some aspects of rural life, like the honeysuckle, and underestimated others, such as the difficulty of farming and the knowledge of local farmers.

Before Lusa can even begin to call herself a goat farmer, Kingsolver orchestrates the plot so that she must seek the expertise of Garnett Walker, the retired local agriculture teacher and former 4-H Club leader. Garnett is famous for his attempts to cross-breed a new strain of chestnut that will withstand the blight and infamous for having overseen the 4-H Club project that led to the county-wide goat surplus. By engaging this crusty old loner in her enterprise, Lusa forges links within Egg Fork that have been broken, connecting Garnett with her niece and nephew, Crys and Lowell, who are his grandchildren but whom he does not know. Garnett is estranged from his wayward son, who has divorced the children's mother, Jewel Widener. Such a gradually revealed connection is only one of the many threads that Kingsolver carefully and cleverly uses to knit Lusa's, Garnett's, and

Deanna's lives together and to link their three seemingly separate plot lines.[10] Lusa's successful venture raising goats depends on interdependence in the community and in the family. To help with the day-to-day physical labor, Lusa hires her nephew, Little Rickie.

Before Lusa can be accepted as a member of the community and the family, she must overcome their local bias against raising goats and their rural prejudices against city people and against farm wives operating outside the domestic sphere. Lusa, who had expected to be "a farmer's partner" when she married Cole (42), finds that his family and their neighbors expect otherwise. But Lusa's fiscal success raising goats goes a long way toward elevating her status in the community, no matter her transgressions of the usual gender roles. Lusa proves herself in ecological terms to be more like the Asian daylilies that bloom throughout Appalachia in July than the Japanese honeysuckle that engulfs the barn—she is non-native, but not invasive. Indeed her arrival, like that of the coyotes in the nearby national forest, begins to right an imbalance in the ecosystem. First, Lusa pulls the Widener farm out of debt with her successful goat venture. Then, she promises a loving home to her niece and nephew whose mother is dying of cancer and whose biological aunts do not want the children because they say Crys acts like a boy and Lowell like a girl.

In the final accounting I think Kingsolver succeeds in showing readers that farmers, indeed everyone, need to be more place-conscious. To use Dirlik's terms, Kingsolver shows readers what a "place-based" imagination has to offer. Her ecologically enlightened characters—Deanna, the wildlife ecologist and forest ranger; Nannie, the organic apple grower; and Lusa, the entomologist turned farmer—prosper because they understand both the human and nonhuman ecology of their bioregion.

Kingsolver is less successful in showing how individuals such as Garnett Walker, the Widener sisters, and the western rancher Eddie Bondo can become less "place-bound." Kingsolver resolves the problems Lusa has relating to her sisters-in-law by revealing their misunderstandings to be based more on misconceptions than absolute ideological differences. By having Lusa decide to change her name to Widener, Kingsolver finesses one "place-bound" issue that concerns the family, Lusa's feminism, which she has exhibited by retaining her maiden name. Lusa takes the Widener name when she decides to commit her life to a farm that she knows the locals will always call the Widener place. Her decision to leave the farm to Crys and Lowell means that the Wideners no longer have to worry that the farm will go out of the family (307).

Physical desire, propelled by pheromones, seems to be Kingsolver's rather too-easy, though biologically explicable, way of bringing ideologically different humans together to debate crucial issues—from Lusa and Cole to Deanna and Eddie. But Kingsolver does not suggest that full understanding, much less an ideological change, necessarily follows dialogue, even if sex is involved. During their short marriage, Lusa and Cole argue daily about the best farming practices and Eddie never buys Deanna's thesis that coyotes breed more prolifically the more they are killed, although he does respect her enough not to hunt coyotes in southern Appalachia. Indeed their relationship ends after he reads her thesis about coyotes. Kingsolver does seem to suggest that physical attraction works best in the ideological conversion of youth. Seventeen-year-old Little Rickie is an easy convert to Lusa's innovative farming practices and an eager listener to her lessons about the world's religions because he is smitten with his beautiful young aunt.

The pairing of Nannie and Garnett is the most unbelievable in the novel. Garnett mellows because of his growing dependence on his spunky seventy-something neighbor, but her Unitarian beliefs, feminist ideals, and organic-farming practices incense him. Garnett, a religious fundamentalist, believes humans have dominion over the earth and so thinks nothing of the consequences of using herbicides to keep his property weed-free and broad-spectrum insecticides to protect his hybrid chestnut seedlings. Garnett is a perfect example of Dirlik's "place-bound" individual: "disguising and suppressing inequalities and oppressions that are internal to place," blaming internal dissension on outside agitators (feminists, Unitarians), and in the face of facts, clinging to fanciful, often faith-based, points of view (Dirlik, 6). Certain he is right, Garnett does not think about how his choices affect others. As a result, he has been at odds with his neighbor Nannie over the needs of her organic orchard (to be free of the insecticides and herbicides he uses in close proximity to her land), and he has withheld from her the discontinued shingles that he has discovered in his barn, which he does not need but which she could use to patch her roof. Despite the heated ideological sparring that goes on between them, Kingsolver wants readers to believe that Nannie's neighborly care for Garnett's health and her frequent appearance in shorts in her orchard combine to spark his physical attraction and a manly desire to protect her. In having Garnett finally decide to give Nannie the shingles, Kingsolver does not go so far as to suggest that their budding friendship will alter their ideological differences about evolution, feminism, or the use of malathion, only that Garnett is becoming less self-centered—a primary step, to be sure, in perceiving one's world ecologically.

Kingsolver's greatest success in this novel is in helping readers to see the human and nonhuman interdependencies in an ecosystem. Kingsolver has said that "this is the most challenging book" she's "ever given" her readers, one whose complexity she believes some reviewers have missed by focusing too much on the humans and not enough on the flora and fauna.[11] Kingsolver understands the tendency of any species to be self-centered and attempts to reach those readers, like Garnett, who persist in anthropocentric thinking. Nannie makes an ironic point by telling Garnett, "I do believe humankind holds a special place in the world. It's the same place held by a mockingbird, in his opinion, and a salamander in whatever he has that resembles a mind of his own. Every creature alive believes this: The center of everything is *me*" (215). The similarity between humans and animals that Kingsolver calls attention to here is repeated in multiple ways throughout the novel.

Prodigal Summer is a metaphor-laden book because Kingsolver is out to change the way readers perceive themselves and their relationship to the natural world. Paul Ricoeur has argued that "a metaphor may be seen as a model for changing our way of looking at things, of perceiving the world. The word 'insight,' very often applied to the *cognitive* import of metaphor, conveys in a very appropriate manner this move from sense to reference" (150). As if to help readers understand the value of metaphor, Kingsolver sets up a situation in which Lusa makes light of the Appalachian people's saying that the "mountains breathe": "she had some respect for the poetry of country people's language, if not for the veracity of their perceptions" (31). After living in the shadow of the mountain and experiencing the air currents, Lusa realizes that their personification is apt: "the inhalations of Zebulon Mountain touched her face all morning, and finally she understood. She learned to tell time with her skin, as morning turned to afternoon and the mountain's breath began to bear gently on the back of her neck. By early evening it was insistent as a lover's sigh, sweetened by the damp woods, cooling her nape and shoulders whenever she paused her work in the kitchen to lift her sweat-damp curls off her neck. She had come to think of Zebulon as another man in her life, larger and steadier than any other companion she had known" (33). In this example, Lusa, the scientist, learns Ricoeur's lesson about metaphor: "poetic language is no less about reality than any other use of language but refers to it by the complex strategy which implies, as an essential component, a suspension and seemingly an abolition of the ordinary reference attached to descriptive language. . . . in another respect, it constitutes the primordial reference to the extent that it suggests, reveals, unconceals—or whatever you say—the deep structures of reality to which we are related as mortals who are born into this world and who *dwell* in it for a while."[12]

The "deep structure" Kingsolver wants to reveal is the complex ecosystem in which humans live but about which they know far too little. In an attempt to disrupt an anthropocentric world view, Kingsolver personifies animals and animalizes people. For example, the coyote pups are "children born empty-headed like human infants," and they live in a "family" (200). The novel concludes with a chapter from a coyote's perspective in which readers experience the acrid odor of crop-dusted farms and the sweet pleasure of Nannie's organic orchard. When the coyote thinks of prey, she does not fixate on Lusa's goats, as Eddie Bondo and some readers might expect, but on squirrels and mice. Similarly, Kingsolver reveals the animalism of humans, both through her metaphors (Eddie marks his "territory" when he urinates off Deanna's porch; Cole's beard is like a "nectar guide" for Lusa's kiss, 26, 38) and the revelation of little known biological facts (women cycle with the moon when exposed to its light, and like female animals they emit a scent when they are fertile). As Lusa points out, smell is a "whole world of love we don't discuss" (237). Through Kingsolver's use of metaphor, she suggests that the natural world could give humans "insight" into their own behavior, and she reminds readers that humans are but one species among many in the world they dwell in. At the same time that Kingsolver gives some animals voices, she does not anthropomorphize animals or romanticize their behavior. For weeks a snake coexists with Deanna and the baby birds she nurtures, preying on the pesky mice in her cabin, only to eat the baby birds at summer's end. At the same time that Kingsolver gives humans animal instincts, she does not strip them of their capacity to reason. The newly widowed Lusa does not have sex with Cole's nephew Little Rickie, despite her powerful attraction to him: "'We're not blood kin,' he argued. 'But we're family,'" she said (416).

Much of the pleasure of this text, which increases on second and third readings, comes from developing an attention to detail and from observing how intricately Kingsolver has connected these details, not just metaphorically but structurally through her braided narratives. Learning to observe and understand interconnections is an important ecological lesson that readers absorb through the novel's form by doing—by actively making unheralded connections—rather than by passively listening to the characters' Rachel Carson-inspired orations about keystone predators, evolution, and broad-spectrum insecticides.[13] Granted these overt lessons emerge organically because Kingsolver's main characters are teachers, but many of the same "lessons" in this novel of lessons about ecology are taught indirectly.

Readers gradually become aware of the human and nonhuman connections among the novel's three seemingly separate but intertwined narratives at the same time that the characters make them aware of interconnections in the southern Appalachian bioregion. In the human world, these connections range from the serendipitous to the poignant. The stained green brocade armchair on Deanna's porch was one of a matched pair once in the Widener family's living room; its mate, still in the Widener farmhouse but moved to the bedroom, has become Lusa's favorite reading chair. Garnett's grandfather felled the huge hollowed out chestnut that serves as Deanna's home away from home in the woods. The old woman who gives Lusa such sage advice at Cole's funeral is Nannie Rawley. Lusa longs for a friend who shares her views, and readers come to see what Lusa does not know by novel's end, that among the locals, whom she has stereotyped as environmentally ignorant, are two women who share her knowledge of and passion for ecology, Deanna and Nannie. As regards the non-human world, for example, by novel's end readers have pieced together information from the three separate narratives to learn that pesky cockleburs abound not because God has made "one mistake in Creation" (213), as Garnett suggests, but because the Carolina parakeets that once ate them are now extinct. However, Kingsolver shows that an ecological imbalance may be corrected. Coyotes are taking the place of the extinct red wolves, Magnolia warblers have returned to the Zebulon National Forest now that their habitat has been protected from clear cutting, bobwhites are also coming back, perhaps as Deanna suggests because of the passages the coyotes are opening in the tight clumps of fescue, and Nannie Rawley's organic orchard is "the best producing orchard in five counties" (420). In *Prodigal Summer* Kingsolver demonstrates that both the survival of the Widener farm and the well-being of the southern Appa-

lachian ecosystem depend on understanding the complex interconnections between human and nonhuman worlds, between natives and
newcomers, between the local and the global.

From *Southern Literary Journal* 39, no. 1 (2006): 83-97. Copyright © 2006 by the University of
North Carolina Press. Used by permission of the publisher.

Acknowledgment
This essay also appears in *Poverty and Progress in the U.S. South Since 1920*, edited by Suzanne W. Jones and Mark Newman (Amsterdam: VU UP, 2006).

Notes
1. According to Judith Plant, "Bioregionalism calls for human society to be more
closely related to nature (hence 'bio') and to be more conscious of its locale, or regions, or life place (thus 'bioregion'). . . . It is a proposal to ground human cultures
within natural systems, to get to know one's place intimately in order to fit human communities to the earth, not distort the earth to our demands" (132). Plant's "Learning to
Live with Differences" appears in *Ecofeminism: Women, Culture, Nature*, ed. Karen J.
Warren (Bloomington: Indiana UP, 1997).

2. Wendell Berry's *The Unsettling of America: Culture and Agriculture* (San
Francisco: Sierra Club Books, 1977) is still considered "the definitive contemporary
statement of agrarian concerns and priorities," and Janisse Ray's recent memoir, *Ecology of a Cracker Childhood* (Minneapolis: Milkweed Editions, 1999), which won the
American Book Award, is required reading in Georgia's public schools and in a number of college environmental studies programs.

3. The novel is set in the fictional town of Egg Fork, in the vicinity of the Virginia-
Kentucky-Tennessee borders.

4. See Kingsolver's essay collection *Small Wonder* (New York: HarperCollins,
2002) and her Foreword to *The Essential Agrarian Reader: The Future of Culture,
Community, and the Land*, ed. Norman Wirzba (Lexington: UP of Kentucky, 2003).
Kingsolver also published an earlier collection of essays, *High Tide in Tucson* (New
York: HarperCollins, 1995).

5. In her acknowledgments (x), Kingsolver cites the source of her coyote research
as Mike Finkel, "The Ultimate Survivor" in *Audubon* (May-June 1999): 52-59. For an
analysis of coyotes in urban and suburban environments, see Mary Battiata, "Among
Us," *Washington Post Magazine* (16 April 2006): 6-11, 17-21.

6. This environmental ethic of care is not gender specific, although to some reviewers it has seemed so, perhaps because of the prominence of these three female pro-

tagonists. See for example, Jeff Giles' review in *Newsweek*, 30 October 2000, 82, and Susan Tekulve's review in *Book*, November 2000, 69. But Deanna's father is enlightened, Little Rickie proves a willing listener to Lusa's new ideas, and early in his career Cole wants to learn new farming methods. For a comprehensive analysis of the land ethic in *Prodigal Summer*, see Peter S. Wenz, "Leopold's Novel: The Land Ethic in Barbara Kingsolver's *Prodigal Summer*," *Ethics and the Environment* 8.2 (2003): 106-125. He argues that Kingsolver echoes Aldo Leopold's call for "a land ethic [that] changes the role of *Homo sapiens* from conqueror of the land-community to plain member and citizen of it" (106). The quotation is from Leopold's *A Sand County Almanac with Essays on Conservation from Round River* (New York: Ballantine, 1970), 240. See also Plant, "Learning to Live with Differences."

7. Wendell Berry, *Citizenship Papers* (Washington, D.C.: Shoemaker and Hoad, 2003), 159. Berry attributes this rule of thumb to agricultural scientists like Sir Albert Howard and Wes Jackson, whose guiding principle is "harmony between local ways of farming and local ecosystems," as opposed to agri-industrialists who assume universal applicability (159).

8. In "Women in Agriculture: The 'New Entrepreneurs,'" *Australian Feminist Studies*, 18.41 (2003), Margaret Alston argues that in order to make women more visible in agriculture, women must change the language and the way they view themselves, must question the lack of women in agricultural leadership positions, and must critically examine their own practices and customs, making sure to value their daughters' desires to be farmers (169-170).

9. Berry, *Citizenship Papers*, 110. In her Foreword to *The Essential Agrarian Reader*, Kingsolver says she repeatedly encountered the belief that all farmers are "political troglodytes and devotees of All-Star wrestling" (x).

10. Garnett's neighbor is Nannie Rawley, the only mother-figure Deanna has ever known. Deanna's father has had a long-term affair with Nannie after Deanna's mother's death in childbirth; he would have married Nannie if she had said yes.

11. "*Prodigal Summer* Questions and Answers," www.Kingsolver.com/faq/answers.asp.

12. Paul Ricoeur, "The Metaphysical Process as Cognition, Imagination, and Feeling" in *On Metaphor*, ed. Sheldon Sacks (Chicago, U of Chicago P, 1979), 151. In suggesting that a metaphor can yield insight about reality, I do not mean to suggest that Kingsolver thinks metaphoric and scientific discourses are the same or are apprehended in the same way. In explaining metaphoric apprehension, which involves making similar what is different, Ricoeur reminds us of the "semantic impertinence or incongruence" that is inherent: "In order that a metaphor obtains, one must continue to identify the previous incompatibility through the new compatibility" (146). I would like to thank Richard Godden for suggesting that I read Ricoeur.

13. This is not to say that these lessons, often delightful, are not enlightening to many readers. My students have said that they have a better understanding of ecology because of this novel.

Works Cited

Alston, Margaret. "Women in Agriculture: The 'New Entrepreneurs.'" *Australian Feminist Studies*, 18.41 (2003): 163-171.

Battiata, Mary. "Among Us." *Washington Post Magazine* 16 April 2006, 6-11, 17-21.

Bone, Martyn. *The Postsouthern Sense of Place in Contemporary Fiction*. Baton Rouge: Louisiana State UP, 2005.

Berry, Wendell. *Citizenship Papers*. Washington, D.C.: Shoemaker and Hoard, 2003.

_____. *The Unsettling of America: Culture and Agriculture*. San Francisco: Sierra Club Books, 1977.

Dirlik, Arif. "Place-based Imagination: Globalism and the Politics of Place." *Places and Politics in an Age of Globalization*. Ed. Roxann Prazniak and Arif Dirlik. Lanham, MD: Rowman and Littlefield Publishers, Inc., 2001.

Finkel, Mike. "The Ultimate Survivor." *Audubon* (May-June 1999): 52-59.

Giles, Jeff. Review of *Prodigal Summer* by Barbara Kingsolver. *Newsweek*, 30 October 2000, 82.

Kingsolver, Barbara. Foreword to *The Essential Agrarian Reader: The Future of Culture, Community, and the Land*. Ed. Norman Wirzba. Lexington: UP of Kentucky, 2003.

_____. *High Tide in Tucson*. New York: HarperCollins, 1995.

_____. *Prodigal Summer*. New York: HarperCollins, 2000.

_____. "*Prodigal Summer* Questions and Answers," www.Kingsolver .com/faq/answers.asp.

_____. *Small Wonder*. New York: HarperCollins, 2002.

Leopold, Aldo. *A Sand County Almanac with Essays on Conservation from Round River*. New York: Ballantine, 1970.

Plant, Judith. "Learning to Live with Differences." *Ecofeminism: Women, Culture, Nature*. Ed. Karen J. Warren. Bloomington: Indiana UP, 1997.

Ray, Janisse. *Ecology of a Cracker Childhood*. Minneapolis: Milkweed Editions, 1999.

Ricoeur, Paul. "The Metaphorical Process as Cognition, Imagination, and Feeling." *On Metaphor*. Ed. Sheldon Sacks. Chicago: U of Chicago P, 1979.

Tekulve, Susan. Review of *Prodigal Summer* by Barbara Kingsolver. *Book*, November 2000, 69.

Wenz, Peter S. "Leopold's Novel: The Land Ethic in Barbara Kingsolver's *Prodigal Summer*." *Ethics and the Environment* 8.2 (2003): 106-125.

Wirzba, Norman. Introduction to *The Essential Agrarian Reader: The Future of Culture, Community, and the Land*. Ed. Norman Wirzba. Lexington: UP of Kentucky, 2003.

RESOURCES

Chronology of Barbara Kingsolver's Life_____

1955	Barbara Kingsolver is born to Dr. Wendell R. Kingsolver and Virginia Lee Henry Kingsolver in Annapolis, Maryland, where Dr. Kingsolver is temporarily working as a Navy doctor.
1956	The Kingsolver family returns to its permanent home in Carlisle, Kentucky.
1963-1964	The family moves to the Congo, where Dr. Kingsolver practices medicine, then returns to Carlisle.
1977	Kingsolver graduates magna cum laude from DePauw University with a degree in biology.
1977-1979	Kingsolver works and travels in Greece, England, and France and then moves to Tucson, Arizona.
1981	Kingsolver completes her master's degree at the University of Arizona.
1981-1985	Kingsolver works as a technical writer in the Office of Arid Lands Studies.
1985	Kingsolver marries Joseph Hoffmann, a chemist; they divorce during the early 1990s.
1985-1987	Kingsolver works as a freelance journalist and writes *The Bean Trees* during bouts of insomnia brought on by pregnancy.
1987	Kingsolver's first daughter, Camille, is born.
1988	*The Bean Trees* is published.
1989	*Holding the Line: Women in the Great Arizona Mine Strike of 1983* and *Homeland, and Other Stories* are published.
1990	*Animal Dreams* is published and wins the PEN/USA West Fiction Award the following year.

1992	*Another America/Otra America*, a collection of poetry, is published.
1993	*Pigs in Heaven* is published.
1995	*High Tide in Tucson: Essays from Now or Never* is published. Kingsolver marries Steven Hopp and is awarded an honorary doctorate by DePauw University.
1996	Kingsolver's second daughter, Lily, is born.
1997	Kingsolver establishes the Bellwether Prize for Fiction, a biannual award for first novels demonstrating a commitment to social change.
1998	*The Poisonwood Bible* is published. It is short-listed for the Pulitzer Prize and the PEN/Faulkner Award.
2000	*Prodigal Summer* is published. Kingsolver is awarded a National Humanities Medal.
2002	*Last Stand: America's Virgin Lands* and *Small Wonder* are published. *Prodigal Summer* is nominated for the International IMPAC Dublin Literary Award.
2004	Kingsolver moves with her family to a farm in southwestern Virginia.
2007	*Animal, Vegetable, Miracle: A Year of Food Life* is published.
2008	Kingsolver delivers the commencement address at Duke University.

Works by Barbara Kingsolver

Long Fiction
The Bean Trees, 1988
Animal Dreams, 1990
Pigs in Heaven, 1993
The Poisonwood Bible, 1998
Prodigal Summer, 2000

Short Fiction
Homeland, and Other Stories, 1989

Nonfiction
Holding the Line: Women in the Great Arizona Mine Strike of 1983, 1989
High Tide in Tucson: Essays from Now or Never, 1995
Last Stand: America's Virgin Lands, 2002 (photographs by Annie Griffiths Belt)
Small Wonder, 2002
Animal, Vegetable, Miracle: A Year of Food Life, 2007 (with Steven L. Hopp and
   Camille Kingsolver)

Poetry
Another America/Otra America, 1992

Edited Work
The Best American Short Stories, 2001

Bibliography

Clarke, Deborah. "Domesticating the Car: Women's Road Trips." *Studies in American Fiction* 32.1 (Spring 2004): 101-28.

DeMarr, Mary Jean. *Barbara Kingsolver: A Critical Companion.* Westport, CT: Greenwood Press, 1999.

Demory, Pamela H. "Into the Heart of Light: Barbara Kingsolver Rereads *Heart of Darkness.*" *Conradiana* 34.3 (Fall 2002): 181-93.

Fagan, Kristina. "Adoption as National Fantasy in Barbara Kingsolver's *Pigs in Heaven* and Margaret Laurence's *The Diviners.*" *Imagining Adoption: Essays on Literature and Culture.* Ed. Marianne Novy. Ann Arbor: University of Michigan Press, 2001. 251-66.

Fleischner, Jennifer, ed. *A Reader's Guide to the Fiction of Barbara Kingsolver: "The Bean Trees," "Homeland, and Other Stories," "Animal Dreams," "Pigs in Heaven."* New York: HarperPerennial, 1994.

Frye, Bob J. "Nuggets of Truth in the Southwest: Artful Humor and Realistic Craft in Barbara Kingsolver's *The Bean Trees.*" *Southwestern American Literature* 26.2 (Spring 2001): 73-83.

Godfrey, Kathleen. "Barbara Kingsolver's Cherokee Nation: Problems of Representation in *Pigs in Heaven.*" *Western American Literature* 36.3 (Fall 2001): 259-77.

Kingsolver, Barbara. "Barbara Kingsolver: Her Fiction Features Ordinary People Heroically Committed to Political Issues." Interview with Lisa See Kendall. *Publishers Weekly* 31 Aug. 1990: 46-47.

_____. Interview. *Backtalk: Women Writers Speak Out.* Ed. Donna Perry. New Brunswick, NJ: Rutgers UP, 1993. 143-69.

_____. Interview. *Conversations with Kentucky Writers.* Ed. L. Elisabeth Beattie. Lexington: University Press of Kentucky, 1996. 151-71.

_____. Interview with Robin Epstein. *The Progressive* 60.2 (1996): 33-38.

_____. "Serendipity and the Southwest: A Conversation with Barbara Kingsolver." Interview. *Bloomsbury Review* Nov.-Dec. 1990: 3+.

Koza, Kimberly A. "The Africa of Two Western Women Writers: Barbara Kingsolver and Margaret Laurence." *Critique* 44.3 (Spring 2003): 284-94.

Kunz, Diane. "White Men in Africa: On Barbara Kingsolver's *The Poisonwood Bible.*" *Novel History: Historians and Novelists Confront America's Past (and Each Other).* Ed. Mark C. Carnes. New York: Simon & Schuster, 2001. 285-97.

Litovitz, Malca. "Huck Finn, Barbara Kingsolver, and the American Dream." *Queen's Quarterly* (Winter 1998): 3-12.

Metteer, Christine. "*Pigs in Heaven*: A Parable of Native American Adoption Under the Indian Child Welfare Act." *Arizona State Law Journal* 28.2 (1996): 589-628.

Michael, Magali Cornier. *New Visions of Community in Contemporary American Fic-*

tion: Tan, Kingsolver, Castillo, Morrison. Iowa City: University of Iowa Press, 2006.

Novy, Marianne. "Nurture, Loss, and Cherokee Identity in Barbara Kingsolver's Novels of Cross-Cultural Adoption." *Reading Adoption: Family and Difference in Fiction and Drama*. Ann Arbor: University of Michigan Press, 2005.

Ryan, Maureen. "Barbara Kingsolver's Lowfat Fiction." *Journal of American Culture* 18.4 (1995): 77-82.

Snodgrass, Mary Ellen. *Barbara Kingsolver: A Literary Companion*. Jefferson, NC: McFarland, 2004.

Wagner-Martin, Linda. *Barbara Kingsolver*. Philadelphia: Chelsea House, 2004.

_____. *Barbara Kingsolver's "The Poisonwood Bible": A Reader's Guide*. New York: Continuum, 2001.

Wenz, Peter S. "Leopold's Novel: The Land Ethic in Barbara Kingsolver's *Prodigal Summer*." *Ethics and the Environment* 8.2 (2003): 106-25.

Wirzba, Norman, ed. *The Essential Agrarian Reader: The Future of Culture, Community, and the Land*. Lexington: University Press of Kentucky, 2003.

CRITICAL INSIGHTS

About the Editor

Thomas Austenfeld is Professor of American Literature and Dean of the Faculty of Letters at the University of Fribourg, Switzerland. He was educated at the University of Münster (Germany) and at the University of Virginia, where he earned a Ph.D. in English and American literature with a dissertation on Robert Lowell. His fifteen-year teaching career in the United States took him to Missouri, Utah, and Georgia before he returned to Europe. Austenfeld is the author of *American Women Writers and the Nazis: Ethics and Politics in Boyle, Porter, Stafford, and Hellman* (2001) and the editor of *Kay Boyle for the Twenty-First Century* (2008) as well as coeditor of *Writing American Women* (2009). He founded the Kay Boyle Society and served as its first president. He has published numerous encyclopedia and reference entries as well as scholarly articles on authors as diverse as Lord Byron, Wallace Stevens, Katherine Anne Porter, Peter Taylor, Thomas Wolfe, Josef Pieper, Derek Walcott, Louise Erdrich, Philip Roth, and Frank Norris. He has contributed bibliographies to *Western American Literature* and bibliographic essays to the annual *American Literary Scholarship*. In more than forty conference papers, he has discussed women writers, literature of the American West, and questions at the intersections of literature and philosophy. His current work centers on a reinterpretation of the significance of ethical reasoning in twentieth-century American texts.

About *The Paris Review*

The Paris Review is America's preeminent literary quarterly, dedicated to discovering and publishing the best new voices in fiction, nonfiction, and poetry. The magazine was founded in Paris in 1953 by the young American writers Peter Matthiessen and Doc Humes, and edited there and in New York for its first fifty years by George Plimpton. Over the decades, the *Review* has introduced readers to the earliest writings of Jack Kerouac, Philip Roth, T. C. Boyle, V. S. Naipaul, Ha Jin, Jay McInerney, and Mona Simpson, and published numerous now classic works, including Roth's *Goodbye, Columbus*, Donald Barthelme's *Alice*, Jim Carroll's *Basketball Diaries*, and selections from Samuel Beckett's *Molloy* (his first publication in English). The first chapter of Jeffrey Eugenides's *The Virgin Suicides* appeared in the *Review*'s pages, as well as stories by Edward P. Jones, Rick Moody, David Foster Wallace, Denis Johnson, Jim Shepard, Jim Crace, Lorrie Moore, Jeanette Winterson, and Ann Patchett.

The Paris Review's renowned Writers at Work series of interviews, whose early installments include legendary conversations with E. M. Forster, William Faulkner, and Ernest Hemingway, is one of the landmarks of world literature. The interviews received a George Polk Award and were nominated for a Pulitzer Prize. Among the more than three hundred interviewees are Robert Frost, Marianne Moore, W. H. Auden, Elizabeth Bishop, Susan Sontag, and Toni Morrison. Recent issues feature conversations with Salman Rushdie, Joan Didion, Stephen King, Norman Mailer, Kazuo Ishiguro, and Umberto Eco. (A complete list of the interviews is available at www.theparisreview.org.) In November 2008, Picador will publish the third of a four-volume series of anthologies of *Paris Review* interviews. The first two volumes have received acclaim. *The New York Times* called the Writers at Work series "the most remarkable and extensive interviewing project we possess."

The Paris Review is edited by Philip Gourevitch, who was named to the post in 2005, following the death of George Plimpton two years earlier. Under Gourevitch's leadership, the magazine's international distribution has expanded, paid subscriptions have risen 150 percent, and newsstand distribution has doubled. A new editorial team has published fiction by Andre Aciman, Damon Galgut, Mohsin Hamid, Gish Jen, Richard Price, Said Sayrafiezadeh, and Alistair Morgan. Poetry editors Charles Simic, Meghan O'Rourke, and Dan Chiasson have selected works by Billy Collins, Jesse Ball, Mary Jo Bang, Sharon Olds, and Mary Karr. Writing published in the magazine has been anthologized in *Best American Short Stories* (2006, 2007, and 2008), *Best American Poetry*, *Best Creative Non-Fiction*, the Pushcart Prize anthology, and *O. Henry Prize Stories*.

The magazine presents two annual awards. The Hadada Award for lifelong contribution to literature has recently been given to William Styron, Joan Didion, Norman Mailer, and Peter Matthiessen in 2008. The Plimpton Prize for Fiction, given to a new voice in fiction brought to national attention in the pages of *The Paris Review*, was presented in 2007 to Benjamin Percy and to Jesse Ball in 2008.

The Paris Review won the 2007 National Magazine Award in photojournalism, and the *Los Angeles Times* recently called *The Paris Review* "an American treasure with true international reach."

Since 1999 *The Paris Review* has been published by The Paris Review Foundation, Inc., a not-for-profit 501(c)(3) organization.

The Paris Review is available in digital form to libraries worldwide in selected academic databases exclusively from EBSCO Publishing. Libraries can contact EBSCO at 1-800-653-2726 for details. For more information on *The Paris Review* or to subscribe, please visit: www.theparisreview.org.

Contributors

Thomas Austenfeld currently serves as Professor of American Literature and Dean of the Faculty of Letters at the University of Fribourg, Switzerland, having previously taught in Virginia, Missouri, and Georgia. His research and publications focus on American women writers and on the West.

Marilyn Kongslie is a graduate of Portland State University. She is a writer and a gardener.

Karen L. Arnold is an independent scholar and writer who received her undergraduate degree from Northern Illinois University and her master's and Ph.D. degrees from the University of Maryland, College Park. She has facilitated Maryland Humanities Council, local library, and NEH-funded reading and discussion series throughout Maryland for more than fifteen years. Currently she teaches in the Johns Hopkins University Osher Adult Education programs and leads the discussion series Literature and Medicine for hospitals in the Baltimore area. She has taught at the University of Lund in Sweden, the U.S. Naval Academy, and the University of Maryland, College Park. She was Poet-in-Residence at Montpelier Cultural Arts Center in Laurel for ten years, and her chapbook *Border Crossings* appeared in 1997.

Katherine Ryder is a graduate of the University of Michigan and the London School of Economics.

John Nizalowski holds a B.A. in English and history from Binghamton University and an M.A. in English from the University of Delaware. He is the author of a multi-genre book titled *Hooking the Sun* (2003), and his scholarly and creative works have appeared in *Puerto del Sol, Weber: The Contemporary West, Bloomsbury Review, ISLE, Frank Waters Studies, The New York Review of Science-Fiction, Fish Drum, The Albany Review,* and elsewhere. His writings have also been anthologized, most notably in *Readings Under the Sign of Nature, The Blueline Reader,* and *Rekindling the Inner Light: The Frank Waters Centennial.* Currently he resides in Grand Junction, Colorado, where he teaches creative writing and mythology at Mesa State College.

Rosemary M. Canfield Reisman was Professor of English and Department Chair at Troy University and is now Adjunct Professor at Charleston Southern University. She coauthored *Contemporary Southern Women Fiction Writers* (1994) and *Contemporary Southern Men Fiction Writers* (1998) and has published numerous essays. She has presented lectures on British and American literature at the University of Hanover, Germany, at the American University in Cairo, and throughout the southeastern United States.

Matthew J. Bolton is an English teacher and the academic dean of Loyola School in New York City. He earned his Ph.D. in English literature in 2005 from the Graduate Center of the City University of New York, where he wrote his dissertation on Robert Browning and T. S. Eliot. He received the T. S. Eliot Society's Fathman Young Scholar

Award for work related to his dissertation. In addition to his doctorate, he holds master's degrees in teaching and in educational administration from Fordham University. His research and writing center on connections between Victorian and modernist literature.

Christine M. Battista is currently completing her doctoral work at Binghamton University, where she teaches courses in American literature, ecofeminism, theories of globalization, and new Americanist studies. She has published an article on the history of music in the Mid-Atlantic region in *The Greenwood Encyclopedia of American Regional Cultures* and has recently completed a book review of R. Radhakrishnan's *History, the Human, and the World Between* for *Modern Fiction Studies*. At present, she is working to complete her dissertation, which involves tracing an ontology of land through an ecofeminist lens in American literature from James Fenimore Cooper to Willa Cather.

Catherine Himmelwright is Instructor in the English Department at Auburn University. Her articles on Barbara Kingsolver and Katherine Anne Porter have appeared in *Southern Literary Journal* and *Mississippi Quarterly.*

Loretta Martin Murrey is Associate Professor of English at Western Kentucky University-Glasgow. Her scholarly interests include southern American literature, especially Kentucky literature, and environmental literature, and her work has appeared in the *Journal of Kentucky Studies*, *Southern Quarterly*, and *Southern Studies: An Interdisciplinary Journal of the South.*

Sheryl Stevenson is Professor Emeritus of English at the University of Akron. Her work has appeared in *Autism and Representation* (2007) and *Critical Perspectives on Pat Barker* (2005), and she has published essays on Djuna Barnes, Stevie Smith, Barbara Kingsolver, and Sarah Waters.

Lee Ann De Reus is Associate Professor of Human Development & Family Studies and Women's Studies at Pennsylvania State University, Altoona. Among other publications, her work has appeared in *Handbook of Feminist Family Studies* (2008), *Strengths and Challenges of New Immigrant Families: Implications for Research, Theory, Education, and Service* (2008), *Sourcebook of Family Theory and Research* (2005), *Journal of Teaching in Marriage and the Family*, *Family Science Review, Post Script: Essays in Film and the Humanities*, and *Journal of Humanistic Education and Development.*

Amanda Cockrell is managing editor of *The Hollins Critic* and teaches creative writing and children's literature at Hollins College. She holds an M.F.A. in creative writing from Hollins College and is the author of several novels, including *Pomegranate Seed* (2001), *The Deer Dancers* trilogy (1995-1996), *The Horse Catchers* trilogy (1999-2001), *The Moonshine Blade* (1988), and *The Legions of the Mist* (1979).

Elaine R. Ognibene is Professor of English at Siena College. Her work has appeared in *The Women and War Reader* (1998), *College English*, *English Journal*, *Teaching Education*, and *College Teaching.*

Kristin J. Jacobson is Assistant Professor of American Literature and Women's Studies at Stockton College. Her articles have appeared in *Legacy, Tulsa Studies in Women's Literature*, and *Genre*, and she is currently at work on a book titled *Domestic Geographies: Neodomestic American Fiction*.

Anne Marie Austenfeld holds an M.A. in English from the University of Virginia and an M.L.I.S. from the University of Alabama. She has taught courses in fine arts at North Georgia College & State University and her work has appeared in the *Journal of Narrative Theory*.

Stephen D. Fox is Professor of English at Gallaudet University. His work has appeared in *Critique* and *American Annals of the Deaf*.

Suzanne W. Jones is Professor of English at the University of Richmond. She is the author of *Race Mixing: Southern Fiction Since the Sixties* (2004) and the editor of *Crossing the Color Line: Readings in Black and White* (2000), *Writing the Woman Artist: Essays on Poetics, Politics, and Portraiture* (1991), and *Growing up in the South: An Anthology of Modern Southern Literature* (1991). She is also the coeditor of *South to a New Place: Region, Literature, Culture* (2002).

Acknowledgments _____

"Barbara Kingsolver" by Marilyn Kongslie and Karen L. Arnold. From *Magill's Survey of American Literature*. Rev. ed. Copyright © 2007 by Salem Press, Inc. Reprinted with permission of Salem Press.

"The *Paris Review* Perspective" by Katherine Ryder. Copyright © 2010 by Katherine Ryder. Special appreciation goes to Christopher Cox and Nathaniel Rich, editors for *The Paris Review*.

"Gardens of Auto Parts: Kingsolver's Merger of American Western Myth and Native American Myth in *The Bean Trees*" by Catherine Himmelwright. From *Southern Literary Journal* 39, no. 2 (2007): 119-139. Copyright © 2007 by the University of North Carolina Press. Used by permission of the publisher. www.uncpress.unc.edu

"The Loner and the Matriarchal Community in Barbara Kingsolver's *The Bean Trees* and *Pigs in Heaven*" by Loretta Martin Murrey. From *Southern Studies* 5, nos. 1 & 2 (1994): 155-164. Copyright © 1994 by The Southern Studies Institute. Reprinted by permission of The Southern Studies Institute.

"Trauma and Memory in Kingsolver's *Animal Dreams*" by Sheryl Stevenson. From *LIT: Literature Interpretation Theory* 11, no. 4 (2001): 327-350. Copyright © 2001 by Taylor & Francis Ltd. (http://www.tandf.co.uk/journals). Reprinted by permission of Taylor & Francis Ltd.

"Exploring the Matrix of Identity in Barbara Kingsolver's *Animal Dreams*" by Lee Ann De Reus. From *Reading the Family Dance: Family Systems Therapy and Literary Study* (2003). Ed. John V. Knapp and Kenneth Womack. Copyright © 2003 by Rosemont Publishing and Printing Corp. Reprinted by permission of Rosemont Publishing and Printing Corp.

"Luna Moths, Coyotes, Sugar Skulls: The Fiction of Barbara Kingsolver" by Amanda Cockrell. From *The Hollins Critic* 38, no. 2 (April 2001): 1-14. Copyright © 2001 by Amanda Cockrell. Reprinted by permission of Amanda Cockrell.

"The Missionary Position: Barbara Kingsolver's *The Poisonwood Bible*" by Elaine R. Ognibene. From *College Literature* 30, no. 3 (2003): 19-36. Copyright © 2003 by *College Literature*. Reprinted by permission of *College Literature*.

"The Neodomestic American Novel: The Politics of Home in Barbara Kingsolver's *The Poisonwood Bible*" by Kristin J. Jacobson. From *Tulsa Studies in Women's Literature* 24, no. 1 (2005): 105-127. Copyright © 2005 by the University of Tulsa. Reprinted by permission of the University of Tulsa.

"The Revelatory Narrative Circle in Barbara Kingsolver's *The Poisonwood Bible*" by Anne Marie Austenfeld. From *JNT: Journal of Narrative Theory* 36, no. 2 (2006): 293-305. Copyright © 2006 by Eastern Michigan University, Department of English. Reprinted by permission of Eastern Michigan University, Department of English.

"Barbara Kingsolver and Keri Hulme: Disability, Family, and Culture" by Ste-

Index

Achebe, Chinua, 212, 247, 257
Agricultural issues, 12, 31, 33, 48, 56, 62, 67, 284, 287, 291, 299
Alaimo, Stacy, 61, 67
All Souls' Day, 135, 142, 148, 173
Allen, Paula Gunn, 101
Alston, Margaret, 299
American Indian cultures. *See* Native American cultures
Angelou, Maya, 120
Animal Dreams (Kingsolver), 4, 25, 39, 120, 124, 130, 135, 142, 148, 153, 158, 180
Animal, Vegetable, Miracle (Kingsolver), 5, 12, 33, 48, 55, 67
Another America/Otra America (Kingsolver), 27, 40, 183
Aprile, Dianne, 116
Archer, Sally, 156, 169
Armstrong, Nancy, 217

Bakhtin, Mikhail, 132, 247
Bal, Mieke, 248
Banks, Russell, 38
Barker, Elspeth, 44
Baym, Nina, 219, 225, 239, 245
Bean Trees, The (Kingsolver), 8, 24, 36, 43, 70, 77, 81, 88, 93, 96, 106, 114, 175
Beattie, L. Elisabeth, 25
Beecher, Catharine E., 222, 243
Bellwether Prize for Fiction, 47
Benhabib, Seyla, 224
Berger, James, 123
Berry, Wendell, 65, 67, 287, 298
Bioregionalism, 56, 287, 298
Bird imagery, 104, 130, 132, 144, 177, 190, 296
Bloom, Sandra, 131

Bondo, Eddie (*Prodigal Summer*), 48, 59, 296
Bone People, The (Hulme), 260, 271, 274, 278
Bone, Martyn, 288
Brandmark, Wendy, 38
Brinkmeyer, Robert, 92
Bromberg, Judith, 45
Bruchac, Joseph, 110
Bruner, Jerome, 148
Butler, Jack, 36

Carson, Rachel, 67
Caruth, Cathy, 124
Cave, Marianne, 254
Charlton, James I., 267
Cherokee Nation, 69, 97, 117
Child loss, 78, 83, 105, 126, 137, 161, 200, 205, 210, 227
Conrad, Joseph, 212
Cooke, Carolyn, 39
Cowley, Malcolm, 18
Cox, Bonnie Jean, 120
Coyotes, 59, 138, 179, 189, 285, 293, 296
Creation myths, 99
Curry, Renee, 254

Daugherty, Tracy, 148
Daurio, Beverly, 42
Day of the Dead, 135, 142, 148, 173
DeMarr, Mary Jean, 24, 46, 153, 248
DeMeester, Karen, 148
Demory, Pamela H., 253
DeVries, Marten W., 142, 148
Dirlik, Arif, 285
Disability, physical, 206, 241, 260
Domestic fiction, 217
Dorban, Joshua, 148
Dreams, 137, 182, 229

Eaton, Heather, 53
Ecofeminism, 40, 53, 61, 66
Ecological issues, 26, 48, 54, 58, 63, 165, 284, 287, 296
Epstein, Robin, 18, 44
Erikson, Erik, 153, 168
Ethnicity. *See* Race and ethnicity issues

Families, 93, 114, 153, 177, 216, 239, 243, 263, 292, 296; and identity formation, 157; Maori, 271, 278; Native American, 29, 119, 281; nontraditional, 107, 140, 170, 234; patriarchal, 45
Farming. *See* Agricultural issues
Father-daughter relationships, 125, 160, 198
Feltey, Kathryn M., 148
Feminism, 20, 37, 40, 55, 145, 156, 168, 241, 244, 247, 264, 293
Fiedler, Leslie A., 91, 96, 267
Finkel, Mike, 60
Fisher, Walter R., 254
Fleischner, Jennifer, 153
Fludernik, Monika, 254
Forgiveness, 166, 199, 210
Foss, Sonja K., 247
Fox, Stephen D., 249
Freeman, Mark, 129

Gardens, 88, 109, 199, 288
Gender roles, 21, 61, 89, 93, 99, 156, 168, 218, 227, 234, 244-245, 292
Genette, Gérard, 250
George, Rosemary Marangoly, 218, 237, 242, 244
Gilman, Charlotte Perkins, 120
Godfrey, Kathleen, 29
Gothic fiction, 70
Graulich, Melody, 90
Gray, Paul, 40, 47

Green, Gayle, 45
Greer, Alice (*The Bean Trees*), 117, 121, 178
Greer, Taylor (*Pigs in Heaven*), 28, 119, 178
Greer, Taylor (*The Bean Trees*), 39, 69, 73, 79, 96, 100, 104, 114, 175
Griffin, Cindy L., 247
Griffin, Susan, 140

Haraway, Donna, 67
Harbine, Newt (*The Bean Trees*), 93
Harris, Susan K., 219
Hartman, Geoffrey H., 124
Heart of Darkness (Conrad), 47, 213, 247, 253, 269
Herman, Judith Lewis, 124, 128, 137
High Tide in Tucson (Kingsolver), 27, 44, 121, 149, 174, 187
Himmelwright, Catherine, 25
Hirsch, Marianne, 121
Hochschild, Adam, 192, 213
Holding the Line (Kingsolver), 8, 23, 37, 148, 176, 251, 256
Holmes, Martha Stoddard, 261
Homeland, and Other Stories (Kingsolver), 25, 38, 176
Homemaking, 217, 227, 233, 238
Hulme, Keri, 47, 260, 271

Identity, 76, 82, 92, 121; development of, 96, 107, 115, 126, 140, 153, 161, 225, 241, 254
Imagery, 92, 130, 144; birds, 104, 130, 132, 144, 177, 190, 296; bones, 129, 139, 173, 274; gardens, 88, 109, 199, 288; nature, 58, 102, 107, 110, 140, 145, 179, 296; water, 95, 137
Indian Child Welfare Act (1978), 28
Indian cultures. *See* Native American cultures
Irigaray, Luce, 67

Jacobson, Kristin J., 246, 253
Jane Eyre (Brontë), 75
Johnson, Michael, 90
Jones, Suzanne W., 31, 47, 63, 67
Josselson, Ruthellen, 169

Kafka, Phillipa, 192
Kaplan, Amy, 221, 242
Kaplan, Cora, 265, 270
Karbo, Karen, 42
Kegan, Robert, 157
Kendall, Lisa See, 39
Kingsolver, Barbara; awards and honors, 8, 40; critical reception of works, 11, 29, 36, 40, 45, 105, 153, 264, 270, 294, 298; education, 7; influences on, 19; on *The Poisonwood Bible*, 256; political views, 8, 12, 18, 23, 27, 32, 44, 54, 187, 266; on writing, 17, 148, 251; writing career, 25
Kingsolver, Wendell (father), 19
Knapp, John V., 157
Kolodny, Annette, 88
Kunz, Diane, 253

Landowski, Lusa (*Prodigal Summer*), 31, 47, 61, 188, 286, 289, 293
Language, 71, 128, 134, 184, 192, 198, 200, 204, 209, 241, 263, 295
Leavitt, Sarah A., 243
Le Guin, Ursula K., 144
Lehmann-Haupt, Christopher, 41
Lewis, R. W. B., 95
Little Women (Alcott), 47, 216, 234, 242
Lorde, Audre, 147
Lorentzen, Lois Ann, 53
Lumumba, Patrice, 30, 185, 197, 204, 243

McDowell, Linda, 235
Maori culture, 271, 277

Marcia, James E., 157
Markstrom-Adams, Carol, 158
Martin, Biddy, 225, 244
Massey, Doreen, 237
Matriarchal communities, 26, 104, 114, 120
Memory, 125, 130, 135, 140, 163, 181
Mesic, Penelope, 48
Messent, Peter, 248
Michael, Magali Cornier, 29
Miller, J. Hillis, 135
Mitchell, David T., 261
Mohanty, Chandra Talpade, 225, 244
Morrison, Toni, 221, 239, 243
Mother-daughter relationships, 106, 117, 121, 160, 223
Motherhood, 106, 115, 119, 177
Mourning, 134, 141, 181, 190
Mrs. Dalloway (Woolf), 135, 148
Murphy, Patrick D., 64
Muteness, 72, 263, 271

Names and naming, 4, 82, 95, 100, 114, 116, 120, 144, 176, 235, 265, 267, 293
Narration and narrators, 39, 45, 70, 79, 125, 128, 183, 195, 198, 208, 220, 246, 250, 254
Native American cultures, 26, 40, 96, 99, 102, 110, 162, 281
Nature imagery, 58, 102, 107, 110, 140, 145, 179, 296
Neely, Alan, 44
Neuhaus, Denise, 38
Noline, Codi (*Animal Dreams*), 26, 39, 125, 128, 133, 137, 141, 146, 152, 158, 164, 170, 173, 180
Noline, Doc Homer (*Animal Dreams*), 26, 126, 138, 160, 165, 180
Norman, Liane Ellison, 45
Nünning, Ansgar, 246

Ognibene, Elaine R., 252
Outsiders, 94, 99, 120, 133, 159, 183, 261, 289

Palgi, Phyllis, 148
Paradise (Morrison), 239
Pearlman, Mickey, 113
Peeler, David P., 18
Perdue, Theda, 99
Peregrina, Loyd (*Animal Dreams*), 26, 134, 162, 165, 181
Perry, Donna, 17, 27
Phelps Dodge Mining Company, 23, 37
Pigs in Heaven (Kingsolver), 4, 28, 40, 114, 118, 177, 281
Poisonwood Bible, The (Kingsolver), 4, 8, 12, 29, 183, 193, 212, 262, 275; critical reception, 47; narrators, 220, 247, 252; as neodomestic novel, 217, 229; settings, 221
Pratt, Minnie Bruce, 235, 244
Predators, 60, 179, 189, 285
Pregnancy, 94, 114, 120, 137, 145, 161, 179, 190
Price, Adah (*The Poisonwood Bible*), 184, 198, 202, 228, 249, 263, 266, 275
Price, Leah (*The Poisonwood Bible*), 184, 198, 201, 226, 233, 245, 249, 262
Price, Nathan (*The Poisonwood Bible*), 30, 44, 183, 186, 193, 197, 202, 209, 262, 275
Price, Orleanna (*The Poisonwood Bible*), 184, 195, 223, 227, 238, 249, 253
Price, Rachel (*The Poisonwood Bible*), 184, 207, 229, 232, 239, 245, 249
Price, Ruth May (*The Poisonwood Bible*), 185, 201, 205, 227, 250
Prodigal Summer (Kingsolver), 8, 20, 31, 47, 54, 57, 64, 67, 188, 284, 290, 295

Race and ethnicity issues, 70, 74, 81, 162, 223, 234, 264, 279
Rawley, Nannie (*Prodigal Summer*), 31, 63, 188, 293, 299
Ray, Janisse, 283, 298
Religion, 44, 183, 193, 242, 287
Ricoeur, Paul, 295, 299
Riley, Jeanette, 251
Rituals, 102, 106, 132, 141, 148, 194, 277
Romines, Ann, 241
Rubenstein, Roberta, 140
Ryan, Maureen, 29, 42

Sanctuary Movement, 22, 131, 251
Schlissel, Lillian, 90, 110
Schoeffel, Melissa, 29
Shapiro, Laura, 41, 118
Silent Spring (Carson), 67
Slotkin, Richard, 110
Small Wonder (Kingsolver), 8, 24, 32, 48, 54, 64
Smith, Henry Nash, 96
Snodgrass, Mary Ellen, 46
Snyder, Sharon L., 261
Southwest (U.S. region), 22, 70, 173; writers, 33
Spirituality, 98, 106, 144, 195, 212, 271
Stafford, Tim, 44
Star Woman myth, 99, 108
Steinberg, Marc W., 38
Stout, Janis, 90
Stowe, Harriet Beecher, 222, 243
Strehle, Susan, 30
Swartz, Patti Capel, 26

Things Fall Apart (Achebe), 247, 269
Tischler, Barbara L., 38
Tobacco farming, 62, 67, 286
Tompkins, Jane, 89
Trauma studies, 124
Twins, 132, 144, 178, 183, 198, 262

Wagner-Martin, Linda, 21, 26, 47, 251, 255
Walker, Alice, 120
Walker, Garnett (*Prodigal Summer*), 31, 48, 63, 188, 291
Warner, Susan, 148
Warren, Karen J., 54, 66
Water imagery, 95, 137
Welch, Sharon D., 145
Welter, Barbara, 241
Wenz, Peter S., 67, 299

Wirzba, Norman, 290
Wolfe, Deanna (*Prodigal Summer*), 31, 57, 61, 188, 285, 290
Wright, Gwendolyn, 238
Wrong, Michela, 213
Wuthering Heights (Brontë), 70

Young, Elizabeth, 41

Zimmerman, Michael, 56